# SIDNEY LANIER

## POEMS AND LETTERS

# SIDNEY LANIER

## POEMS AND LETTERS

WITH AN INTRODUCTION AND NOTES BY
CHARLES R. ANDERSON

THE JOHNS HOPKINS PRESS
BALTIMORE AND LONDON

# CONTENTS

# PREFACE

THE CENTENNIAL EDITION OF SIDNEY LANIER in ten volumes, based on the voluminous manuscript collections at Johns Hopkins University, was first published in 1945; it has been reissued, in part (1963-1969), and will be kept in print to serve the needs of libraries, institutions, and individuals desiring the complete scholarly edition of Lanier's writings. The purpose of the present volume of selections, using the text and notes of the Centennial Edition, is to make the best of Lanier available to the widest possible audience. For reasons that will be made clear in the Introduction, Lanier's literary career was confined to a few fevered years, and as a result his poetry is very uneven in quality. For the general reader, therefore, a winnowing of the best is highly desirable.

The twenty-five poems chosen here include all of his really successful ones, though they comprise only a small part of the corpus. They are arranged in chronological order, except that four early ones are placed in a separate group at the end. The poems are followed by detailed notes, giving the history of composition and publication of each poem and other pertinent data. They are prefaced by an introductory essay written especially for this volume, surveying Lanier's entire career as a writer, with commentary on the major poems.

For the letters, I have chosen those which relate to Lanier's professional life, in music and literature, or to the circumstances and experiences that were in conflict with that career. In a few cases the opening or closing paragraphs of letters to his family, dealing with domestic matters, have been deleted (the omissions being indicated by . . .). Seventy-four letters have been selected, preceded by a chronological table and with the detailed annotations from the Centennial Edition retained so that they can be placed in the proper narrative context.

Charles R. Anderson

*The Johns Hopkins University*

# SIDNEY LANIER

## POEMS AND LETTERS

# INTRODUCTION

"I HAD the pleasure of seeing him but once, when he called on me at Elmwood," wrote James Russell Lowell, "but the image of his shining presence is among the friendliest in my memory." Those who knew Sidney Lanier well have testified to the rare quality of his character and to the charm of his personality. But this tribute by a comparative stranger is the happiest phrase ever used of him, and it aptly symbolizes the figure that emerges from the second half of this book. There are many standards for measuring the value of letters, but on one point there seems to be general agreement, namely, that they should reflect the writer. In his correspondence Lanier revealed himself with unusual candor. Even in a small selection of his letters, such as this, the autobiographical picture is a remarkably vivid one, especially of the inner man—the life of the emotions and the spirit, essential to understanding a musician and lyric poet.*

The life and song of Sidney Lanier were so intimately related, and the frustrations that beset his ambition for achievement as an artist so moving, that the tendency has been to lose the poems in the poet. In the last analysis, of course, all poetry must be understood and evaluated on its own merits, quite independently of its relation to biography. But since one function of the editor, as distinguished from the critic, is to set the author's works in an adequate frame of facts, a survey of Lanier's poetic career will provide a proper approach to the poems themselves. The purpose of this introduction is to supplement the letters by filling out the external narrative of his life as an artist.

Many a lyric poet dying at Lanier's age or earlier has left behind a fuller measure of his worth, but few have been faced with so many obstacles in a life of less than forty years. Plunged into four years of war and imprisonment, on the threshold of maturity, he emerged at the age of twenty-three crippled with a fatal disease and conditioned by the economic blight that paralyzed the South during ten years of Reconstruction. Illness and poverty blocked his progress at every stage, rising to a climax in the last five desperate years; and they increased that isolation

---

* This essay has been drawn from my much longer Introduction to the *Poems,* in Volume I of the Centennial Edition. There one may find citation of authoritative sources for all my statements, but such scholarly documentation seemed unsuited to a reader's edition. All of Lanier's poems and prose mentioned here may be found in Volumes I–VI, definitive text and full annotations; all of his letters, cited or quoted here, in Volumes VII–X. The Centennial Edition is also provided with detailed introductions, a bibliography, and a general index.

1

from the contemporary world of letters which he felt to be such a handicap. But though this is the best-known part of his frustration, it is by no means the whole story. More disastrous, perhaps, was the proclivity to scatter his talents and energies in several fields, increased by the untoward circumstances of his life but also coming from originally divided aims. As early as his college days he was unable to decide between music and poetry as his natural bent, and the choice was further complicated by his yearning for an academic career. The failure to choose, which resulted from outward pressure and from lack of inward discipline, accounts in great measure for his failure to achieve more largely as poet, musician, or scholar.

During the twenty years of his mature life, first one and then another of these aspirations dominated him. The creation of poetry, though the most continuous single aim, was sometimes subordinated and on occasions thrust altogether into the background. The majority of his poems were written in two periods, of four and five years respectively, between stretches largely devoted to other fields.* And even in times of his greatest productivity he was disabled by illness, harassed by economic necessity, and distracted by his activities as a professional musician and an amateur scholar.

These were the hostile forces that prevented the full expression of his message to mankind—the gospel of love and beauty that was to redeem a world sick with materialism. That Lanier was aware of this thwarting is evidenced in the three projected volumes of his last years, unfinished "outlines" for as many more poems as he had written in a lifetime, and especially in the note of pathos sounded in the final jotting: "For I deemed it was safer not to depart from hence before I had acquitted my conscience with the composition of some poems in obedience to the dream." The wonder of it is that he accomplished as much as he did; the tragedy, not that he died young, but that after many delays he died at the beginning of his period of greatest development, in originality and in sureness of technique. The loss to poetry is implicit in the progress of these last years and the unfinished plans that he left.

Lanier's poetic career began late. Referring in a letter of August 15, 1876, to "Corn," "The Symphony," and "Psalm of the West," all written during the previous two years, he said: "These are my first poems, excepting short songs which have appeared in *Scribner's* and *Lippincott's*." In the deepest sense this was true, for it was not until he was thirty-two years

---

* In the two periods of his greatest productivity he wrote 104 out of a total of 164 poems. The first period, 1865–1868 (46 minor poems), came to an end when he turned to law; the second, 1874–1878 (58 major poems), ended when he turned to the academic life.

old that he gave himself with full seriousness to the composition of poetry, and few verses of importance date before this time. In a literal sense it was far from true, for he had written as many poems before "Corn" (1874) as he was to write thereafter. But the work of these last crowded years is that on which his reputation rests, and the several abortive starts of the earlier period need be mentioned only briefly here.

Of the fifty-odd poems written while he was at college, during the Civil War, and in the years immediately following, none showed real promise. They consisted of light lyrics addressed to friends and sweethearts, occasional pieces, and uninspired imitations. First he was attracted by the gloomy introspection of Byron and Poe, then by the sentimentalism of the German writers he learned about from Carlyle-Novalis and Jean Paul Richter—the latter being formative influences that also vitiated his novel, *Tiger-Lilies,* and plagued him to the end. (The only one of the great romanticists to exert any abiding influence of a sanative sort on Lanier was Keats, and that came later.) At last, during the grim winter of 1868, as the evils of Reconstruction began to bear down on the South, for the first time Lanier's own experience of life gave him something to say—something that brought life into his poetry. (His war experiences had been consistently bypassed or romanticized.) Several poems from this period seem worth salvaging, and they are included in a group at the end of the present selection. In "The Raven Days," with its anguished remonstrance, and in "Tyranny," where his bitterness has burned down to irony, he achieved a certain lyricism. But as the paralysis spread throughout his native region, Lanier too became lethargized. The poems ceased, and a second novel, which was to record the catastrophe of Reconstruction, was abandoned. In January came a hemorrhage from the lungs, the first sure evidence that he had tuberculosis; in May the Academy of which he was principal shut down because of the economic depression.

With illness, debt, no employment, and a child expected (he had married in December 1867), his fortunes reached bottom. And not the least part of his depression came from the conclusion that he must give up his hopes of authorship, probably forever, and turn to some more certain means of livelihood. The irony of all this could hardly be more pointed. For the very adverse circumstances that made this change necessary had produced his most interesting poems; and it was just at this time that he made his first acquaintance with an established poet, Paul Hayne, who had read one of these recent lyrics and sent him a warm letter of encouragement. Exactly when the decision was made to become a lawyer instead of a poet is not known, but it was reflected poignantly in "Life and Song," written during the summer of 1868. This was not only his best poem to date but his first real success, being reprinted in periodicals in Baltimore and New York after its original publication in an Atlanta magazine. It has been a favorite with anthologists, as a symbol of the union between his life and his art—a plea that he might live his poems if he could not write them. By the end of 1868 he had begun the study of law in his father's office in Macon, Georgia.

The next five years constitute a pathetic gap in Lanier's career as a poet. His difficulty in adjusting himself to necessity is reflected in his letters and in the only two serious poems of this period, "Nirvana" and "June Dreams, In January." Far more interesting to students of literature, and more relevant to Lanier's first major poem, are the verses in dialect he amused himself by writing during spare hours in the law office. They appeared at a time (1871) when the "Pike County" ballads of Bret Harte and John Hay had started something of a vogue, but it seems clear that Lanier hit upon this literary type independently. The distinguishing feature of his dialect poems is not their humor but their moral earnestness. Though he chose a light form, his theme was serious. The poems draw strength from their concern with the region Lanier knew and loved—the problems involved in the transition from cotton plantations to diversified farming—and so form a link between the earlier Reconstruction poems and his more exalted treatment of the same theme in "Corn." The best one, "Thar's More in the Man Than Thar Is in the Land," was reprinted in newspapers all over the country, and is included in the present volume. In all of them the portrayal of Cracker character and speech, which he had known since boyhood, is sharp and precise. But it is Lanier's grappling with realities in the world around him, a trait all too rare in his poetry, that gives these poems their importance for the modern reader.

During most of the Macon period (1868–1873), the struggle had been less between poetry and law than between law and health. After a particularly long and severe illness, which sent him to Texas for the winter, he took stock of his prospects. The bravery of his decision to launch himself in the precarious profession of an artist lay in the fact that it was based not upon the recovery of his health but, on the contrary, upon the realization of how few years he had left to live. The practical feature of his plan was that he should support himself by playing in an orchestra while he wrote his books. In December 1873 he began his career as first flute in the Peabody Orchestra of Baltimore. During that winter most of his energies were devoted to music.

Lanier's real career as a poet did not begin until the summer of 1874, when he returned to Georgia after the lonely months in Baltimore. His vision of the blighted South was now sharpened by the contrasting progress of his adopted city. Writing to a friend (October 9, 1874) of the genesis of "Corn," he said: "I have been struck with alarm, in seeing the numbers of deserted old homesteads and gullied hills in the older counties of Georgia." The earlier poems on this theme came back to him, but this time he desired to carry these same "prosaic matters up to a loftier plane." When he had chosen for the symbol of this tragedy the illiterate small farmer, his treatment had been comic. If he should now choose the old-school planter, it would be sentimental. Wisely, instead, he turned his eyes to the land itself. Taking his family to board during the summer at Sunnyside, just north of Macon, he was surrounded by farms whose prosperity had come from planting corn instead of the single traditional money-crop, cotton. Here then was the new life that could spring from the old soil. Lanier's best poems invariably came when he drew from deeply felt experiences to embody themes over which he had long brooded. Having determined the previous spring to break away from conventional poetic form, he chose now as his model the dignity of the Cowleyan ode and began experimenting in the direction of that musical irregularity that was to distinguish his best work. From his long devotion to Keats, and from his recent reading of Chaucer and Shakespeare, he drew the language and imagery needed to heighten his timely drama to one of universal significance. The result was the most original poem he had written.

When "Corn" appeared in the February 1875 issue of *Lippincott's Magazine* it was an immediate success, partly because of the sponsorship of Gibson Peacock, editor of the Philadelphia *Evening Bulletin*. From obscurity Lanier emerged into national prominence. During the next three years this magazine bought fifteen of his poems, at higher prices than he ever received elsewhere, gave him several good commissions for prose, and issued through its publisher a selected volume of his poetry. The house of Lippincott launched Lanier on his career.

Even more ambitious was the next important poem, "The Symphony," which also had its roots deep in his past. Its theme grew out of a much longer one, "The Jacquerie." This earlier poem was begun in 1868 at the time Lanier started studying law, was worked on for many years as his hopeful masterpiece, but was never finished. It was to be a novel in verse, based on a remarkable peasant uprising in fourteenth-century France, which he had read about in Froissart's *Chronicles* and Michelet's *Histoire de France*. He referred to it in a letter of November 15, 1874, as "the first time that the big hungers of *the People* appear in our modern civilization." The reason he abandoned his long-cherished narrative poem is made clear in this last significant reference to it. Though he seems in sympathy with the insurrection in which "Trade arose and overthrew Chivalry," the second half of his comment is directed against the deadening spirit of commercialism in his own day: "Thus in the reversals of time, it is *now* the *gentlemen* who must arise & overthrow Trade." His theme had shifted from the oppressed peasants of medieval France to the evils of materialism in modern America, the plight of the industrial and urban poor. So in a sense "The Symphony" was a revision of "The Jacquerie." And when he wrote to Peacock (March 24, 1875) that a new poem in which he discussed "various deep social questions of the times" had taken hold of him "like a real James River Ague," this must not be thought of as a spontaneous growth of the two months that had passed since the publication of "Corn." Like all his best work, it had been long maturing.

"The Symphony" is less a plea for a fairer distribution of the world's goods on socialistic principles than for a broader and deeper love of humanity, by which the poor may be given a larger life in nature and in art. Next to love, and making an equation with it, music was to Lanier the religion of the new age which would redeem it from trade, and "The Symphony" was his first major effort to relate the two arts between which his life was divided. Much of the imagery of the poem is drawn from his enthusiastic experiences as an orchestral player during the previous two seasons, though there is no attempt to parallel the structural design of a symphonic composition. Instead, this is a sort of counterpart to program music, as though the impression made on him by a symphony had been translated into words which would in turn re-create for the reader the original music. The experiment has the fascination and the hazards of all efforts to interpret one art in terms of another. "The Symphony" was Lanier's first deeply religious poem. It was also the first important American poem protesting against economic tyranny and the enslavement of the spirit by commercialism.

When "The Symphony" was published in *Lippincott's*, June 1875, several critics who praised its timeliness and originality linked it with "Corn," giving a cumulative lift to his reputation. And as the earlier poem had brought him acquaintance with the Baltimore *literati*, through the Wednesday Club of which he later became a member, so now the second brought him an invitation to the Century Club, where he met the intellectual and artistic leaders of New York. More important still were the personal relationships that resulted from the publication of these two poems—especially those with Gibson Peacock, his indefatigable sponsor, and Bayard Taylor, the best literary friend and critic he was ever to have. A true measure of this progress in the popular mind can be found in the casual aside in the New York *World*, June 7, 1875, describing him as "that new and happy singer, SIDNEY LANIER, [who] rapidly mounts the wave of recognition like a strong swimmer as he is." In the ears of one who, less than a year before, had begun his career completely unknown, this must have sounded pleasantly like fame.

Unfortunately, Lanier was not able at first to take full advantage of his success, for at this juncture one of his old enemies, the need of money, slowed down his creative activities. The second half of 1875 was spent writing a travel book on Florida, and as a result of this, other pot-boilers were offered him. The first half of 1876 was largely spent on two long poems, written on commission: "The Centennial Meditation of Columbia," the invitation coming through the good offices of Taylor, and "Psalm of the West," requested by the editor of *Lippincott's* for the special July 4th issue. The former, though it raised a storm of controversy at first, enhanced his reputation in the end. The latter (for which he was paid $300, the highest fee he ever got for a poem) consolidated his position as the leading author of his new publisher. Though they do not rank with his best poems, they kept him before the public and made the name of Sidney Lanier one to conjure with in American letters. If the Cantata was a song of reconciliation between South and North, the "Psalm" was a hymn of devotion to his country. Lanier was now a recognized poet, and a national rather than a sectional one.

The creative activity of these first years in Baltimore did not spend itself entirely in the composition of the long poems just discussed. In addition, Lanier wrote some twenty-five poems between 1874 and 1876, most of which found their way into the magazines—*Scribner's* and *Harper's,* as well as *Lippincott's.* In the midst of his work on "Psalm of the West" he wrote to a friend, March 20, 1876: "As for me, life has resolved simply into a time during which I want to get upon paper as many as possible of the poems with which my heart is stuffed like a schoolboy's pocket." And there was variety as well as quantity in the product of these years. Two of them were experiments in the portrayal of Negro character and dialect, written in collaboration with his brother Clifford. Two others dealt with the plight of the artist in the modern world. By far the greatest number were sonnets and short lyrics, celebrating his love for Mary Day Lanier. The finest of these was "Evening Song," written to be set to music by Dudley Buck, who had composed the score for his Cantata.

This is an appropriate time for a summing up in Lanier's career, as the end of 1876 marks a turning point. In November the firm of J. B. Lippincott issued a volume containing the ten poems that had appeared in their magazine during the past two years. For the first time, critics and reading public had an opportunity to survey his work in collected form. The volume seems to have had a small-to-normal sale; and for a first book of poems it had a fairly wide and generally favorable reception from the periodical press. Reviewers were almost unanimous in granting him a "rich poetic nature" and in speaking of him as "the most promising of our rising poets." Although "The Symphony" received considerable praise, "Corn" proved the favorite of the critics. With one accord they pointed to the subtropical luxurance of the deep South as the chief source of Lanier's strength, in both theme and style, and he was soon to prove them right in their diagnosis. But they qualified this praise by pointing

out the overrichness and obscurity, even in his best poems, resulting from
a want of discipline. His friend Bayard Taylor put a finger on the real
problem in a long *Tribune* article (November 21, 1876), declaring that
the author's "redundancy and apparent *abandon* to the starts and bolts of
Fancy" were in singular contrast to the maturity of his ideas: "But just
such technical splendors of poetry require the firmest hand, the finest ear,
the most delicate sense of art. It is still too soon to decide whether Mr.
Lanier's true course is to train or carefully prune this luxuriance." The
benefit Lanier derived from this advice is demonstrated in his major
poems of the next few years.

A week before the *Tribune* review appeared, in fact, Lanier had written
to Taylor (November 13), just as his *Poems* came from the press, that
he already felt himself entering a new period of development:

I can't tell you with what ravishing freedom and calmness I find myself
writing, in these days, nor how serene and sunny the poetic region seems
to lie, in front, like broad upland fields and slopes. . . . I hope to have
out another volume soon, of work which will show a much quieter technique than this one.

He failed to add that he was confined to his bed with an illness now entering its fifth month and daily growing more serious. The way in which
his recurring attacks coincide with his periods of greatest progress seems
like some malignant fate trying to rob him of his few pitiful moments of
success, until it becomes clear that excitement and overwork were almost
invariably the immediate causes. And in the present collapse of his health
another familiar old enemy had played a part—economic need and worry.
Anxious to realize his dream of establishing a permanent home, he had
brought his family north in June 1876. But the failure of two money-
making schemes on which he had relied left him in debt and with no
means of support. Stranded penniless at a farm in West Chester, Pennsylvania, his strength ebbed, he fell ill, and depression of spirit followed.
As illness and worry reacted on each other, his situation became desperate.
At last, just as the heartening reviews of his first volume of poems began
to come in, his physician ordered him to a warmer climate for the winter
as his only chance for life. With a gift from an anonymous friend he set
out for Florida, December 2, accompanied by his wife.

Lanier's resilience was as remarkable as his courage. Within less than
a month of his arrival in Tampa he wrote of his improvement (January
11, 1877), declaring: "I 'bubble song' continually during these heavenly
days, and it is as hard to keep me from my pen as a toper from his tipple."
Thus began the most prolific period of his entire career. The first two
poems he wrote in Florida form a pair: "The Stirrup-Cup," announcing
with quiet bravery his resignation to death if that is necessary, and

"Tampa Robins," voicing his intention to sing blithely while life remained. These were the beginning of a spray of songs which he sent out to the magazines, finding new vehicles in *Appleton's, Leslie's,* and the *Galaxy.* In this manner his name was kept before the public, his purse modestly replenished, and his spirit revived. Though none of the dozen poems that came out of his four months in Florida rank with his best, they are important as indications of considerable poetic creativity and of a new trend, growing out of a combination of two new influences, one from within and one from without.

As Lanier struggled back to life, the sunshine and profusion of this subtropical land began to vitalize his poetry as well. Here we find orange groves and robins, "bosky avenues" and mocking birds, bees rioting in the "huge nectary" of jessamine vines that wreathe the live-oaks, green parakeets, palm trees, and pelicans poised above the shallows. Here also are wide expanses of sky and sea on the sunny beaches, followed significantly by a yearning from the "drear sand-levels" back to the more familiar landscape of his native Georgia. Nature had figured in Lanier's writings from the beginning, largely in the etherealizing manner of Tennyson. But in Florida, as the world of eye and ear thronged upon his outward senses, it was informed with a new spirit that came from his discovery of a kindred author whom he had somehow missed all these years. It was Emerson who stung him fertile, to borrow a phrase from "The Bee," a poem whose setting comes from just such a personal experience of nature as those which abound in the essays and poems of his new teacher. From these he first became aware of the vast spiritual background of the sensuous world and of the essential kinship of each and all, which produced the religious tranquility of "A Florida Sunday," the best fruit of these months of convalescence. "Emerson, whom I have been reading all winter," he wrote to Taylor (May 25), "gives me immeasurable delight because he does not propound to me disagreeable systems and hideous creeds but simply walks along high and bright ways where one loves to go with him." And in discovering Emerson, he found himself as a poet. Lanier's true vein lay not in social protest, nor in celebrating the national spirit, nor even, except subordinately, in the marriage of music and words. It lay in his religious interpretation of nature. This was the most important thing that happened to him in Florida, though it was another year before he realized it in a memorable poem and one worthy of his great discovery.

Lanier returned to Baltimore in the fall of 1877 after an absence of eighteen months. His health was now considerably restored, and except for a few brief setbacks he was free from serious illness for the next two years. As as result, his life during this period was fuller of activity than usual, but with an unfortunate scattering of energies. Sorely disappointed in his several efforts to find permanent employment, notably a government clerkship in Washington, he finally abandoned hopes of earning an adequate living. Joined by his family, he settled down in Baltimore, resigned to making what sporadic income he could as musician, author, and lecturer—depending on aid from his father and brother for the rest. In the winter of 1877–1878 he resumed his old post as first flute in the Peabody Orchestra, began teaching in the local schools, and in the spring gave a series of lectures on literature at the Peabody Institute. He also squandered a great deal of time on hapless schemes for literary textbooks before hitting upon a series of books for boys that really helped to keep the pot boiling. Although he managed to write poems too, in the midst of this busy life, it is small wonder that out of a dozen composed between the spurt of creativity in Florida and the summer of 1878 only three are important. "The Harlequin of Dreams" was the best sonnet Lanier ever wrote, "Song of the Chattahoochee" his most anthologized lyric, and "The Revenge of Hamish" his first experiment in the running rhythm of logaoedic dactyls.

"Another freer treatment of the same rhythm by me," Lanier said modestly of "The Marshes of Glynn," ". . . reads well if a man understands the long roll of dactyls in which it is written" (letters of October 20 and December 21, 1878). This is one of the two or three finest poems he ever wrote, yet little is known of its composition except that it was his contribution to an anonymous anthology, *A Masque of Poets,* and that it was sent off "hot from the mint" on July 13, 1878. It would be ingenuous to think of "The Marshes of Glynn" as a perfunctory piece composed on order or an experiment to illustrate a prosodical theory. It is, instead, a product of the slow convergence of several forces that rank as the most important in his entire career as a poet. From scattered bits of evidence, its evolution can be traced over a period of about three years.

Lanier had been intimately acquainted with the coastal regions of Georgia for a long time. In a letter of April 18, 1875, for example, he speaks of it as an idyllic land for a battered soul, with its "unbroken forest of oaks, of all manner of clambering and twining things and of pines," its "divine atmosphere . . . unspeakably bland, bringing strange secrets rather of leaves than of flowers." His guide book *Florida* (1876) contains romantic descriptions of the moss-hung oaks and "manifold vine-growths," of the trees as religious symbols, offering a refuge from "the fever of the unrest of trade." The next winter in Tampa similar scenery filters into several poems written there. Again, fresh from reading Emerson, he jots down in a notebook his contemplations after a forest stroll when, in semimystical mood, he had begun to "glide out of the idea that this multiform beauty is familiar, that it is a clump of trees and vines and flowers." Tentatively he suggests that its real meaning is "Silence,"

"Mystery," "Revelation"—but his fumblings remained in prose. Emerson had sensitized him to the spiritual values in nature, but at that time Lanier lacked the serenity needed to produce the poem that was stirring within him, and the gestation period was long.

One reason Lanier was so late in discovering that he was primarily a religious poet was his concern over his own unorthodoxy. Doubts as to his beliefs appear from maturity on, and during the last decade of his life his attack on creeds grew to be a major issue. The contrasting orthodoxy of family and friends made him feel that he was without any religion. But the experiences of his winter in Florida touched the deeper springs of his transcendental longings, and it is in the marsh hymns that flowed from this that we first see the high priest of nature at his devotions. Yet Lanier was concerned with the music of poetry as well as with its spiritual meaning, and Emerson's halting rhythms could not give form to his vision. One more influence was necessary before he could fashion to his harp the rhapsodic chords of "The Marshes of Glynn."

In the winter of 1878 Lanier discovered for the first time the poetry of Walt Whitman. Writing on February 3 to Taylor, from whose library he had borrowed the volume, he declared:

LEAVES OF GRASS was a real refreshment to me—like rude salt spray in your face—in spite of its enormous fundamental error that a thing is good because it is natural, and in spite of the world-wide difference between my own conceptions of art and its author's.

Three months later, when his scant budget allowed him to purchase this coveted volume, he wrote to the Good Gray Poet revealing candidly the excitement of his discovery: "It is not known to me where I can find another modern song at once so large and so naive . . . , propounded in such strong and beautiful rhythms." Indeed, in spite of obvious differences between them, they had much in common, especially their interest in new and freer forms. Perhaps the greatest likeness is between Whitman's practice and Lanier's theory, as set forth in several radical suggestions for the extension of conventional rhythms in *The Science of English Verse.* But the rhythmic freedom of *Leaves of Grass* may have had some influence on the range and sweep of his experimental "Marshes of Glynn." Lanier was also a musician interested in the "colors" of verse, not only rhyme and alliteration but consonant-sequence and vowel-distribution, qualities he had admired in Tennyson and Swinburne. Out of all this came the orchestral effects he needed to give shape to his vision of religious values that he had found in the forests and marshes of the southern coast. In spite of the many influences that went into the making of "The Marshes of Glynn," it was essentially original, the poem of his aesthetic and spiritual maturity.

Lanier had found his true "church," and having sounded his prelude, he planned a whole book of hymns that would chant his new gospel. Neither the "Marshes" nor any of the hymns that followed served to advance his reputation during his lifetime. (The "Marshes" was buried in a "no-name" anthology of mediocre verse; and of the other hymns, all but one were published posthumously.) However, they were of the first importance in maturing him as an artist, and they are the foundation on which his fame must rest. The last three years of his life were subject to many interruptions—from work, illness, and the crossing of his purposes by new ideas he did not have time to assimilate. It is only in his recessional, "Sunrise," that all his powers of rhapsody again found adequate expression. His last important poem, it is the only real companion piece to "The Marshes of Glynn," and much that has been said of the one applies to the other.

Lanier's final illness, which continued through more than a year with mounting intensity, began in the second half of 1880. By December he was prostrated with a temperature of 104 degrees, yet it was while he lay all but extinguished with the fire of this fever that he penciled the faint script of "Sunrise." In spite of its beauty of phrase and rhythm it does not come up to the technical achievement of "The Marshes of Glynn." But even more than the earlier hymn, "Sunrise" is a summing up of Lanier as both man and poet. Here his courage in facing death has become triumphant acceptance; the social gospel of "The Symphony" has been transmuted into a chant for a better world, sung with the conviction of poetic vision rather than with the querulousness of the reformer; the adoration of nature has been exalted into unqualified worship of the sun as the divine source of life—and as the promise of immortality. For "Sunrise" is pagan only in its explicit language and imagery. The manuscripts now available make clear for the first time the poem's underlying Christianity, though it was a far cry from the current orthodoxy. Lanier created his own symbol for God, an original and daring one for that day, and he realized it grandly in "Sunrise."

That this major poem was never submitted to a publisher is explained by Lanier's intention of using it to lead off his projected book of "Hymns of the Marshes." He completed only one other long poem for this volume, "The Cloud," but this is a troubled poem and a labored one, belonging with the group that grew out of his reading in science and religion. Although there were no further hymns, there were shorter songs of the marshes, five of which were written out and a dozen more left in outline form. All of the finished ones are interesting, especially the two included in the present volume, "Marsh Song—At Sunset" and "A Ballad of Trees and the Master." The unfinished songs are mere brush strokes and musical notations to record fleeting impressions on eye and ear.

From 1879 to 1881 Lanier's life was harried in the extreme. He was seriously ill more than half the time. For the rest, his strength was sapped by manifold activities. In addition to schoolteaching and orchestra playing, he gave several long courses of lectures at Johns Hopkins University, edited *The Boy's Froissart* and three other juveniles, did a lot of hackwork for the magazines, and wrote *The Science of English Verse*—his only prose of lasting value. Though he managed to complete a half-dozen important poems in spite of this press of work, much of his writing during these last years is so fragmentary—memoranda for poems he never found time to finish—as to furnish only a hint of his direction. The fortunate survival of at least a dozen prose drafts later actually worked into poems indicates just how meaningful to the poet were jottings that show small promise to the reader. Lanier's plans for three projected volumes can now be sketched from the evidence of these surviving "Poem Outlines" (*Centennial Edition, I*, 251–284), supported by the few poems he completed in each category. The first was his "Hymns of the Marshes," now expanded to include the Fields and the Mountains, especially suggestive being the notations made at his camp in North Carolina during the final illness—his songs against death.

The religious tone of these reveals their connection with the second unfinished volume, "Credo and Other Poems," several actually bearing alternate titles. Though few of the outlines in this group approach true lyricism, the impact of scientific thought on Lanier was deeply significant, and if he had lived to resolve this discordant note the result might have been stronger if less harmonious music than the concord of his more confident songs. Like other intelligent Victorians he was swept into the controversy between science and religion, excited by the widening of the boundaries of the mind but disturbed by the doubts that were unsettling old beliefs. (For a full account of Lanier's part in this see the *Centennial Edition, I*, lxvi–lxxvi.) The half-dozen completed poems in this group, several of which are included in the present selection, are but a token of what might have followed. "Remonstrance," his attack on creeds, was rejected by *Lippincott's* specifically because of its unorthodoxy, which may explain why more of the poems planned for the "Credo" volume were never completed. "The Cloud," likewise rejected, is the result of his agonizing over what he took to be the implications of evolution for man, its halting rhythms echoing his confusion. "Opposition," the best of these poems, has an interesting history. In a lecture at the Peabody Institute in 1878 Lanier allowed himself a casual aside to announce a new concept that was stirring his imagination: "From the string stretched in one direction, plucked in another, to the world in space executing its rhythmic revolution . . . , OPPOSITION has revealed itself as underlying rhythm." The next year he expanded this into the most poetic chapter of

*The Science of English Verse*—"Rhythm in Nature"—citing Herbert
Spencer's *First Principles* as his authority, then adding: "Perhaps this
view may be made, without strain, to bind together even facts so remote
from each other as the physical and the moral . . . the fret, the sting, the
thwart, the irreconcilable me as against all other me's, the awful struggle
for existence . . . may also result in rhythm." This is one of Lanier's
most interesting contributions to critical theory. Better still it produced
one of his most interesting poems, "Opposition," his reconciliation of
science, art, and morals—if not religion.

"Opposition" also forms the connecting link between "Credo" and
the third volume of poems that Lanier left unfinished, the "Songs of
Aldhelm." This was to be a collection dealing with the theory and function of poetry, idealizing the old Saxon bishop as the type *poeta,* the
representative not only of poetic authority but of leadership among men.
Of the outlines for poems to go in this volume, two set the scene, with
the poet on a bridge at the edge of town importuning the merchants to
hear him. That Lanier intended to include in his "Songs of Aldhelm"
other poems already written on the same theme is proved by the fortunate
survival of printer's copy for yet another volume, hastily gathered together under the title of "Clover and Other Poems." Several in one
group, headed by "Street-Cries" which echoes the scene at the bridge,
seem like songs that could have been placed in the mouth of Aldhelm:
pleas for a leader in time of crisis, for the abolition of tyranny among men,
and so on. More successful as poems are three that set forth Lanier's
creed—that the poet's function is to serve men by bringing love, beauty,
and wisdom into their lives—"Clover," "The Bee," and "Song of the
Chattahoochee" (only the last of which is included here). In this ideal-
ism Lanier showed his kinship with the preceding generation, especially
Tennyson and Emerson. It was in quite a different direction that he
showed his kinship with the poetry of the future, that of technique—in
his theory, as set forth in *The Science of English Verse,* and to a lesser
extent in his practice, notably the experiments in sound effects that make
his longer poems unique.

More to the taste of modern readers than the orchestral rhapsodies of
the marsh hymns, perhaps, would have been that simpler music of which
there are hints in the subdued lament of "A Ballad of Trees and the
Master." This late poem, Lanier's most spontaneous lyrical utterance, is
in a sense an epitome of his religion and art. And because of its relationship to all three of the projected volumes it makes a fitting capstone to
this account of his poetic career. It is actually incorporated in one manuscript of "Sunrise," as an intercalary song, which shows that Lanier
thought of it as belonging with his "Hymns of the Marshes." That it
interprets the most significant episode of western religious history in a

way equally satisfying to orthodox and unorthodox, places it with "Credo and Other Poems." Its relation to the "Aldhelm" volume is that of practice to theory. For here is the conscious architecture of the musician-poet—its melody the product of a haunting refrain, of strong substantives, of adjectives few and quiet. If Lanier had lived longer he might have produced other examples of this new and simpler poetry.

Such is the story of the poet, to serve as an introduction to his poetry. The story of the man, told in his own words, will be found in the second half of this volume. The posthumously published *Poems* (1884), which contained all of his best work, also included an appreciative biographical sketch, so that for the first time the reading public could judge both the man and the poet. The heroic struggle of Lanier's life, his high moral purpose, and the nobility of his character won the sympathy of almost every reviewer, some even declaring that his life was greater than his poems. In the present selection of letters this story is told fully and movingly: Lanier's early years, set against the background of a South torn by war and broken by Reconstruction; his mature years, happily sharing in the cultural life of Baltimore and the northern cities; the pathos of his struggle to earn a living, to unite his scattered family, to realize his varied talents, to face down death. The purpose of the present volume is to present the poet and the man, each at his best.

POEMS

# Corn

To-day the woods are trembling through and through
With shimmering forms, that flash before my view,
Then melt in green as dawn-stars melt in blue.
The leaves that wave against my cheek caress
Like women's hands; the embracing boughs express
A subtlety of mighty tenderness;
The copse-depths into little noises start,
That sound anon like beatings of a heart,
Anon like talk 'twixt lips not far apart.
The beech dreams balm, as a dreamer hums a song;
Through that vague wafture, expirations strong
Throb from young hickories breathing deep and long
With stress and urgence bold of prisoned spring
And ecstasy of burgeoning.
Now, since the dew-plashed road of morn is dry,
Forth venture odors of more quality
And heavenlier giving. Like Jove's locks awry,
Long muscadines
Rich-wreathe the spacious foreheads of great pines,
And breathe ambrosial passion from their vines.
I pray with mosses, ferns and flowers shy
That hide like gentle nuns from human eye
To lift adoring perfumes to the sky.
I hear faint bridal-sighs of brown and green
Dying to silent hints of kisses keen
As far lights fringe into a pleasant sheen.
I start at fragmentary whispers, blown
From undertalks of leafy souls unknown,
Vague purports sweet, of inarticulate tone.

Dreaming of gods, men, nuns and brides, between
Old companies of oaks that inward lean
To join their radiant amplitudes of green
I slowly move, with ranging looks that pass
Up from the matted miracles of grass

19

Into yon veined complex of space
Where sky and leafage interlace
So close, the heaven of blue is seen
Inwoven with a heaven of green.

I wander to the zigzag-cornered fence
Where sassafras, intrenched in brambles dense,
Contests with stolid vehemence
    The march of culture, setting limb and thorn
As pikes against the army of the corn.

There, while I pause, my fieldward-faring eyes
Take harvests, where the stately corn-ranks rise,
    Of inward dignities
And large benignities and insights wise,
    Graces and modest majesties.
Thus, without theft, I reap another's field;
Thus, without tilth, I house a wondrous yield,
And heap my heart with quintuple crops concealed.

Look, out of line one tall corn-captain stands
Advanced beyond the foremost of his bands,
    And waves his blades upon the very edge
    And hottest thicket of the battling hedge.
Thou lustrous stalk, that ne'er mayst walk nor talk,
    Still shalt thou type the poet-soul sublime
    That leads the vanward of his timid time
    And sings up cowards with commanding rhyme—

Soul calm, like thee, yet fain, like thee, to grow
By double increment, above, below;
    Soul homely, as thou art, yet rich in grace like thee,
    Teaching the yeomen selfless chivalry
    That moves in gentle curves of courtesy;
Soul filled like thy long veins with sweetness tense,
    By every godlike sense
Transmuted from the four wild elements.
    Drawn to high plans,
    Thou lift'st more stature than a mortal man's,
Yet ever piercest downward in the mould
    And keepest hold

Upon the reverend and steadfast earth
            That gave thee birth;
Yea, standest smiling in thy future grave,
            Serene and brave,
With unremitting breath
Inhaling life from death,
Thine epitaph writ fair in fruitage eloquent,
            Thyself thy monument.

            As poets should,
Thou hast built up thy hardihood
With universal food,
      Drawn in select proportion fair
      From honest mould and vagabond air;
From darkness of the dreadful night,
            And joyful light;
      From antique ashes, whose departed flame
      In thee has finer life and longer fame;
From wounds and balms,
From storms and calms,
From potsherds and dry bones
            And ruin-stones.

Into thy vigorous substance thou hast wrought
Whate'er the hand of Circumstance hath brought;
      Yea, into cool solacing green hast spun
      White radiance hot from out the sun.
So thou dost mutually leaven
Strength of earth with grace of heaven;
      So thou dost marry new and old
      Into a one of higher mould;
      So thou dost reconcile the hot and cold,
            The dark and bright,
And many a heart-perplexing opposite,
            And so,
      Akin by blood to high and low,
Fitly thou playest out thy poet's part,
Richly expending thy much-bruisèd heart
      In equal care to nourish lord in hall
            Or beast in stall:
Thou took'st from all that thou might'st give to all.

O steadfast dweller on the selfsame spot
Where thou wast born, that still repinest not—
Type of the home-fond heart, the happy lot!—
     Deeply thy mild content rebukes the land
     Whose flimsy homes, built on the shifting sand
Of trade, for ever rise and fall
With alternation whimsical,
     Enduring scarce a day,
     Then swept away
By swift engulfments of incalculable tides
Whereon capricious Commerce rides.

Look, thou substantial spirit of content!
Across this little vale, thy continent,
     To where, beyond the mouldering mill,
     Yon old deserted Georgian hill
Bares to the sun his piteous aged crest
          And seamy breast,
     By restless-hearted children left to lie
     Untended there beneath the heedless sky,
     As barbarous folk expose their old to die.
Upon that generous-rounding side,
          With gullies scarified
     Where keen Neglect his lash hath plied,
Dwelt one I knew of old, who played at toil,
And gave to coquette Cotton soul and soil.
     Scorning the slow reward of patient grain,
     He sowed his heart with hopes of swifter gain,
     Then sat him down and waited for the rain.
He sailed in borrowed ships of usury—
A foolish Jason on a treacherous sea,
Seeking the Fleece and finding misery.
     Lulled by smooth-rippling loans, in idle trance
     He lay, content that unthrift Circumstance
     Should plough for him the stony field of Chance.
Yea, gathering crops whose worth no man might tell,
He staked his life on games of Buy-and-Sell,
And turned each field into a gambler's hell.
     Aye, as each year began,
     My farmer to the neighboring city ran;

Passed with a mournful anxious face
Into the banker's inner place;
Parleyed, excused, pleaded for longer grace;
  Railed at the drought, the worm, the rust, the grass;
  Protested ne'er again 'twould come to pass;
  With many an *oh* and *if* and *but alas*
Parried or swallowed searching questions rude,
And kissed the dust to soften Dives's mood.
At last, small loans by pledges great renewed,
  He issues smiling from the fatal door,
  And buys with lavish hand his yearly store
  Till his small borrowings will yield no more.
Aye, as each year declined,
With bitter heart and ever-brooding mind
He mourned his fate unkind.
  In dust, in rain, with might and main,
  He nursed his cotton, cursed his grain,
  Fretted for news that made him fret again,
Snatched at each telegram of Future Sale,
And thrilled with Bulls' or Bears' alternate wail—
In hope or fear alike for ever pale.
  And thus from year to year, through hope and fear,
  With many a curse and many a secret tear,
  Striving in vain his cloud of debt to clear,
      At last
He woke to find his foolish dreaming past,
  And all his best-of-life the easy prey
  Of squandering scamps and quacks that lined his way
    With vile array,
From rascal statesman down to petty knave;
Himself, at best, for all his bragging brave,
A gamester's catspaw and a banker's slave.
  Then, worn and gray, and sick with deep unrest,
  He fled away into the oblivious West,
    Unmourned, unblest.

Old hill! old hill! thou gashed and hairy Lear
Whom the divine Cordelia of the year,
E'en pitying Spring, will vainly strive to cheer—
  King, that no subject man nor beast may own,
  Discrowned, undaughtered and alone—

Yet shall the great God turn thy fate,
And bring thee back into thy monarch state
   And majesty immaculate.
Lo, through hot waverings of the August morn,
  Thou givest from thy vasty sides forlorn
  Visions of golden treasuries of corn—
Ripe largesse lingering for some bolder heart
That manfully shall take thy part,
   And tend thee,
   And defend thee,
With antique sinew and with modern art.

1874                                                    *1875*

## The Symphony

" O Trade! O Trade! would thou wert dead!
The Time needs heart—'tis tired of head:
We're all for love," the violins said.
" Of what avail the rigorous tale
Of bill for coin and box for bale?
Grant thee, O Trade! thine uttermost hope:
Level red gold with blue sky-slope,
And base it deep as devils grope:
When all's done, what hast thou won
Of the only sweet that's under the sun?
Ay, canst thou buy a single sigh
Of true love's least, least ecstasy? "
Then, with a bridegroom's heart-beats trembling,
All the mightier strings assembling
Ranged them on the violins' side
As when the bridegroom leads the bride,
And, heart in voice, together cried:
" Yea, what avail the endless tale
Of gain by cunning and plus by sale?
Look up the land, look down the land—
The poor, the poor, the poor, they stand

Wedged by the pressing of Trade's hand
Against an inward-opening door
That pressure tightens evermore:
They sigh a monstrous foul-air sigh
For the outside leagues of liberty,
Where Art, sweet lark, translates the sky
Into a heavenly melody.
' Each day, all day ' (these poor folks say),
' In the same old year-long, drear-long way,
We weave in the mills and heave in the kilns,
We sieve mine-meshes under the hills,
And thieve much gold from the Devil's bank tills,
To relieve, O God, what manner of ills?—
The beasts, they hunger, and eat, and die;
And so do we, and the world's a sty;
Hush, fellow-swine: why nuzzle and cry?
*Swinehood hath no remedy*
Say many men, and hasten by,
Clamping the nose and blinking the eye.
But who said once, in the lordly tone,
*Man shall not live by bread alone*
*But all that cometh from the Throne?*
    Hath God said so?
    But Trade saith *No*:
And the kilns and the curt-tongued mills say *Go*:
*There's plenty that can, if you can't: we know.*
*Move out, if you think you're underpaid.*
*The poor are prolific; we're not afraid;*
    *Trade is trade.' "*
Thereat this passionate protesting
    Meekly changed, and softened till
It sank to sad requesting
    And suggesting sadder still:
" And oh, if men might some time see
How piteous-false the poor decree
That trade no more than trade must be!
Does business mean, *Die, you—live, I?*
Then ' Trade is trade ' but sings a lie:
'Tis only war grown miserly.
If business is battle, name it so:

War-crimes less will shame it so,
And widows less will blame it so.
Alas: for the poor to have some part
In yon sweet living lands of Art,
Makes problem not for head, but heart.
Vainly might Plato's brain revolve it:
Plainly the heart of a child could solve it."

And then, as when from words that seem but rude
We pass to silent pain that sits abrood
Back in our heart's great dark and solitude,
So sank the strings to gentle throbbing
Of long chords change-marked with sobbing—
Motherly sobbing, not distinctlier heard
Than half wing-openings of the sleeping bird,
Some dream of danger to her young hath stirred.

Then stirring and demurring ceased, and lo!
Every least ripple of the strings' song-flow
Died to a level with each level bow
And made a great chord tranquil-surfaced so,
As a brook beneath his curving bank doth go
To linger in the sacred dark and green
Where many boughs the still pool overlean
And many leaves make shadow with their sheen.
  But presently
A velvet flute-note fell down pleasantly
Upon the bosom of that harmony,
And sailed and sailed incessantly,
As if a petal from a wild-rose blown
Had fluttered down upon that pool of tone
And boatwise dropped o' the convex side
And floated down the glassy tide
And clarified and glorified
The solemn spaces where the shadows bide.
From the warm concave of that fluted note
Somewhat, half song, half odor, forth did float,
As if a rose might somehow be a throat:
" When Nature from her far-off glen
Flutes her soft messages to men,

The flute can say them o'er again;
Yea, Nature, singing sweet and lone,
Breathes through life's strident polyphone
The flute-voice in the world of tone.
     Sweet friends,
       Man's love ascends
     To finer and diviner ends
     Than man's mere thought e'er comprehends.
     For I, e'en I,
       As here I lie,
     A petal on a harmony,
Demand of Science whence and why
Man's tender pain, man's inward cry,
When he doth gaze on earth and sky?
     I am not overbold:
       I hold
     Full powers from Nature manifold.
I speak for each no-tonguèd tree
That, spring by spring, doth nobler be,
And dumbly and most wistfully
His mighty prayerful arms outspreads
Above men's oft-unheeding heads,
And his big blessing downward sheds.
I speak for all-shaped blooms and leaves,
Lichens on stones and moss on eaves,
Grasses and grains in ranks and sheaves;
Broad-fronded ferns and keen-leaved canes,
And briery mazes bounding lanes,
And marsh-plants, thirsty-cupped for rains,
And milky stems and sugary veins;
For every long-armed woman-vine
That round a piteous tree doth twine;
For passionate odors, and divine
Pistils, and petals crystalline;
All purities of shady springs,
All shynesses of film-winged things
That fly from tree-trunks and bark-rings;
All modesties of mountain-fawns
That leap to covert from wild lawns,
And tremble if the day but dawns;

All sparklings of small beady eyes
Of birds, and sidelong glances wise
Wherewith the jay hints tragedies;
All piquancies of prickly burs,
And smoothnesses of downs and furs
Of eiders and of minevers;
All limpid honeys that do lie
At stamen-bases, nor deny
The humming-birds' fine roguery,
Bee-thighs, nor any butterfly;
All gracious curves of slender wings,
Bark-mottlings, fibre-spiralings,
Fern-wavings and leaf-flickerings;
Each dial-marked leaf and flower-bell
Wherewith in every lonesome dell
Time to himself his hours doth tell;
All tree-sounds, rustlings of pine-cones,
Wind-sighings, doves' melodious moans,
And night's unearthly under-tones;
All placid lakes and waveless deeps,
All cool reposing mountain-steeps,
Vale-calms and tranquil lotos-sleeps;—
Yea, all fair forms, and sounds, and lights,
And warmths, and mysteries, and mights,
Of Nature's utmost depths and heights,
—These doth my timid tongue present,
Their mouthpiece and leal instrument
And servant, all love-eloquent.
I heard, when 'All for love' the violins cried:
So, Nature calls through all her system wide,
Give me thy love, O man, so long denied.
Much time is run, and man hath changed his ways,
Since Nature, in the antique fable-days,
Was hid from man's true love by proxy fays,
False fauns and rascal gods that stole her praise.
The nymphs, cold creatures of man's colder brain,
Chilled Nature's streams till man's warm heart was fain
Never to lave its love in them again.
Later, a sweet Voice Love thy neighbor said;

Then first the bounds of neighborhood outspread
Beyond all confines of old ethnic dread.
Vainly the Jew might wag his covenant head:
' *All men are neighbors,*' so the sweet Voice said.
So, when man's arms had circled all man's race,
The liberal compass of his warm embrace
Stretched bigger yet in the dark bounds of space;
With hands a-grope he felt smooth Nature's grace,
Drew her to breast and kissed her sweetheart face:
Yea man found neighbors in great hills and trees
And streams and clouds and suns and birds and bees,
And throbbed with neighbor-loves in loving these.
But oh, the poor! the poor! the poor!
That stand by the inward-opening door
Trade's hand doth tighten ever more,
And sigh their monstrous foul-air sigh
For the outside hills of liberty,
Where Nature spreads her wild blue sky
For Art to make into melody!
Thou Trade! thou king of the modern days!
    Change thy ways,
    Change thy ways;
Let the sweaty laborers file
    A little while,
    A little while,
Where Art and Nature sing and smile.
Trade! is thy heart all dead, all dead?
And hast thou nothing but a head?
I'm all for heart," the flute-voice said,
And into sudden silence fled,
Like as a blush that while 'tis red
Dies to a still, still white instead.

    Thereto a thrilling calm succeeds,
Till presently the silence breeds
A little breeze among the reeds
That seems to blow by sea-marsh weeds:
Then from the gentle stir and fret
Sings out the melting clarionet,

Like as a lady sings while yet
Her eyes with salty tears are wet.
" O Trade! O Trade! " the Lady said,
" I too will wish thee utterly dead
If all thy heart is in thy head.
For O my God! and O my God!
What shameful ways have women trod
At beckoning of Trade's golden rod!
Alas when sighs are traders' lies,
And heart's-ease eyes and violet eyes
      Are merchandise!
O purchased lips that kiss with pain!
O cheeks coin-spotted with smirch and stain!
O trafficked hearts that break in twain!
—And yet what wonder at my sisters' crime?
So hath Trade withered up Love's sinewy prime,.
Men love not women as in olden time.
Ah, not in these cold merchantable days
Deem men their life an opal gray, where plays
The one red Sweet of gracious ladies'-praise.
Now, comes a suitor with sharp prying eye—
Says, *Here, you Lady, if you'll sell, I'll buy:*
*Come, heart for heart—a trade? What! weeping? why?*
Shame on such wooers' dapper mercery!
I would my lover kneeling at my feet
In humble manliness should cry, *O sweet!*
*I know not if thy heart my heart will greet:*
*I ask not if thy love my love can meet:*
*Whate'er thy worshipful soft tongue shall say,*
*I'll kiss thine answer, be it yea or nay:*
*I do but know I love thee, and I pray*
*To be thy knight until my dying day.*
Woe him that cunning trades in hearts contrives!
Base love good women to base loving drives.
If men loved larger, larger were our lives;
And wooed they nobler, won they nobler wives."

There thrust the bold straightforward horn
To battle for that lady lorn,

With heartsome voice of mellow scorn,
Like any knight in knigthood's morn.
 " Now comfort thee," said he,
   " Fair Lady.
For God shall right thy grievous wrong,
And man shall sing thee a true-love song,
Voiced in act his whole life long,
   Yea, all thy sweet life long,
     Fair Lady.
Where's he that craftily hath said,
The day of chivalry is dead?
I'll prove that lie upon his head,
   Or I will die instead,
     Fair Lady.
Is Honor gone into his grave?
Hath Faith become a caitiff knave,
And Selfhood turned into a slave
   To work in Mammon's Cave,
     Fair Lady?
Will Truth's long blade ne'er gleam again?
Hath Giant Trade in dungeons slain
All great contempts of mean-got gain
   And hates of inward stain,
     Fair Lady?
For aye shall name and fame be sold,
And place be hugged for the sake of gold,
And smirch-robed Justice feebly scold
   At Crime all money-bold,
     Fair Lady?
Shall self-wrapt husbands aye forget
Kiss-pardons for the daily fret
Wherewith sweet wifely eyes are wet—
   Blind to lips kiss-wise set—
     Fair Lady?
Shall lovers higgle, heart for heart,
Till wooing grows a trading mart
Where much for little, and all for part,
   Make love a cheapening art,
     Fair Lady?

Shall woman scorch for a single sin
That her betrayer can revel in,
And she be burnt, and he but grin
    When that the flames begin,
        Fair Lady?
Shall ne'er prevail the woman's plea,
*We maids would far, far whiter be*
*If that our eyes might sometimes see*
    *Men maids in purity,*
        Fair Lady?
Shall Trade aye salve his conscience-aches
With jibes at Chivalry's old mistakes—
The wars that o'erhot knighthood makes
    For Christ's and ladies' sakes,
        Fair Lady?
Now by each knight that e'er hath prayed
To fight like a man and love like a maid,
Since Pembroke's life, as Pembroke's blade,
    I' the scabbard, death, was laid,
        Fair Lady,
I dare avouch my faith is bright
That God doth right and God hath might,
Nor time hath changed His hair to white,
    Nor His dear love to spite,
        Fair Lady.
I doubt no doubts: I strive, and shrive my clay,
And fight my fight in the patient modern way
For true love and for thee—ah me! and pray
    To be thy knight until my dying day,
        Fair Lady."
Made end that knightly horn, and spurred away
Into the thick of the melodious fray.


And then the hautboy played and smiled,
And sang like any large-eyed child,
Cool-hearted and all undefiled.
    "Huge Trade!" he said,
    "Would thou wouldst lift me on thy head,
And run where'er my finger led!
Once said a Man—and wise was He—

*Never shalt thou the heavens see,*
*Save as a little child thou be."*
Then o'er sea-lashings of commingling tunes
The ancient wise bassoons,
   Like weird
   Gray-beard
Old harpers sitting on the high sea-dunes,
   Chanted runes:
" Bright-waved gain, gray waved loss,
The sea of all doth lash and toss,
One wave forward and one across:
But now 'twas trough, now 'tis crest,
And worst doth foam and flash to best,
   And curst to blest.

" Life Life! thou sea-fugue, writ from east to west,
   Love, Love alone can pore
   On thy dissolving score
   Of harsh half-phrasings,
     Blotted ere writ,
   And double erasings
     Of chords most fit.
Yea, Love, sole music-master blest,
May read thy weltering palimpsest.
To follow Time's dying melodies through,
And never to lose the old in the new,
And ever to solve the discords true—
   Love alone can do.
And ever Love hears the poor-folks' crying,
And ever Love hears the women's sighing,
And ever sweet knighthood's death-defying,
And ever wise childhood's deep implying,
But never a trader's glozing and lying.

" And yet shall Love himself be heard,
Though long deferred, though long deferred:
O'er the modern waste a dove hath whirred:
Music is Love in search of a word."

1875                                              *1875*

# Evening Song

Look off, dear Love, across the sallow sands,
  And mark yon meeting of the sun and sea;
How long they kiss, in sight of all the lands!
    Ah, longer, longer, we.

Now in the sea's red vintage melts the sun,
  As Egypt's pearl dissolved in rosy wine,
And Cleopatra Night drinks all. 'Tis done!
    Love, lay thine hand in mine.

Come forth, sweet stars, and comfort Heaven's heart;
  Glimmer, ye waves, round else unlighted sands;
O Night, divorce our sun and sky apart—
    Never our lips, our hands.

1876                                         *1877*

# The Stirrup-Cup

Death, thou'rt a cordial old and rare:
Look how compounded, with what care!
Time got his wrinkles reaping thee
Sweet herbs from all antiquity.

David to thy distillage went,
Keats, and Gotama excellent,
Omar Khayyám, and Chaucer bright,
And Shakspere for a king-delight.

Then, Time, let not a drop be spilt:
Hand me the cup whene'er thou wilt;
'Tis thy rich stirrup-cup to me;
I'll drink it down right smilingly.

1877                                         *1877*

## Tampa Robins

The robin laughed in the orange-tree:
" Ho, windy North, a fig for thee:
While breasts are red and wings are bold
And green trees wave us globes of gold,
Time's scythe shall reap but bliss for me
—Sunlight, song, and the orange-tree.

" Burn, golden globes in leafy sky,
My orange-planets: crimson, I
Will shine and shoot among the spheres
(Blithe meteor that no mortal fears)
And thrid the heavenly orange-tree
With orbits bright of minstrelsy.

" If that I hate wild winter's spite—
The gibbet trees, the world in white,
The sky but gray wind over a grave—
Why should I ache, the season's slave?
I'll sing from the top of the orange-tree
*Gramercy, winter's tyranny.*

" I'll south with the sun, and keep my clime;
My wing is king of the summer-time;
My breast to the sun his torch shall hold;
And I'll call down through the green and gold
*Time, take thy scythe, reap bliss for me,*
*Bestir thee under the orange-tree.*"

1877                                    *1877*


## A Florida Sunday

From cold Norse caves or buccaneer Southern seas
    Oft come repenting tempests here to die;
Bewailing old-time wrecks and robberies,
    They shrive to priestly pines with many a sigh,
Breathe salutary balms through lank-lock'd hair
    Of sick men's heads, and soon—this world outworn—
Sink into saintly heavens of stirless air,
    Clean from confessional. One died, this morn,

And willed the world to wise Queen Tranquil: she,
    Sweet sovereign Lady of all souls that bide
In contemplation, tames the too bright skies
    Like that faint agate film, far down descried,
Restraining suns in sudden thoughtful eyes
    Which flashed but now.  Blest distillation rare
Of o'er-rank brightness filtered waterwise
    Through all the earths in heaven—thou always fair,
Still virgin bride of e'er-creating thought—
Dream-worker, in whose dream the Future's wrought—
Healer of hurts, free balm for bitter wrongs—
Most silent mother of all sounding songs—
Thou that dissolvest hells to make thy heaven—
Thou tempest's heir, that keep'st no tempest leaven—
But after winds' and thunders' wide mischance
Dost brood, and better thine inheritance—
Thou privacy of space, where each grave Star
As in his own still chamber sits afar
To meditate, yet, by thy walls unpent,
Shines to his fellows o'er the firmament—
Oh! as thou liv'st in all this sky and sea
That likewise lovingly do live in thee,
So melt my soul in thee, and thine in me,
Divine Tranquillity!


Gray Pelican, poised where yon broad shallows shine,
Know'st thou, that finny foison all is mine
In the bag below thy beak—yet thine, not less?
For God, of His most gracious friendliness,
Hath wrought that every soul, this loving morn,
Into all things may be new-corporate born,
And each live whole in all: I sail with thee,
Thy Pelican's self is mine; yea, silver Sea,
In this large moment all thy fishes, ripples, bights,
Pale in-shore greens and distant blue delights,
White visionary sails, long reaches fair
By moon-horn'd strands that film the far-off air,
Bright sparkle-revelations, secret majesties,
Shells, wrecks and wealths, are mine; yea, Orange-trees,

That lift your small world-systems in the light,
Rich sets of round green heavens studded bright
With globes of fruit that like still planets shine,
Mine is your green-gold universe; yea, mine,
White slender Lighthouse fainting to the eye
That wait'st on yon keen cape-point wistfully,
Like to some maiden spirit pausing pale,
New-wing'd, yet fain to sail
Above the serene Gulf to where a bridegroom soul
Calls o'er the soft horizon—mine thy dole
Of shut undaring wings and wan desire—
Mine, too, thy later hope and heavenly fire
Of kindling expectation; yea, all sights,
All sounds, that make this morn—quick flights
Of pea-green paroquets 'twixt neighbor trees,
Like missives and sweet morning inquiries
From green to green, in green—live oaks' round heads,
Busy with jays for thoughts—grays, whites and reds
Of pranked woodpeckers that ne'er gossip out,
But alway tap at doors and gad about—
Robins and mocking-birds that all day long
Athwart straight sunshine weave cross-threads of song,
Shuttles of music—clouds of mosses gray
That rain me rains of pleasant thoughts alway
From a low sky of leaves—faint yearning psalms
Of endless metre breathing through the palms
That crowd and lean and gaze from off the shore
Ever for one that cometh nevermore—
Palmettos ranked, with childish spear-points set
Against no enemy—rich cones that fret
High roofs of temples shafted tall with pines—
Green, grateful mangroves where the sand-beach shines—
Long lissom coast that in and outward swerves,
The grace of God made manifest in curves—
All riches, goods and braveries never told
Of earth, sun, air and heaven—now I hold
Your being in my being; I am ye,
And ye myself; yea, lastly, Thee,
God, whom my roads all reach, howe'er they run,
My Father, Friend, Belovèd, dear All-One,

Thee in my soul, my soul in Thee, I feel,
Self of my self. Lo, through my sense doth steal
Clear cognizance of all selves and qualities,
Of all existence that hath been or is,
Of all strange haps that men miscall of chance,
And all the works of tireless circumstance:
Each borders each, like mutual sea and shore,
Nor aught misfits his neighbor that's before,
Nor him that's after—nay, through this still air,
Out of the North come quarrels, and keen blare
Of challenge by the hot-breath'd parties blown;
Yet break they not this peace with alien tone,
Fray not my heart, nor fright me for my land,
—I hear from all-wards, allwise understand,
The great bird Purpose bears me twixt her wings,
And I am one with all the kinsmen things
That e'er my Father fathered. Oh, to me
All questions solve in this tranquillity:
E'en this dark matter, once so dim, so drear,
Now shines upon my spirit heavenly-clear:
Thou, Father, without logic, tellest me
How this divine denial true may be,
—How *All's in each, yet every one of all*
*Maintains his Self complete and several.*

1877                                    *1877*


# From the Flats

What heartache—ne'er a hill!
Inexorable, vapid, vague, and chill
The drear sand-levels drain my spirit low.
With one poor word they tell me all they know;
Whereat their stupid tongues, to tease my pain,
Do drawl it o'er again and o'er again.
They hurt my heart with griefs I cannot name:
  Always the same, the same.

Nature hath no surprise,
No ambuscade of beauty 'gainst mine eyes
From brake or lurking dell or deep defile;
No humors, frolic forms—this mile, that mile;
No rich reserves or happy-valley hopes
Beyond the bends of roads, the distant slopes.
Her fancy fails, her wild is all run tame:
Ever the same, the same.

Oh, might I through these tears
But glimpse some hill my Georgia high uprears,
Where white the quartz and pink the pebble shine,
The hickory heavenward strives, the muscadine
Swings o'er the slope, the oak's far-falling shade
Darkens the dogwood in the bottom glade,
And down the hollow from a ferny nook
Bright leaps a living brook!

1877                                    *1877*


## The Mocking Bird

Superb and sole, upon a plumèd spray
    That o'er the general leafage boldly grew,
    He summ'd the woods in song; or typic drew
The watch of hungry hawks, the lone dismay
Of languid doves when long their lovers stray,
    And all birds' passion-plays that sprinkle dew
    At morn in brake or bosky avenue.
Whate'er birds did or dreamed, this bird could say.
Then down he shot, bounced airily along
The sward, twitched-in a grasshopper, made song
    Midflight, perched, primped, and to his art again.
    Sweet Science, this large riddle read me plain:
        How may the death of that dull insect be
        The life of yon trim Shakspere on the tree?

1877                                    *1877*

# Song of the Chattahoochee

Out of the hills of Habersham,
    Down the valleys of Hall,
I hurry amain to reach the plain,
Run the rapid and leap the fall,
Split at the rock and together again,
Accept my bed, or narrow or wide,
And flee from folly on every side
With a lover's pain to attain the plain
    Far from the hills of Habersham,
    Far from the valleys of Hall.

All down the hills of Habersham,
    All through the valleys of Hall,
The rushes cried *Abide, abide,*
The willful waterweeds held me thrall,
The laving laurel turned my tide,
The ferns and the fondling grass said *Stay,*
The dewberry dipped for to work delay,
And the little reeds sighed *Abide, abide,*
    *Here in the hills of Habersham,*
    *Here in the valleys of Hall.*

High o'er the hills of Habersham,
    Veiling the valleys of Hall,
The hickory told me manifold
Fair tales of shade, the poplar tall
Wrought me her shadowy self to hold,
The chestnut, the oak, the walnut, the pine,
Overleaning, with flickering meaning and sign,
Said, *Pass not, so cold, these manifold*
    *Deep shades of the hills of Habersham,*
    *These glades in the valleys of Hall.*

And oft in the hills of Habersham,
    And oft in the valleys of Hall,
The white quartz shone, and the smooth brook-stone
Did bar me of passage with friendly brawl,

And many a luminous jewel lone
—Crystals clear or a-cloud with mist,
Ruby, garnet and amethyst—
Made lures with the lights of streaming stone
   In the clefts of the hills of Habersham,
   In the beds of the valleys of Hall.

   But oh, not the hills of Habersham,
   And oh, not the valleys of Hall
Avail: I am fain for to water the plain.
Downward the voices of Duty call—
Downward, to toil and be mixed with the main,
The dry fields burn, and the mills are to turn,
And a myriad flowers mortally yearn,
And the lordly main from beyond the plain
   Calls o'er the hills of Habersham,
   Calls through the valleys of Hall.

1877                                    *1877?, 1883*


## The Harlequin of Dreams

Swift through some trap mine eyes have never found,
   Dim-panelled in the painted scene of sleep,
   Thou, giant Harlequin of Dreams, dost leap
Upon my spirit's stage. Then sight and sound,
Then space and time, then language, mete and bound,
   And all familiar forms that firmly keep
   Man's reason in the road, change faces, peep
Betwixt the legs, and mock the daily round.
Yet thou canst more than mock: sometimes my tears
   At midnight break through bounden lids—a sign
   Thou hast a heart; and oft thy little leaven
Of dream-taught wisdom works me bettered years.
   In one night witch, saint, trickster, fool divine,
     I think thou'rt Jester at the Court of Heaven!

1878?                                    *1878*

## The Revenge of Hamish

It was three slim does and a ten-tined buck in the bracken lay;
　And all of a sudden the sinister smell of a man,
　Awaft on a wind-shift, wavered and ran
Down the hill-side and sifted along through the bracken and
　passed that way.

Then Nan got a-tremble at nostril; she was the daintiest doe;
　In the print of her velvet flank on the velvet fern
　She reared, and rounded her ears in turn.
Then the buck leapt up, and his head as a king's to a crown
　did go

Full high in the breeze, and he stood as if Death had the form
　of a deer;
　And the two slim does full lazily stretching arose,
　For their day-dream slowlier came to a close,
Till they woke and were still, breath-bound with waiting and
　wonder and fear.

Then Alan the huntsman sprang over the hillock, the hounds
　shot by,
　The does and the ten-tined buck made a marvellous bound,
　The hounds swept after with never a sound,
But Alan loud winded his horn, in sign that the quarry was nigh.

For at dawn of that day proud Maclean of Lochbuy to the hunt
　had waxed wild,
　And he cursed at old Alan till Alan fared off with the hounds
　For to drive him the deer to the lower glen-grounds:
" I will kill a red deer," quoth Maclean, " in the sight of the
　wife and the child."

So gayly he paced with the wife and the child to his chosen
　stand;
　But he hurried tall Hamish the henchman ahead: " Go
　turn,"—
　Cried Maclean—" if the deer seek to cross to the burn,
Do thou turn them to me: nor fail, lest thy back be red as thy
　hand."

Now hard-fortuned Hamish, half blown of his breath with the
    height of the hill,
    Was white in the face when the ten-tined buck and the does
    Drew leaping to burn-ward; huskily rose
His shouts, and his nether lip twitched, and his legs were o'er-
    weak for his will.

So the deer darted lightly by Hamish and bounded away to the
    burn.
    But Maclean never bating his watch tarried waiting below
    Still Hamish hung heavy with fear for to go
All the space of an hour; then he went, and his face was
    greenish and stern,

And his eye sat back in the socket, and shrunken the eyeballs
    shone,
    As withdrawn from a vision of deeds it were shame to see.
    " Now, now, grim henchman, what is't with thee? "
Brake Maclean, and his wrath rose red as a beacon the wind
    hath upblown.

" Three does and a ten-tined buck made out," spoke Hamish,
    full mild,
    " And I ran for to turn, but my breath it was blown, and they
    passed;
    I was weak, for ye called ere I broke me my fast."
Cried Maclean: " Now a ten-tined buck in the sight of the wife
    and the child

I had killed if the gluttonous kern had not wrought me a snail's
    own wrong! "
    Then he sounded, and down came kinsmen and clansmen all:
    " Ten blows, for ten tine, on his back let fall,
And reckon no stroke if the blood follow not at the bite of
    thong! "

So Hamish made bare, and took him his strokes; at the last he
    smiled.
    " Now I'll to the burn," quoth Maclean, " for it still may be,
    If a slimmer-paunched henchman will hurry with me,
I shall kill me the ten-tined buck for a gift to the wife and the
    child! "

Then the clansmen departed, by this path and that; and over
  the hill
  Sped Maclean with an outward wrath for an inward shame;
  And that place of the lashing full quiet became;
And the wife and the child stood sad; and bloody-backed
  Hamish sat still.

But look! red Hamish has risen; quick about and about turns he.
  " There is none betwixt me and the crag-top! " he screams
  under breath.
  Then, livid as Lazarus lately from death,
He snatches the child from the mother, and clambers the crag
  toward the sea.

Now the mother drops breath; she is dumb, and her heart goes
  dead for a space,
  Till the motherhood, mistress of death, shrieks, shrieks
  through the glen,
  And that place of the lashing is live with men,
And Maclean, and the gillie that told him, dash up in a desperate race.

Not a breath's time for asking; an eye-glance reveals all the
  tale untold.
  They follow mad Hamish afar up the crag toward the sea,
  And the lady cries: " Clansmen, run for a fee! —
Yon castle and lands to the two first hands that shall hook him
  and hold

Fast Hamish back from the brink! "—and ever she flies up
  the steep,
  And the clansmen pant, and they sweat, and they jostle and
  strain.
  But, mother, 'tis vain; but, father, 'tis vain;
Stern Hamish stands bold on the brink, and dangles the child
  o'er the deep.

Now a faintness falls on the men that run, and they all stand
  still.
  And the wife prays Hamish as if he were God, on her knees,
  Crying: " Hamish! O Hamish! but please, but please
For to spare him! " and Hamish still dangles the child, with a
  wavering will.

On a sudden he turns; with a sea-hawk scream, and a gibe, and
a song,
Cries: " So; I will spare ye the child if, in sight of ye all,
Ten blows on Maclean's bare back shall fall,
And ye reckon no stroke if the blood follow not at the bite of
the thong! "

Then Maclean he set hardly his tooth to his lip that his tooth
was red,
Breathed short for a space, said: " Nay, but it never shall be!
Let me hurl off the damnable hound in the sea! "
But the wife: " Can Hamish go fish us the child from the sea,
if dead?

Say yea!—Let them lash *me*, Hamish? "—" Nay! "—" Hus-
band, the lashing will heal;
But, oh, who will heal me the bonny sweet bairn in his grave?
Could ye cure me my heart with the death of a knave?
Quick! Love! I will bare thee—so—kneel! " Then Maclean
'gan slowly to kneel

With never a word, till presently downward he jerked to the earth.
Then the henchman—he that smote Hamish—would tremble
and lag;
" Strike, hard! " quoth Hamish, full stern, from the crag;
Then he struck him, and " One! " sang Hamish, and danced
with the child in his mirth.

And no man spake beside Hamish; he counted each stroke with
a song.
When the last stroke fell, then he moved him a pace down
the height,
And he held forth the child in the heartaching sight
Of the mother, and looked all pitiful grave, as repenting a wrong.

And there as the motherly arms stretched out with the thanks-
giving prayer—
And there as the mother crept up with a fearful swift pace,
Till her finger nigh felt of the bairnie's face—
In a flash fierce Hamish turned round and lifted the child in
the air,

And sprang with the child in his arms from the horrible height
    in the sea,
    Shrill screeching, "Revenge!" in the wind-rush; and pallid
      Maclean,
    Age-feeble with anger and impotent pain,
Crawled up on the crag, and lay flat, and locked hold of dead
    roots of a tree—

And gazed hungrily o'er, and the blood from his back drip-
    dripped in the brine,
    And a sea-hawk flung down a skeleton fish as he flew,
    And the mother stared white on the waste of blue,
And the wind drove a cloud to seaward, and the sun began to
    shine.

1878                                                              *1878*

# The Marshes of Glynn

Glooms of the live-oaks, beautiful-braided and woven
With intricate shades of the vines that myriad-cloven
    Clamber the forks of the multiform boughs,—
      Emerald twilights,—
      Virginal shy lights,
Wrought of the leaves to allure to the whisper of vows,
When lovers pace timidly down through the green colon-
      nades
    Of the dim sweet woods, of the dear dark woods,
    Of the heavenly woods and glades,
That run to the radiant marginal sand-beach within
    The wide sea-marshes of Glynn;—

Beautiful glooms, soft dusks in the noon-day fire,—
Wildwood privacies, closets of lone desire,
Chamber from chamber parted with wavering arras of
      leaves,—
Cells for the passionate pleasure of prayer to the soul that
      grieves,
    Pure with a sense of the passing of saints through the wood,
    Cool for the dutiful weighing of ill with good;—

O braided dusks of the oak and woven shades of the vine,
While the riotous noon-day sun of the June-day long did shine,
Ye held me fast in your heart and I held you fast in mine;
  But now when the noon is no more, and riot is rest,
  And the sun is a-wait at the ponderous gate of the West,
    And the slant yellow beam down the wood-aisle doth seem
    Like a lane into heaven that leads from a dream,—
Ay, now, when my soul all day hath drunken the soul of the oak,
And my heart is at ease from men, and the wearisome sound
            of the stroke
Of the scythe of time and the trowel of trade is low,
And belief overmasters doubt, and I know that I know,
And my spirit is grown to a lordly great compass within,
That the length and the breadth and the sweep of the
          marshes of Glynn
Will work me no fear like the fear they have wrought me
          of yore
When length was fatigue, and when breadth was but bitter-
          ness sore,
And when terror and shrinking and dreary unnamable pain
Drew over me out of the merciless miles of the plain,—
  Oh, now, unafraid, I am fain to face
  The vast sweet visage of space.
  To the edge of the wood I am drawn, I am drawn,
Where the gray beach glimmering runs, as a belt of the dawn,
    For a mete and a mark
    To the forest-dark:—
      So:
    Affable live-oak, leaning low,—
Thus—with your favor—soft, with a reverent hand,
(Not lightly touching your person, Lord of the land!)
Bending your beauty aside, with a step I stand
    On the firm-packed sand,
      Free
By a world of marsh that borders a world of sea.
Sinuous southward and sinuous northward the shimmering
          band
Of the sand-beach fastens the fringe of the marsh to the folds
         of the land.

Inward and outward to northward and southward the beach-
lines linger and curl
As a silver-wrought garment that clings to and follows the firm
sweet limbs of a girl.
Vanishing, swerving, evermore curving again into sight,
Softly the sand-beach wavers away to a dim gray looping of
light.
And what if behind me to westward the wall of the woods
stands high?
The world lies east: how ample, the marsh and the sea and
the sky!
A league and a league of marsh-grass, waist-high, broad in
the blade,
Green, and all of a height, and unflecked with a light or a
shade,
Stretch leisurely off, in a pleasant plain,
To the terminal blue of the main.

Oh, what is abroad in the marsh and the terminal sea?
Somehow my soul seems suddenly free
From the weighing of fate and the sad discussion of sin,
By the length and the breadth and the sweep of the marshes
of Glynn.
Ye marshes, how candid and simple and nothing-withholding
and free
Ye publish yourselves to the sky and offer yourselves to the
sea!
Tolerant plains, that suffer the sea and the rains and the sun,
Ye spread and span like the catholic man who hath mightily
won
God out of knowledge and good out of infinite pain
And sight out of blindness and purity out of a stain.

As the marsh-hen secretly builds on the watery sod,
Behold I will build me a nest on the greatness of God:
I will fly in the greatness of God as the marsh-hen flies
In the freedom that fills all the space 'twixt the marsh and
the skies:
By so many roots as the marsh-grass sends in the sod
I will heartily lay me a-hold on the greatness of God:
Oh, like to the greatness of God is the greatness within
The range of the marshes, the liberal marshes of Glynn.

And the sea lends large, as the marsh: lo, out of his plenty
the sea
Pours fast: full soon the time of the flood-tide must be:
Look how the grace of the sea doth go
About and about through the intricate channels that flow
Here and there,
Everywhere,
Till his waters have flooded the uttermost creeks and the low-
lying lanes,
And the marsh is meshed with a million veins,
That like as with rosy and silvery essences flow
In the rose-and-silver evening glow.
Farewell, my lord Sun!
The creeks overflow: a thousand rivulets run
'Twixt the roots of the sod; the blades of the marsh-grass
stir;
Passeth a hurrying sound of wings that westward whirr;
Passeth, and all is still; and the currents cease to run;
And the sea and the marsh are one.

How still the plains of the waters be!
The tide is in his ecstasy.
The tide is at his highest height:
And it is night.

And now from the Vast of the Lord will the waters of sleep
Roll in on the souls of men,
But who will reveal to our waking ken
The forms that swim and the shapes that creep
Under the waters of sleep?
And I would I could know what swimmeth below when the
tide comes in
On the length and the breadth of the marvellous marshes
of Glynn.

1878                                          *1878*

## Remonstrance

Opinion, let me alone: I am not thine.
   Prim Creed, with categoric point, forbear
To feature me my Lord by rule and line.
   Thou canst not measure Mistress Nature's hair,
     Not one sweet inch: nay, if thy sight is sharp,
     Would'st count the strings upon an angel's harp?
      Forbear, forbear.

Oh let me love my Lord more fathom deep
   Than there is line to sound with: let me love
My fellow not as men that mandates keep:
   Yea, all that's lovable, below, above,
     That let me love by heart, by heart, because
     (Free from the penal pressure of the laws)
      I find it fair.

The tears I weep by day and bitter night,
   Opinion! for thy sole salt vintage fall.
—As morn by morn I rise with fresh delight,
   Time through my casement cheerily doth call
     " Nature is new, 'tis birthday every day,
     Come feast with me, let no man say me nay,
      Whate'er befall."

So fare I forth to feast: I sit beside
   Some brother bright: but, ere good-morrow's passed,
Burly Opinion wedging in hath cried
   " Thou shalt not sit by us, to break thy fast,
     Save to our Rubric thou subscribe and swear—
     *Religion hath blue eyes and yellow hair:*
      She's Saxon, all."

Then, hard a-hungered for my brother's grace
   Till well-nigh fain to swear his folly's true,
In sad dissent I turn my longing face
   To him that sits on the left: " Brother,—with you? "
     —" Nay, not with me, save thou subscribe and swear
     *Religion hath black eyes and raven hair:*
      Nought else is true."

Debarred of banquets that my heart could make
  With every man on every day of life,
I homeward turn, my fires of pain to slake
  In deep endearments of a worshipped wife.
    " I love thee well, dear Love," quoth she, " and yet
    Would that thy creed with mine completely met,
        As one, not two."


Assassin! Thief! Opinion, 'tis thy work.
  By Church, by throne, by hearth, by every good
That's in the Town of Time, I see thee lurk,
  And e'er some shadow stays where thou hast stood.
    Thou hand'st sweet Socrates his hemlock sour;
    Thou sav'st Barabbas in that hideous hour,
        And stabb'st the good


Deliverer Christ; thou rack'st the souls of men;
  Thou tossest girls to lions and boys to flames;
Thou hew'st Crusader down by Saracen;
  Thou buildest closets full of secret shames;
    Indifferent cruel, thou dost blow the blaze
    Round Ridley or Servetus; all thy days
        Smell scorched; I would


—Thou base-born Accident of time and place—
  Bigot Pretender unto Judgment's throne—
Bastard, that claimest with a cunning face
  Those rights the true, true Son of Man doth own
    By Love's authority—thou Rebel cold
    At head of civil wars and quarrels old—
        Thou Knife on a throne—


I would thou left'st me free, to live with love,
  And faith, that through the love of love doth find
My Lord's dear presence in the stars above,
  The clods below, the flesh without, the mind
    Within, the bread, the tear, the smile.
    Opinion, damned Intriguer, gray with guile,
        Let me alone.

1878                                    *1883*

## How Love Looked for Hell

To heal his heart of long-time pain
One day Prince Love for to travel was fain
　　With Ministers Mind and Sense.
" Now what to thee most strange may be? "
Quoth Mind and Sense. " All things above,
One curious thing I first would see—
　　Hell," quoth Love.

Then Mind rode in and Sense rode out:
They searched the ways of man about.
　　First frightfully groaneth Sense,
" Tis here, 'tis here," and spurreth in fear
To the top of the hill that hangeth above
And plucketh the Prince: " Come, come, 'tis here "—
　　" Where? " quoth Love—

" Not far, not far," said shivering Sense
As they rode on. " A short way hence,
　　—But seventy paces hence:
Look, King, dost see where suddenly
This road doth dip from the height above?
Cold blew a mouldy wind by me— "
　　(" Cold? " quoth Love.)

" As I rode down, and the River was black,
And yon-side, lo! an endless wrack
　　And rabble of souls," sighed Sense,
" Their eyes upturned and begged and burned
In brimstone lakes, and a Hand above
Beat back the hands that upward yearned— "
　　" Nay! " quoth Love—

" Yea, yea, sweet Prince; thyself shalt see,
Wilt thou but down this slope with me;
　　'Tis palpable," whispered Sense.
—At the foot of the hill a living rill
Shone, and the lilies shone white above;
" But now 'twas black, 'twas a river, this rill— "
　　(" Black? " quoth Love.)

" Ay, black, but lo! the lilies grow,
And yon-side where was woe, was woe,
　　—Where the rabble of souls " (cried Sense)
" Did shrivel and turn and beg and burn,
Thrust back in the brimstone from above—
Is banked of violet, rose, and fern: "
　　　" How? " quoth Love:

" For lakes of pain, yon pleasant plain
Of woods and grass and yellow grain
　　Doth ravish the soul and sense:
And never a sigh beneath the sky,
And folk that smile and gaze above— "
" But saw'st thou here, with thine own eye,
　　　Hell? " quoth Love—

" I saw true hell with mine own eye,
True hell, or light hath told a lie,
　　True, verily," quoth stout Sense.
Then Love rode round and searched the ground,
The caves below, the hills above:
" But I cannot find where thou hast found
　　　Hell," quoth Love.

There, while they stood in a green wood
And marvelled still on Ill and Good,
　　Came suddenly Minister Mind.
" In the heart of sin doth hell begin:
'Tis not below, 'tis not above,
It lieth within, it lieth within ":
　　　(" Where? " quoth Love.)

" I saw a man sit by a corse;
*Hell's in the murderer's breast: remorse!*
　　Thus clamored his mind to his mind:
Not fleshly dole is the sinner's goal,
Hell's not below, nor yet above,
'Tis fixed in the ever-damnèd soul— "
　　　" Fixed? " quoth Love—

" Fixed: follow me, would'st thou but see:
He weepeth under yon willow tree,
    Fast chained to his corse," quoth Mind.
Full soon they passed, for they rode fast,
Where the piteous willow bent above.
" Now shall I see at last, at last,
        Hell," quoth Love.

There when they came Mind suffered shame:
" These be the same and not the same,"
    A-wondering whispered Mind.
Lo, face by face two spirits pace
Where the blissful willow waves above:
One saith: " Do me a friendly grace— "
        (" Grace! " quoth Love.)

" Read me two Dreams that linger long,
Dim as returns of old-time song
    That flicker about the mind.
I dreamed (how deep in mortal sleep!)
I struck thee dead, then stood above,
With tears that none but dreamers weep ";
        " Dreams," quoth Love;

" In dreams, again, I plucked a flower
That clung with pain and stung with power,
    Yea, nettled me, body and mind."
" 'Twas the nettle of sin, 'twas medicine;
No need nor seed of it here Above;
In dreams of hate true loves begin."
        " True," quoth Love.

" Now strange," quoth Sense, and " Strange," quoth Mind,
" We saw it, and yet 'tis hard to find,
    —But we saw it," quoth Sense and Mind.
Stretched on the ground, beautiful-crowned
Of the piteous willow that wreathed above,
—" But I cannot find where ye have found
        Hell," quoth Love.

1878?                          1884

# Opposition

Of fret, of dark, of thorn, of chill,
    Complain no more; for these, O heart,
Direct the random of the will
    As rhymes direct the rage of art.

The lute's fixt fret, that runs athwart
    The strain and purpose of the string,
For governance and nice consort
    Doth bar his wilful wavering.

The dark hath many dear avails:
    The dark distills divinest dews;
The dark is rich with nightingales,
    With dreams, and with the heavenly Muse.

Bleeding with thorns of petty strife,
    I'll ease (as lovers do) my smart
With sonnets to my lady Life
    Writ red in issues from the heart.

What grace may lie within the chill
    Of favor frozen fast in scorn!
When Good's a freeze, we call it Ill!
    This rosy Time is glacier-born.

Of fret, of dark, of thorn, of chill,
    Complain thou not, O heart; for these
Bank-in the current of the will
    To uses, arts, and charities.

1879                                          *1880*

# Owl Against Robin

Frowning, the owl in the oak complained him
Sore, that the song of the robin restrained him
Wrongly of slumber, rudely of rest.
" From the north, from the east, from the south and the west,
Woodland, wheat-field, corn-field, clover,
Over and over and over and over,
Five o'clock, ten o'clock, twelve, or seven,
Nothing but robin-songs heard under heaven:
    How can we sleep?

" *Peep!* you whistle, and *cheep! cheep! cheep!*
Oh, peep, if you will, and buy, if 'tis cheap,
And have done; for an owl must sleep.
Are ye singing for fame, and who shall be first?
Each day's the same, yet the last is worst,
And the summer is cursed with the silly outburst
Of idiot red-breasts peeping and cheeping
By day, when all honest birds ought to be sleeping.
Lord, what a din! And so out of all reason.
Have ye not heard that each thing hath its season?
Night is to work in, night is for play-time;
        Good heavens, not day-time!

" A vulgar flaunt is the flaring day,
The impudent, hot, unsparing day,
That leaves not a stain nor a secret untold,—
Day the reporter,—the gossip of old,—
Deformity's tease,—man's common scold—
Poh! Shut the eyes, let the sense go numb
When day down the eastern way has come.
'Tis clear as the moon (by the argument drawn
From Design) that the world should retire at dawn.
Day kills.  The leaf and the laborer breathe
Death in the sun, the cities seethe,
The mortal black marshes bubble with heat
And puff up pestilence; nothing is sweet
Has to do with the sun: even virtue will taint
(Philosophers say) and manhood grow faint
In the lands where the villainous sun has sway
Through the livelong drag of the dreadful day.
What Eden but noon-light stares it tame,
Shadowless, brazen, forsaken of shame?
For the sun tells lies on the landscape,—now
Reports me the *what*, unrelieved with the *how*,—
As messengers lie, with the facts alone,
Delivering the word and withholding the tone.

" But oh, the sweetness, and oh, the light
Of the high-fastidious night!
Oh, to awake with the wise old stars—
The cultured, the careful, the Chesterfield stars,

That wink at the work-a-day fact of crime
And shine so rich through the ruins of time
That Baalbec is finer than London; oh,
To sit on the bough that zigzags low
> By the woodland pool,
And loudly laugh at man, the fool
That vows to the vulgar sun; oh, rare,
To wheel from the wood to the window where
A day-worn sleeper is dreaming of care,
And perch on the sill and straightly stare
Through his visions; rare, to sail
Aslant with the hill and a-curve with the vale,—
To flit down the shadow-shot-with-gleam,
Betwixt hanging leaves and starlit stream,
Hither, thither, to and fro,
Silent, aimless, dayless, slow
(*Aimless? Field-mice?* True, they're slain,
But the night-philosophy hoots at pain,
Grips, eats quick, and drops the bones
In the water beneath the bough, nor moans
At the death life feeds on). Robin, pray
> Come away, come away
To the cultus of night. Abandon the day.
Have more to think and have less to say.
And *cannot* you walk now? Bah! don't hop!
> Stop!
Look at the owl, scarce seen, scarce heard,
O irritant, iterant, maddening bird! "

1879                                          *1881*


# The Cloud

Sail on, sail on, fair cousin Cloud;
Oh, loiter hither from the sea.
> Still-eyed and shadow-brow'd,
Steal off from yon far-drifting crowd,
And come and brood upon the marsh with me.

Yon laboring low horizon-smoke,
Yon stringent sail, toil not for thee
      Nor me: did heaven's stroke
The whole deep with drown'd commerce choke,
No pitiless tease of risk or bottomry

Would to thy rainy office close
Thy will, or lock mine eyes from tears
      Part wept for traders'-woes,
Part for that ventures mean as those
In issue bind such sovereign hopes and fears.

Stern Cloud, thy downward countenance stares
Blank on the blank-faced marsh, and thou
      Mindest of dark affairs;
Thy substance seems a warp of cares;
Like late wounds run the wrinkles on thy brow.

Well may'st thou pause, and gloom, and stare,
A visible conscience; I arraign
      Thee, criminal Cloud, of rare
Contempts on Mercy, Right, and Prayer,
Of murders, arsons, thefts, of nameless stain.

Yet though life's logic grow as gray
As thou, my soul's not in eclipse.
      Cold Cloud, but yesterday
Thy lightning slew a child at play,
And then a priest with prayers upon his lips

For his enemies, and then a bright
Lady that did but ope the door
      Upon the stormy night
To let a beggar in,—strange spite,—
And then thy sulky rain refused to pour

Till thy quick torch a barn had burned
Where twelve months' store of victual lay
      A widow's sons had earned,
Which done, thy floods of rain returned,—
The river raped their little herd away.

What myriad righteous errands high
Thy flames *might* run on! In that hour
    Thou slewest the child, oh why
Not rather slay Calamity,
Breeder of Pain and Doubt, infernal Power?

Or why not plunge thy blades about
Some maggot politician throng
    Swarming to parcel out
The body of a land, and rout
The maw-conventicle, and ungorge Wrong?

> *What the cloud doeth,*
> *The Lord knoweth,*
> *The cloud knoweth not.*
> *What the artist doeth,*
> *The Lord knoweth;*
> *Knoweth the artist not?*

Well-answered! O dear artists, ye
—Whether in forms of curve or hue
    Or tone, your gospels be—
Say wrong, *This work is not of me,*
*But God:* it is not true, it is not true.

Awful is Art, because 'tis free.
The artist trembles o'er his plan,
    Where men his Self must see.
Who made a song or picture, he
Did it, and not another, God nor man.

My Lord is large, my Lord is strong:
Giving, He gave: my me is mine.
    How poor, how strange, how wrong,
To dream He wrote the little song
I made to Him with love's unforced design!

Oh, not as clouds dim laws have plann'd
To strike down Good and fight for Ill,
    Oh, not as harps that stand
In the wind and sound the wind's command:
Each artist—gift of terror!—owns his will.

For thee, Cloud,—if thou spend thine all
Upon the South's o'er-brimming sea
    That needs thee not; or crawl
To the dry provinces, and fall
Till every convert clod shall give to thee

Green worship; if thou grow or fade,
Bring mad delight or misery,
    Fly east or west, be made
Snow, hail, rain, wind, grass, rose, light, shade;—
What is it all to thee? There is no thee.

Pass, kinsman Cloud, now fair and mild:
Discharge the will that's not thine own.
    I work in freedom wild,
But work, as plays a little child,
Sure of the Father, Self, and Love, alone.

1880                                          *1882*


## Marsh Song—At Sunset

Over the monstrous shambling sea,
    Over the Caliban sea,
Bright Ariel-cloud, thou lingerest:
Oh wait, oh wait, in the warm red West,—
    Thy Prospero I'll be.

Over the humped and fishy sea,
    Over the Caliban sea,
O cloud in the West, like a thought in the heart
Of pardon, loose thy wing and start,
    And do a grace for me.

Over the huge and huddling sea,
    Over the Caliban sea,
Bring hither my brother Antonio,—Man,—
My injurer: night breaks the ban;
    Brother, I pardon thee.

1880?                                          *1882*

## A Sunrise Song

Young palmer sun, that to these shining sands
    Pourest thy pilgrim's tale, discoursing still
Thy silver passages of sacred lands,
    With news of Sepulchre and Dolorous Hill,

Canst thou be he that, yester-sunset warm,
    Purple with Paynim rage and wrack-desire,
Dashed ravening out of a dusty lair of storm,
    Harried the west, and set the world on fire?

Hast thou perchance repented, Saracen Sun?
    Wilt warm the world with peace and dove-desire?
Or wilt thou, ere this very day be done,
    Blaze Saladin still, with unforgiving fire?

1880                                        *1881*


## A Ballad of Trees and the Master

Into the woods my Master went,
    Clean forspent, forspent.
Into the woods my Master came,
    Forspent with love and shame.
But the olives they were not blind to Him,
The little gray leaves were kind to Him:
The thorn-tree had a mind to Him
    When into the woods He came.

Out of the woods my Master went,
    And He was well content.
Out of the woods my Master came,
    Content with death and shame.
When Death and Shame would woo Him last,
From under the trees they drew Him last:
'Twas on a tree they slew Him—last
    When out of the woods He came.

    1880                                    *1880*

## Sunrise

In my sleep I was fain of their fellowship, fain
Of the live-oak, the marsh, and the main.
The little green leaves would not let me alone in my sleep;
Up-breathed from the marshes, a message of range and of sweep,
Interwoven with wafture of wild sea-liberties, drifting,
    Came through the lapped leaves sifting, sifting,
    Came to the gates of sleep.
Then my thoughts, in the dark of the dungeon-keep
Of the Castle of Captives hid in the City of Sleep,
    Upstarted, by twos and by threes assembling:
    The gates of sleep fell a-trembling
Like as the lips of a lady that forth falter *yes*,
    Shaken with happiness:
    The gates of sleep stood wide.

I have waked, I have come, my beloved! I might not abide:
I have come ere the dawn, O beloved, my live-oaks, to hide
    In your gospelling glooms,—to be
As a lover in heaven, the marsh my marsh and the sea my sea.

    Tell me, sweet burly-bark'd, man-bodied Tree
    That mine arms in the dark are embracing, dost know
From what fount are these tears at thy feet which flow?
They rise not from reason, but deeper inconsequent deeps.
    Reason's not one that weeps.
    What logic of greeting lies
Betwixt dear over-beautiful trees and the rain of the eyes?

O cunning green leaves, little masters! like as ye gloss
All the dull-tissued dark with your luminous darks that emboss
    The vague blackness of night into pattern and plan,
        So,
    (But would I could know, but would I could know,)
With your question embroid'ring the dark of the question of
    man,—

So, with your silences purfling this silence of man
While his cry to the dead for some knowledge is under the ban,
    Under the ban,—
        So, ye have wrought me
Designs on the night of our knowledge,—yea, ye have taught me,
                So,
    That haply we know somewhat more than we know.


Ye lispers, whisperers, singers in storms,
Ye consciences murmuring faiths under forms,
Ye ministers meet for each passion that grieves,
Friendly, sisterly, sweetheart leaves,
Oh, rain me down from your darks that contain me
Wisdoms ye winnow from winds that pain me,—
Sift down tremors of sweet-within-sweet
That advise me of more than they bring,—repeat
Me the woods-smell that swiftly but now brought breath
From the heaven-side bank of the river of death,—
Teach me the terms of silence,—preach me
The passion of patience,—sift me,—impeach me,—
        And there, oh there
    As ye hang with your myriad palms upturned in the air,
        Pray me a myriad prayer.


        My gossip, the owl,—is it thou
    That out of the leaves of the low-hanging bough,
        As I pass to the beach, art stirred?
        Dumb woods, have ye uttered a bird?


            *      *      *      *      *


Reverend Marsh, low-couched along the sea,
    Old chemist, rapt in alchymy,
        Distilling silence,—lo,
That which our father-age had died to know—
The menstruum that dissolves all matter—thou
Hast found it: for this silence, filling now
The globèd clarity of receiving space,
This solves us all: man, matter, doubt, disgrace,

Death, love, sin, sanity,
Must in yon silence's clear solution lie.
Too clear! That crystal nothing who'll peruse?
The blackest night could bring us brighter news.
    Yet precious qualities of silence haunt
    Round these vast margins, ministrant.
Oh, if thy soul's at latter gasp for space,
With trying to breathe no bigger than thy race
Just to be fellow'd, when that thou hast found
No man with room, or grace, enough of bound
To entertain that New thou tell'st, thou art,—
'Tis here, 'tis here, thou canst unhand thy heart
    And breathe it free, and breathe it free,
By rangy marsh, in lone sea-liberty.

The tide's at full: the marsh with flooded streams
Glimmers, a limpid labyrinth of dreams.
Each winding creek in grave entrancement lies,
A rhapsody of morning-stars. The skies
    Shine scant with one forked galaxy,—
The marsh brags ten: looped on his breast they lie.

Oh, what if a sound should be made!
Oh, what if a bound should be laid
To this bow-and-string tension of beauty and silence a-spring,—
To the bend of beauty the bow, or the hold of silence the string!
I fear me, I fear me yon dome of diaphanous gleam
    Will break as a bubble o'er-blown in a dream,—
Yon dome of too-tenuous tissues of space and of night,
    Over-weighted with stars, over-freighted with light,
    Over-sated with beauty and silence, will seem
        But a bubble that broke in a dream,
    If a bound of degree to this grace be laid,
        Or a sound or a motion made.

But no: it is made: list! somewhere,—mystery, where?
        In the leaves? in the air?
    In my heart? is a motion made:
'Tis a motion of dawn, like a flicker of shade on shade.
In the leaves, 'tis palpable: low multitudinous stirring
Upwinds through the woods; the little ones, softly conferring,

Have settled, my lord's to be looked for; so; they are still;
   But the air and my heart and the earth are a-thrill,—
And look where the wild duck sails round the bend of the river,—
     And look where a passionate shiver
     Expectant is bending the blades
   Of the marsh-grass in serial shimmers and shades,—
   And invisible wings, fast fleeting, fast fleeting,
         Are beating
The dark overhead as my heart beats,—and steady and free
   Is the ebb-tide flowing from marsh to sea
       (Run home, little streams,
    With your lapfulls of stars and dreams);—
   And a sailor unseen is hoisting a-peak,
   For list, down the inshore curve of the creek
    How merrily flutters the sail,—
   And lo, in the east! Will the East unveil?
   The East is unveiled, the East hath confessed
A flush: 'tis dead; 'tis alive: 'tis dead, ere the West
Was aware of it: nay, 'tis abiding, 'tis unwithdrawn:
    Have a care, sweet Heaven! 'Tis Dawn.

     \*     \*     \*     \*     \*

Now a dream of a flame through that dream of a flush is up-
      rolled:
To the zenith ascending, a dome of undazzling gold
Is builded, in shape as a bee-hive, from out of the sea:
The hive is of gold undazzling, but oh, the Bee,
   The star-fed Bee, the build-fire Bee,
    —Of dazzling gold is the great Sun-Bee
   That shall flash from the hive-hole over the sea.

Yet now the dew-drop, now the morning gray,
Shall live their little lucid sober day
Ere with the sun their souls exhale away.
Now in each pettiest personal sphere of dew
The summ'd morn shines complete as in the blue
Big dew-drop of all heaven: with these lit shrines
O'er-silvered to the farthest sea-confines,
The sacramental marsh one pious plain
Of worship lies. Peace to the ante-reign
Of Mary Morning, blissful mother mild,
Minded of nought but peace, and of a Child.

Not slower than Majesty moves, for a mean and a measure
Of motion,—not faster than dateless Olympian leisure
Might pace with unblown ample garments from pleasure to
        pleasure,—
The wave-serrate sea-rim sinks, unjarring, unreeling,
    Forever revealing, revealing, revealing,
Edgewise, bladewise, halfwise, wholewise,—'tis done!
        Good-morrow, lord Sun!
    With several voice, with ascription one,
    The woods and the marsh and the sea and my soul
Unto thee, whence the glittering stream of all morrows doth roll,
Cry good and past-good and most heavenly morrow, lord Sun.

O Artisan born in the purple,—Workman Heat,—
Parter of passionate atoms that travail to meet
And be mixed in the death-cold oneness,—innermost Guest
At the marriage of elements,—fellow of publicans,—blest
King in the blouse of flame, that loiterest o'er
The idle skies yet laborest fast evermore—

        *       *       *       *       *

Thou, in the fine forge-thunder, thou, in the beat
Of the heart of a man, thou Motive,—Laborer Heat:
Yea, Artist, thou, of whose art yon sea's all news,
With his inshore greens and manifold mid-sea blues,
Pearl-glint, shell-tint, ancientest perfectest hues
    Ever shaming the maidens,—lily and rose
    Confess thee, and each mild flame that glows
In the clarified virginal bosoms of stones that shine,
        It is thine, it is thine:
Thou chemist of storms, whether driving the winds a-swirl
Or a-flicker the subtiler essences polar that whirl
In the magnet earth,—yea, thou with a storm for a heart,
Rent with debate, many-spotted with question, part
From part oft sundered, yet ever a globèd light,
Yet ever the artist, ever more large and bright
Than the eye of a man may avail of:—manifold One,
I must pass from thy face, I must pass from the face of the Sun:
Old Want is awake and agog, every wrinkle a-frown;
The worker must pass to his work in the terrible town:

But I fear not, nay, and I fear not the thing to be done;
  I am strong with the strength of my lord the Sun:
How dark, how dark soever the race that must needs be run,
      I am lit with the Sun.

    Oh, never the mast-high run of the seas
          Of traffic shall hide thee,
Never the hell-colored smoke of the factories
          Hide thee,
Never the reek of the time's fen-polities
          Hide thee,
And ever my heart through the night shall with knowledge
      abide thee,
And ever by day shall my spirit, as one that hath tried thee,
Labor, at leisure, in art,—till yonder beside thee
      My soul shall float, friend Sun,
          The day being done.

1880                                            *1882*

## Tyranny

        Spring-germs, spring-germs,
    I charge you by your life, go back to death.
    This glebe is sick, this wind is foul of breath.
        Stay: feed the worms.

        Oh! every clod
    Is faint, and falters from the war of growth
    And crumbles in a dreary dust of sloth,
        Unploughed, untrod.

        What need, what need,
    To hide with flowers the curse upon the hills,
    Or sanctify the banks of sluggish rills
        Where vapors breed?

        And—if needs must—
    Advance, O Summer-heats! upon the land,
    And bake the bloody mould to shards and sand
        And barren dust.

Before your birth,
Burn up, O Roses! in your natal flame.
Good Violets, sweet Violets, hide shame
Below the earth.

Ye silent Mills,
Reject the bitter kindness of the moss.
O Farms! protest if any tree emboss
The barren hills.

Young Trade is dead,
And swart Work sullen sits in the hillside fern
And folds his arms that find no bread to earn,
And bows his head.

Spring-germs, spring-germs,
Albeit the towns have left you place to play,
I charge you, sport not.  Winter owns to-day,
Stay:  feed the worms.

1868                                                    *1868*


# The Raven Days

Our hearths are gone out, and our hearts are broken,
    And but the ghosts of homes to us remain,
And ghostly eyes and hollow sighs give token
    From friend to friend of an unspoken pain.

O, Raven Days, dark Raven Days of sorrow,
    Bring to us, in your whetted ivory beaks,
Some sign out of the far land of To-morrow,
    Some strip of sea-green dawn, some orange streaks.

Ye float in dusky files, forever croaking—
    Ye chill our manhood with your dreary shade.
Pale, in the dark, not even God invoking,
    We lie in chains, too weak to be afraid.

O Raven Days, dark Raven Days of sorrow,
  Will ever any warm light come again?
Will ever the lit mountains of To-morrow
  Begin to gleam across the mournful plain?

1868                                    *1868*


## Life and Song

If life were caught by a clarionet,
  And a wild heart, throbbing in the reed,
Should thrill its joy and trill its fret
  And utter its heart in every deed,

Then would this breathing clarionet
  Type what the poet fain would be;
For none o' the singers ever yet
  Has wholly lived his minstrelsy,

Or clearly sung his true, true thought,
  Or utterly bodied forth his life,
Or out of Life and Song has wrought
  The perfect one of man and wife;

Or lived and sung, that Life and Song
  Might each express the other's all,
Careless if life or art were long
  Since both were one, to stand or fall:

So that the wonder struck the crowd,
  Who shouted it about the land:
*His song was only living aloud,*
  *His work a singing with his hand!*

1868                                    *1868*

## Thar's More in the Man Than
## Thar Is in the Land

I knowed a man, which he lived in Jones,
Which Jones is a county of red hills and stones,
And he lived pretty much by gittin' of loans,
And his mules was nuthin' but skin and bones,
And his hogs was flat as his corn-bread pones,
And he had 'bout a thousand acres o' land.

This man—which his name it was also Jones—
He swore that he'd leave them old red hills and stones,
Fur he couldn't make nuthin' but yallerish cotton,
And little o' *that*, and his fences was rotten,
And what little corn he had, *hit* was boughten,
And dinged ef a livin' was in the land.

And the longer he swore the madder he got,
And he riz and he walked to the stable lot,
And he hollered to Tom to come thar and hitch,
Fur to emigrate somewhar whar land was rich,
And to quit rasin' cock-burrs, thistles and sich,
And a wastin' ther time on the cussed land.

So him and Tom they hitched up the mules,
Pertestin' that folks was mighty big fools
That 'ud stay in Georgy ther lifetime out,
Jest scratchin' a livin' when all of 'em mought
Git places in Texas whar cotton would sprout
By the time you could plant it in the land.

And he driv by a house whar a man named Brown
Was a livin', not fur from the edge o' town,
And he bantered Brown fur to buy his place,
And said that bein' as money was skace,
And bein' as sheriffs was hard to face,
Two dollars an acre would git the land.

They closed at a dollar and fifty cents,
And Jones he bought him a waggin and tents,
And loaded his corn, and his wimmin, and truck,
And moved to Texas, which it tuck
His entire pile, with the best of luck,
To git thar and git him a little land.

But Brown moved out on the old Jones farm,
And he rolled up his breeches and bared his arm,
And he picked all the rocks from off'n the groun',
And he rooted it up and he plowed it down,
Then he sowed his corn and his wheat in the land.

Five years glid by, and Brown, one day
(Which he'd got so fat that he wouldn't weigh),
Was a settin' down, sorter lazily,
To the bulliest dinner you ever see,
When one o' the children jumped on his knee
And says, " Yan's Jones, which you bought his land."

And thar was Jones, standin' out at the fence,
And he hadn't no waggin, nor mules, nor tents,
Fur he had left Texas afoot and cum
To Georgy to see if he couldn't git sum
Employment, and he was a lookin' as hum-
Ble as ef he had never owned any land.

But Brown he axed him in, and he sot
Him down to his vittles smokin' hot,
And when he had filled hisself and the floor
Brown looked at him sharp and riz and swore
That, " whether men's land was rich or poor
Thar was more in the *man* than thar was in the *land*."

1869-1871?                                        *1871*

# NOTES TO THE POEMS

# ABBREVIATIONS

| | |
|---|---|
| *HA* | Huntington Library and Art Gallery, San Marino, Cal. |
| *CL* | Charles D. Lanier Collection, Johns Hopkins University. |
| *HL* | Henry W. Lanier Collection, Johns Hopkins University. |
| *RL* | Robert S. Lanier Collection, Johns Hopkins University. |
| *SL* | Mrs. Sidney Lanier, Jr., Collection, Johns Hopkins University. |
| *ET* | Miss Eleanor Turnbull, Baltimore, Md. |
| *JT* | Clifford Lanier Collection, owned by John Tilley, Montgomery, Ala. |
| *JU* | Johns Hopkins University, Baltimore, Md. |
| *Clover* | Printer's Copy of "Clover and Other Poems," 1879, 84 pp., Henry W. Lanier Collection. |
| *Ledger* | Lanier's literary journal, 1865–1877, Henry W. Lanier Collection. |
| *MDL* | Mary Day Lanier, as editor of Lanier's poems. |
| *1884* | *Poems of Sidney Lanier,* ed. by his wife, New York: Charles Scribner's Sons. |
| *1891* | Same as above, with seven additional poems. |
| *1916* | Same as above, with two additional poems. |
| *1877* | *Poems by Sidney Lanier,* Philadelphia: J. B. Lippincott & Co. |
| *1895* | *Select Poems of Sidney Lanier,* ed. by Morgan Callaway, New York: Charles Scribner's Sons. |
| *Starke* | Aubrey Starke, *Sidney Lanier: A Biographical and Critical Study,* Chapel Hill, N.C., 1933. |

N. B. References to volume and page without other identification (e.g., I, 293, etc.) are to the poems and prose in the *Centennial Edition of Sidney Lanier,* I-VI. Letters referred to by date (and the notes thereto) may be found in the *Centennial Edition,* VII-X. (Some of them are also printed in the present volume.)

## CORN (19-24)

Written at Sunnyside, near Griffin, Ga., July, 1874 (receipt of a copy is acknowledged in Paul Hayne's letter of July 30); revised in Brooklyn, Oct., 1874 (see letter of Oct. 25), again slightly in *1877* and afterwards.

Published in *Lippincott's*, XV, 216-219 (Feb., 1875); reprinted in the Philadelphia *Evening Bulletin*, Jan. 20, 1875, and copied in other newspapers; reprinted with revisions in *1877*, 9-19; and with further changes in *1884*, 53-59.

Text: *CL* copy of *1877*, corrected in Lanier's handwriting (the text used in *1884*). Two MSS and a rough draft of the opening lines survive; for a full collation of variants see pp. 293-296, vol. I.

" Corn," Lanier's best poem to date, was the first to bring him anything like a national reputation. No account of its composition is preserved in his letters, but a credible story of its origin has been recorded by a friend and neighbor at Sunnyside (see J. M. Kell, *Recollections of a Naval Life*, Washington, 1900, pp. 296-297, conveniently recounted in Starke, 182.) The region was a prosperous farming section of middle Georgia, about 60 miles above Macon, where the cultivation of corn had replaced the conventional money-crop of cotton, described by Lanier later as: " that ample stretch of generous soil, where the Appalachian ruggednesses calm themselves into pleasant hills before dying quite away into the sea-board levels, [where] a man can find such temperances of heaven and earth—enough of struggle with nature to draw out manhood, with enough of bounty to sanction the struggle—that a more exquisite co-adaptation of all blessed circumstances for man's life need not be sought " (quoted from " The New South," an essay concerned with the same economic problem, see V, 357). With this inspiration, Lanier made a serious plea for the same agricultural reform in the South that he had advocated three years before in his dialect verses (cf. especially I, 38-39 with I, 22-25, 194-196). Confident that he had written an important poem, he went to New York at the end of August to arrange for its publication. It was rejected by *Scribner's* and the *Atlantic*, and an ambitious scheme to publish it as an illustrated booklet fell through (letters of Sept. 4, 8, 13, 17, Oct. 3, 14). After submitting it to friends for criticism, chiefly Hayne and L. E. Bleckley, he made a complete revision and finally sold it to *Lippincott's*, who upon publication doubled the price originally offered and sent him a check for $50 (Bleckley's analysis is given in note 117, 1874; see letters of Oct. 25, Dec. 1, 1874, and Jan. 24, 1875; also J. F. Kirk's letter of Jan. 16, 1875). Upon its appearance in mid January it met with instant success, especially because of the editorials of Gibson Peacock in the Philadelphia *Evening Bulletin* (see letters of Jan. 18, 24, 26, and notes 25, 28). Through this new friend, who did much to sponsor Lanier's career from this time on, he also met Charlotte Cushman and Bayard Taylor and made his entry into the world of established artists. One ironical result was that this first successful poem brought him the commission to write a travel book, *Florida*, his first sustaining pay for literary work (Mar. 24, 1875, to his wife). " Corn " is further interesting as Lanier's initial effort to break away from conventional verse-forms, in pursuance of plans announced in a letter of the previous spring (Mar. 15, 1874).

### THE SYMPHONY (24-33)

Written in Baltimore, Mar. 20-28, 1875 (see letters of Mar. 24 and 28);
revised in 1876 and again in 1879.
Published in *Lippincott's*, XV, 677-684 (June, 1875); reprinted without
change in *Dwight's Journal of Music*, XXXV, 41-42 (June 26, 1875); reprinted
with revisions in *1877*, 20-38; and with further revisions in *1884*, 60-70.
Text: Printer's Copy, 19 pp., *CL*, originally prepared for inclusion in *Clover*
but omitted (see letter of May 16, 1879). This is clearly Lanier's latest revision
and was used in *1884*. For a full collation of variants see pp. 298-300, vol. I.
*Lippincott's* paid Lanier $100 for "The Symphony" (see J. F. Kirk's letter of
Apr. 4, 1875). Elizabeth Stuart Phelps used l. 3 as a text for her poem, "What
the Violin Said," published in the New York *Daily Graphic*, VIII, 910 (Oct.
27, 1875). The second of Lanier's long ambitious poems to be published, "The
Symphony" won him the friendship of Bayard Taylor through a copy sent by
Gibson Peacock (who had recently become Lanier's sponsor because of his
admiration of "Corn"): and it prompted the first serious consideration of
Lanier's poetry by a literary critic of national reputation, G. H. Calvert's article
in the *Golden Age*, V, 4-5 (June 12, 1875). The poem epitomizes Lanier's
life-long devotion to music, which he was convinced would "revolutionize the
world" through harmony and love, and his continuing conviction that the
blight on modern life was the tyranny of commercialism, here with the added
note of social protest because of its oppression of the poor (see Introduction).
The allusion in ll. 42-43 is to *Matthew* iv:4; in l. 178, to *Matthew* xix:19;
in l. 182, to *Luke* x:29 ff.; in ll. 333-334, to *Luke* xviii:17. The reference
in ll. 311-312 is apparently intended to be to Sir Philip Sidney, who, because of
his sister's marriage, was sometimes referred to as "Pembroke's brother"; the
description fits the character and career of Sidney, a favorite of Lanier's, but does
not apply to any of the Earls of Pembroke.

### EVENING SONG (34)

Written at West Chester, Pa., early autumn of 1876.
Published in *Lippincott's*, XIX, 91 (Jan., 1877); reprinted without change
in Philadelphia *Evening Bulletin* (no file discovered, but undated clipping in
*CL*); in Epes Sargent, *Harper's Cyclopaedia of British and American Poetry*
(New York, 1881), 916; and in *1884*, 151.
Text: Sargent. MS *HA* is a fragment of ll. 1-2, *O Love, look off across
yon sallow sands / To where.* Dudley Buck's letter of Nov. 7, 1876, indicates
that l. 5 originally read, *Now in the sea's red cordial melts the Sun.* No other
variants known.
Written to be set to music, in response to a request from Dudley Buck, Aug.
21, 1876, for "an 'Evening Song,' a sort of 'Ueber allen Gipfeln ist Ruh' but
longer." On Nov. 7 Buck wrote, "I composed your song last night at 'one
heat,'" suggesting one alteration which Lanier made (see above) and a change
of title to "On the Sea Shore." (See note 117, Letters of 1876; for Buck, note
to "Centennial Meditation," pp. 345-346, vol. I.) A posthumous printing in
*Independent*, XLIX, 1489 (Nov. 18, 1897), apparently from a MS in the
possession of H. C. Wysham, gives the title as "On the Shore." It was published

with Buck's music under the title *Sunset*, and has been set to music by several other composers, including Henry Hadley. The figure in the second stanza, an allusion to the tradition that Cleopatra dissolved a pearl in the drink with which she toasted Antony's health, had been used ten years before in "Night" (161). This lyric, addressed to Lanier's wife, is one of his best and has been a favorite with anthologists. He was paid $10 for it by *Lippincott's* (see letter to Peacock, Dec. 31, 1876).


## THE STIRRUP-CUP (34)

Written in Tampa, Jan., 1877 (so dated in *MDL's* handwriting on MS *CL^b*).
Published in *Scribner's*, XIV, 28 (May, 1877); reprinted with one variant line and one stanza rejected in *1884*, 45.
Text: *Clover* 42, MS (the text used in *1884*). Three other MSS survive; for the rejected stanza and a full collation of variants see pp. 311-312, vol. I.
Lanier was paid $20 for it (see letter from *Scribner's*, Jan. 19, 1877, which indicates that the title was originally "Life's Stirrup-Cup"). This poem, written a few weeks after he went to Florida by order of his doctor, reveals Lanier's courageous facing of the prospect of death. The names alluded to include some of those he had listed the previous summer in "Clover"; the following year he added further names in "The Crystal."


## TAMPA ROBINS (35)

Written in Tampa, Jan.-Feb., 1877 (the issue of *Lippincott's* containing it was out by Feb. 18, according to a letter from Emma Stebbins).
Published in *Lippincott's*, XIX, 355 (Mar., 1877), as "Redbreast in Tampa"; reprinted with revisions and one additional stanza in *1884*, 28.
Text: *Clover* 16-17, MS, a revision with new title (the text used in *1884*). A MS rough draft of the first stanza also survives, verso a draft of "The Stirrup-Cup," dated Jan., 1877; for a full collation of variants see p. 313, vol. I.
This poem and the complementary "Stirrup-Cup" are statements of Lanier's attitude toward life and death, the figure of Time appearing in both but with reversed applications; the MS mentioned above suggests that they were written at about the same time.


## A FLORIDA SUNDAY (35-38)

Apparently written in Florida winter-spring, 1877 (dated by *MDL* "Tampa," where Lanier remained until Apr. 5; his letter of June 13, 1877, refers to it as printed).
Published in *Frank Leslie's Sunday Magazine*, II, 72-73 (July, 1877); reprinted without change, except for correction of misprint, in *1884*, 142-145.
Text: *Leslie's* (with correction of misprint, *joys* for *jays*, l. 64, by authority of Lanier's letter of June 13, 1877, which added: "the punctuation is also quite mutilated in some places," though only one such correction seemed necessary—the colon supplied, 5th line from the end). No variants known.
During the winter of 1877 Lanier made his first serious reading of Emerson (see letter of May 25), whose influence is apparent not only in specific lines

(see the concluding couplet) but in the central idea of the poem: the spiritual
unity behind nature and the essential kinship of each and all. Based upon a
personal religious experience (cf. the autobiographical allusion in ll. 5-6), it
foreshadows " The Marshes of Glynn " and " Sunrise." The influence of Keats
may be seen in the delight in color and sound (and cf. the specific echo of the
" Ode on a Grecian Urn " in ll. 16-17).

## FROM THE FLATS (38-39)

Probably written in Tampa, spring of 1877 (see *1884*, 26; Lanier left Florida
on Apr. 5).
Published in *Lippincott's*, XX, 115 (July, 1877); reprinted without change
in Epes Sargent, *Harper's Cyclopaedia of British and American Poetry* (New
York, 1881), 917; and with one line altered in *1884*, 26, but restored in *1910*.
Text: Sargent (with omission of comma after " beauty," l. 10). One MS
survives, entitled " From a Flat Land "; for a full collation of variants, see
pp. 313-314, vol. I.
Lanier's letter of July 12, 1872, is a prose counterpart of this poem. See also
his comment in the Peabody lecture on *Phoenix*: " A modern poet would never
have described a Happy Land as an unbroken plain where no mountains stand;
the picture of a landscape without broken ground is to our eyes intolerable "
(III, 48, note 2).

## THE MOCKING BIRD (39)

Probably written in Brunswick, Ga., Apr.-May, 1877 (see letters of Apr. 26,
July 23, Aug. 1, and note 62, 1877).
Published in *Galaxy*, XXIV, 161 (Aug., 1877); reprinted with changes in
*1884*, 27.
Text: *Clover* 12, MS (the text used in *1884* with *prinked* for *primped*, l. 11).
An earlier version survives in MS; for a full collation of variants see p. 314,
vol. I.
A note in *1884*, 243, quotes from a lost college note-book Lanier's jotting:
" A poet is the mocking-bird of the spiritual universe. In him are collected all
the individual songs of all individual natures." (See also " To Our Mocking
Bird" and note, p. 358, vol. I.)

## SONG OF THE CHATTAHOOCHEE (40-41)

Written in Baltimore, end of Nov., 1877 (see letters of Nov. 27, 30, and note
103).
Said to have been published in *Scott's Magazine* in 1877 (see *1884*, iii, and
F. V. N. Painter, *Poets of the South*, New York, 1903, p. 227); first verified
publication in *Independent*, XXXV, 1601 (Dec. 20, 1883), from which it was
reprinted with correction of two misprints in *1884*, 24-25.
Text: *Clover* 6-10, MS (the text used in the posthumous prints). Capitals
have been supplied in ll. 13, 15, 17. The variants from the " early printing,"
as preserved in Painter, 184-186, are given on pp. 316-317, vol. I.

The evidence concerning the first publication of this poem is confusing. Lanier's letters of Nov. 27, 30, 1877, state that it was "written for a little paper at West Point, Ga.," just being started by a friend of his, and sent off on the former date; but no such periodical has been found. Painter says (p. 227) that it was "first published in *Scott's Magazine*, Atlanta, Georgia, from which it is here taken. It at once became popular, and was copied in many newspapers throughout the South. It was subsequently revised, and the changes, which are pointed out below, are interesting as showing the development of the poet's artistic sense." He then reproduced this different early version; though he does not specifically date this printing, he speaks of it (p. 94) as being two or three years after 1875; and *1884*, iii, dates it specifically as "Scott's Magazine, 1877." But the only periodical bearing this title that has been discovered, *Scott's Monthly Magazine*, ceased to exist in 1869, and a search of its files fails to reveal Lanier's poem. The *Macon Daily Telegraph and Messenger* for 1877-1878 has also been searched for a possible reprinting. Here the matter rests.

The theme of the poem is suggested in a passage in "Sketches of India," written in the autumn of 1875, describing a waterfall where the river Nerbadá "leaps out eagerly toward the low lands he is to fertilize, like a young poet anxious to begin his work of grace in the world" (see VI, 277, Centennial edition). The Chattahoochee River Lanier was familiar with from his summers spent at Marietta, Ga. It is described in *1895*, 78, as follows: "The Chattahoochee River rises in Habersham County, in northeast Georgia, and, intersecting Hall County, flows southwestward to West Point, then southward until it unites with the Flint River at the southwestern extremity of Ga." Lanier's most popular poem, it has frequently been praised for its technical skill. A note by W. H. Ward, accompanying its publication in the *Independent*, said that it was "written just as he was formulating to himself the principles of poetic art." One commentator has suggested that Coleridge's "Song of Glycine" was the musical source of the poem, a fact which "throws light on Lanier's method of poetic composition, suggesting that his poems had their genesis in music rather than in idea" (Philip Graham, "A Note on Lanier's Music," University of Texas *Studies in English*, XVII, 111, 1937). The most common comparison has been to Tennyson's "The Brook," a poem from which Lanier quoted in a letter of Feb. 3, 1878. (An elaborate analysis of its versification is made by C. W. Kent, "A Study of Lanier's Poems," *PMLA*, VII, 33-63, Apr., 1892; see also Introduction.)

## THE HARLEQUIN OF DREAMS (41)

Apparently written in Baltimore, winter of 1878 (from evidence of publication date; possibly one of the two poems referred to in Lanier's letter to Peacock, Jan. 6, 1878).

Published in *Lippincott's*, XXI, 439 (Apr., 1878); reprinted without change in Epes Sargent, *Harper's Cyclopaedia of British and American Poetry* (New York, 1881), 917, and in *1884*, 85.

Text: Sargent. No variants known. (Originally included in *Clover* 49, as indicated in "Subjects for Illustration," but now missing. MS *CL* is a copy, apparently in the handwriting of W. R. Thayer.)

The best of Lanier's sonnets, this is one of half-a-dozen written during the first part of 1878, probably growing out of his studies in Renaissance sonneteers for the Bird lectures (see III, viii). It was singled out for special praise by the London *Spectator* (undated clipping, *JU*).

## THE REVENGE OF HAMISH (42-46)

Probably written in Baltimore, winter of 1878.

Published in *Appleton's Journal*, V [n. s.], 395-396 (Nov., 1878); reprinted with slight revision in *1884*, 33-38.

Text: *Clover* 20-27, MS and early print (the versions followed in *1884* with one careless error). *Appleton's* has four variants, two of which are significant: *and her little keen ears made turn* for *and rounded her ears in turn* (l. 7); and *all unweeting, stood watching and* for *never baiting his watch tarried* (l. 30).

Written as an experiment in logaœdic dactyls, growing out of Lanier's metrical studies for the Bird lectures (see letter of Oct. 20, 1878, and III, vii-viii). It was based on an episode in William Black's novel, *Macleod of Dare*, Chap. III, printed serially in *Harper's*, XVI, 412-413 (Feb., 1878), which it follows identically in plot, though the name of the henchman is borrowed from another character (*1895*, 79, states that Lanier discussed the source of the poem with his friend J. R. Tait). Charles Mackay's poem, " Maclaine's Child " (*Poetical Works*, London, 1876, 99-101) is similar in plot, but was clearly not a source for Lanier. " The Revenge of Hamish," the most ambitious narrative poem he ever completed, has the spirit if not the form of medieval balladry, and was included in Henry F. Randolph's *The Book of Latter-Day Ballads* (New York, 1888), 187-194, along with selections from Whittier, Lowell, Bret Harte, Tennyson, Browning, Meredith, Morris, Rossetti, and others. For a recent criticism see Yves Bourgeois, " Sidney Lanier et le Goffic," *Revue Anglo-Americaine*, VIII, 431-432 (June, 1931). He was paid $30 for it by *Appleton's* (letter from O. B. Bunce, Mar. 15, 1878).

## THE MARSHES OF GLYNN (46-49)

Written in Baltimore, probably summer of 1878 (see letter of July 13).

Published in *A Masque of Poets* (Boston, 1878), 88-94; reprinted without change in H. W. Longfellow's *Poems of Places. America. Southern States* (Boston, 1879), 252-257; and with revisions in *1884*, 14-18, as IV of " Hymns of the Marshes."

Text: *1884*. The authority for this version is conjectural but strong. All of the changes in the twelve lines that show variants are distinct improvements in artistic form or in meaning, and are such as Lanier himself would have made. The poem is marked on the Chronological List in *MDL's* handwriting (*CL*) as " 1878-1879," indicating a revision in the latter year; and it was originally included in *Clover* 11-19, printer's copy of a projected volume made up in May, 1879 (these pages are now missing, but the contents are proved by the accompanying table of " Subjects for Illustration "). Hence it is reasonable to assume that Lanier made a revision, which was the one followed in *1884*. (The variants in the earlier prints are given on p. 317, vol. I.)

The marshes of Glynn County are on the coast of Georgia, near Brunswick, and persistent legend has tried to connect the composition of the poem with the locale, as early as 1875 (see Starke, 279 and note 9). Lanier had known the region thoroughly for many years, his latest visit being in the spring of 1877 returning from Florida (see letter to Taylor, Apr. 26); and it is possible that he may have written the first two stanzas at this time, as the most convincing account reports (see Mattie T. Northen in the Atlanta *Journal*, May 19, 1929, supposedly quoting from a lost letter from Lanier to Mrs. Jas. H. Couper, a

Brunswick friend). All that can be established with certainty on this point is that the poem grew out of Lanier's actual experience of the region. A foreshadowing of the opening lines may be found in an unpublished prose jotting (*Ledger* 602-603), made before he left Tampa:

" In among the trees in Florida. Here walking one presently finds a host of contrasts exhaling from one's contemplation of the forest, one glides out of the idea that this multiform beauty is familiar, that it is a clump of trees and vines and flowers: No, it is Silence, which, denied access to man's ear, has caught form, and set forth its fervent appeal to man's eye: it is Music, in a siesta; it is Conflict, dead, and reappearing as Beauty: it is amiable Mystery, grown communicative: it is Nature, with her finger on her lip,—gesture of double significance, conveying to one, that one may kiss her, if one will say nothing about it: it is Tranquillity, suavely waving aside men's excuses for wars, . . . it is Trade, done into a flower, and blossoming as perfect type of honest *quid pro quo*, in the lavish good measure of that interchange whereby the undersides of leaves use man's breath and return him the same in better condition, paying profitable usuries for what the lender could not help loaning: it is a Reply, in all languages, but untranslateable in any, to the multitudinous interrogations . . . of students who dimly behold the unknowable world of the something unexplainably sweet beyond the immediate field of thought, itself yet far from being crossed,—interrogations of business-men, who, with little time for thinking of the things beyond their routines, yet occasionally desire some little concise revelation of the enormous Besides and Overplus which they suspect to lie beyond all Trade,—interrogations of the pleasure-seeker who cannot but hope that there will be Something Else, when the ball is over at the hotel,—interrogations of the sick man, petulantly wondering if he shall ever find companions who will not shudder when he coughs, nor coddle him with pitying absurdities . . . ."

On Apr. 20, 1878, he was invited by G. P. Lathrop to contribute to an anthology in the " No Name " Series being published by Roberts Brothers, Boston. Lanier's reply has not been found, but it seems clear that " The Marshes of Glynn " was written specifically as his contribution to *A Masque of Poets*. Just when he began the composition of it is not known, but probably not many weeks before the known date of its completion in mid July (letter of July 13 says he has just sent it off " hot from the mint "). Part of it is said to have been written on the schoolhouse steps at Pen Lucy, the academy of R. M. Johnston, where Lanier was teaching at this time (see VII, xxxviii, and notes 95 and 96). At any rate, it was published in Nov., 1878, and attracted some little attention in spite of its anonymity. (For an account of the contents and the reception of *A Masque of Poets* see A. H. Starke, " An Omnibus of Poets," *Colophon*, IV, part 16, Mar., 1934.)

Like " The Revenge of Hamish " (112), it was another experiment in log  œdic dactyls, growing out of his metrical studies in the " Physics of Poetry," in process of composition during the summer of 1878 (see II, viii-xiii). Another influence, especially in the rhythmical freedom of the long, loose lines, came from Whitman, whose poetry he had read for the first time in Jan., 1878, and a copy of whose *Leaves of Grass* he had bought on May 5 (see Lanier's letter of that date to Whitman). The treatment of nature and the touches of mysticism reflect the medieval poets he had been reading during this year (see letter to Peacock, Dec. 21, 1878; cf. the closing paragraphs of the seventh Peabody lecture and the quotation from his own poem in the twelfth Johns Hopkins lecture, III, 39-40, 334). Beyond all this, however, it is essentially original and typical of its author, " the poem of Lanier's spiritual maturity " according to Starke, and generally conceded to be one of his very best.

## REMONSTRANCE  (50-51)

Written in Baltimore, summer of 1878.

Published posthumously in *Century*, XXV, 819-820 (Apr., 1883) ; reprinted with correction of one misprint (*clods* for *clouds*) in *1884*, 86-88.

Text: *Clover* 50-55, MS, numbered I of " Street-Cries " (with *lovable* for *loveable*, l. 11, as in *1884*, which followed this text). This MS shows one alteration, *struggling* > *hideous* (l. 48) ; no other variants known.

Though not published by Lanier, this poem was submitted to *Lippincott's* but rejected because of its attack on orthodoxy (see letter of Aug. 24, 1878, and note to " How Love Looked for Hell," below) ; his intention to publish is further indicated by its inclusion in *Clover*. *MDL* was paid $75 for it by *Century* with the comment, " How did such a poem escape publication? " (letters to her from R. W. Gilder, Dec. 23, 1882, and Apr. 4, 1883).

In theme this poem fits with the Poem Outlines grouped under the heading "Credo and Other Poems" (pp. 262-275, vol. I) ; indeed, the germ of it has been preserved in just such unfinished form (MS *JT,* a copy made in 1883 by J. A. Fisher), entitled " Free ":

> Opinion, let me alone—
> Damned be he (cried the Saxon) that doth not believe
> That Christ had black eyes and black hair.
> Damned be he (cried the Spaniard) that doth not believe
> That Christ had black eyes and black hair.
> Who is he that will fasten creeds before mine eyes, &c.

The allusions in l. 55 are to Nicholas Ridley, an English bishop, and Michael Servetus, a Spanish scientific and theological writer, both burned at the stake during the Inquisition.

## HOW  LOVE  LOOKED  FOR  HELL  (52-54)

Probably written in Baltimore, summer of 1878.

Published posthumously in *Century*, XXVII, 733-734 (Mar., 1884) ; reprinted without change in *1884*, 89-92.

Text: *Clover* 57-64, MS, numbered III of " Street-Cries " (with punctuation supplied in ll. 10, 20, 21, 34, 35, 63, 84, 111—the text used in *1884*). MS *CL* is a rough draft of the first stanza, unrhymed, with minor variants.

Probably one of the three poems mentioned in Lanier's letter of July 13, 1878, as just sent off " hot from the mint "; one of these was " The Marshes of Glynn," another seems to have been " Remonstrance," and this the third—it being the only poem of this period (dated " 1878-1879 " in *1884*) not specifically accounted for. It is possibly the unnamed poem submitted to the *North American Review* and rejected in a letter of Aug. 25, 1878. At any rate, Lanier's intention to publish it is indicated by its inclusion in *Clover*. *MDL* was paid $85 by *Century* for this poem (and " A Song of Love "; see letter to her from R. W. Gilder, Oct. 1, 1883), presumptive evidence that it was not actually published in Lanier's lifetime.

The germ of the poem is contained in a prose note in the *Ledger* 330-331, undated but *c*. 1874: " In all times and peoples, the same old gigantic Tale appears, in never-exhausted forms, how that Love went down into Hell, and rose again: Ishtar, Venus, Proserpine, Eurydice, Virgil, Dante, Goethe's Faust, Bailey's Festus, Christ. This is indeed the Story of Life. Childhood, pure Love, goes down into the fires and smokes of youth,—that time when desires burn, when we plunge ourselves into great [*illegible*] darknesses of sins, when we scorch our hearts with insane rushings through the fires of life, when we are beasts and revel in the brutalities that make our faces grave forever afterward, when we scorn our mothers (and would die ten deaths, afterwards in later life, if we might blot it out) when we laugh at our fathers, when we are simply a pitchy flame of Self. In Manhood, we rise again,—those of us who do not die eternally in the youth stage. (Poem). S. L." (Cf. the implied theme of the poem, that evil is the absence of good, with Lanier's later philosophy in " Opposition.")


## OPPOSITION (55)

Written in Baltimore, probably in the spring of 1879.

Published in *Good Company*, IV, 444 (Jan., 1880) ; reprinted without change in *1884*, 51.

Text: *Good Company*. Two MSS and a draft of the idea, dated Tampa, 1877, survive; for a full collation of variants see pp. 317-318, vol. I.

The conception apparently dates from 1877. The opening line echoes l. 80 of " To Bayard Taylor," written in Dec. 1878. The inclusion of this poem (under the title " The fret that's fixed across the Lute " and marked " MS ") on a list drawn up by Lanier apparently in preparation for his projected volume *Clover* indicates that it was probably written by May, 1879. MS *ET* is dated " 1879 / 180 St. Paul St.," Lanier's residence until Sept. 25, 1879, and hence must have been written before he went on his vacation to Rockingham Springs on July 18. The theme of the poem—that both rhythm and moral development stem from " opposition "—had been expounded in his Peabody lectures in the winter of 1879 and was further elaborated in his *Science of English Verse* written the following summer, and elsewhere. This theory, his most important contribution to literary criticism, grew out of his reading in contemporary science (see vol. I, Introduction). "Opposition" is Lanier's most philosophical poem and one of his most significant to recent critics, being chosen by Conrad Aiken, for example, as the single poem to represent its author in his Modern Library Anthology, *American Poetry, 1671-1928* (New York, 1929).


## OWL AGAINST ROBIN (55-57)

Written in Boston, June 2, 1879; revised at Rockingham Springs, Va., July-Aug. (see Lanier's letter of June 4, MS *JU*, and letter from *Scribner's* Aug. 14).

Published in *Scribner's*, XXII, 453-454 (July, 1881) ; reprinted without change in *1884*, 47-49.

Text: *Scribner's*. Two MSS survive; for a full collation of variants see pp. 318-320, above.

In accepting the poem *Scribner's* wrote: " We have handed it to the artist to see what he can do with the illustrations." These did not materialize, but

negotiation concerning them may explain the delay of two years between acceptance and publication. This is a rare example of humor in Lanier's poems other
than the dialect verse. It probably represents a good-natured reversal of his
own trouble in sleeping during nights of illness.

"Baalbec" (l. 51) was an ancient city of Syria, near Damascus, the center
of worship of the sun-god Baal.


## THE CLOUD (57-60)

Probably written in Baltimore, June, 1880 (see letter of June 15).

Published posthumously in *Century*, XXV, 222-223 (Dec., 1882), as "Individuality"; reprinted without change, except for addition of eight lines, in
*1884*, 10-13, as "Hymns of the Marshes / II / Individuality."

Text: MS *CL*, entitled "Hymns of the Marshes / II / The Cloud," signed
"Sidney Lanier," undated but in his late handwriting (apostrophe added l. 21;
capitals ll. 50, 61). No authority has been found for the variants in the posthumous prints, and the title there used seems to have been an earlier one (see
Lanier's letter of June 15, 1880, and the alteration on MS *JT*). MS *CL* is
apparently the latest revision. For a full collation, including the variants in two
MSS, see pp. 322-323, vol. I.

Although not published by Lanier, it was submitted to *Lippincott's* in a letter
of June 15, 1880 (containing an explanation of its genesis and meaning); it
was also intended for inclusion in his projected volume, "Hymns of the
Marshes." *MDL* was paid $75 for it by *Century* (letter to her of Jan. 19, 1882),
presumptive evidence that it had not been previously published.

This poem reveals, more fully than any other by Lanier, his interest in the
conflict between evolution and religion, between scientific determinism and the
responsibility of the individual. There also survives a similar prose jotting
(MS *CL*), which shows how Lanier frequently made memoranda without being
certain whether he intended to use them in prose or poetry, and which points
up the relationship of "The Cloud" to the theme of "Personality" developed
in the lectures at Johns Hopkins, winter, 1881 (see IV, 6). It is written on a
blank envelop, with a note at the top: "J. H. The Sacred Difference between
me and you. The Modern Personality." Then beneath: "Marsh Hymns. It
is at this difference, as I understand it, that Evolution stop[s]: See Fiske in
Jany Atlantic, Darwin, Spencer &c. You cannot account for it. Here it would
seem the direct hand of God is involved [?] in world's economy. The incon-
ceivably thyself. . . . Tennyson ["De Profundis"]." On the reverse side: "The
mystery in us which calls itself I. No man would voluntarily exchange per-
sonalities: nature has taken care of this sacred difference. (Shakspere's Sonnet)
Vedder's picture. Whitman's mistake: he has only sung the average man: the
reserve of *me* he has overridden in the most shocking manner. This force,
what becomes of it on the principle of conservation? You cannot account for
origin. A new function [*illegible*]. . . ." (See Introduction.)


## MARSH SONG—AT SUNSET (60)

Probably written in Baltimore, late autumn of 1880 (dated "Fall of 1880" in
the handwriting of *MDL* on a MS list of Lanier's poems, *CL*; see also note 124,
letters of 1880).

Published posthumously in *Our Continent*, I, 4 (Feb. 15, 1882); reprinted without change in *1884*, 13, as III of " Hymns of the Marshes."

Text: *Our Continent*. No other text known except a draft of five lines included in an early version of "The Cloud" (see p. 322, vol. I).

Not published by Lanier, but apparently intended for inclusion in his projected volume, " Hymns of the Marshes." The allusions to Shakespeare's *The Tempest*, without which the poem is unintelligible, will be readily identified by the student.

## A SUNRISE SONG (61)

Written in Baltimore, Nov.-Dec., 1880 (probably one of the " two little Songs just sent," mentioned in letter to W. H. Ward, Dec. 6, inclosing " A Ballad of Trees and the Master ").

Published in *Independent*, XXXIII, 1 (Apr. 28, 1881); reprinted without change in *1891*, 152.

Text: *Independent*. No variants known.

Apparently intended for inclusion in Lanier's projected volume, " Hymns of the Marshes."

## A BALLAD OF TREES AND THE MASTER (61)

Written in Baltimore on or shortly before Dec. 1, 1880 (see note 124, Letters of 1880).

Published in *Independent*, XXXII, 1 (Dec. 23, 1880); reprinted without change in *1884*, 141.

Text: *Independent*. No variants known.

The finest of Lanier's lyrics and probably the most perfect poem he ever wrote, it was composed at one sitting in " fifteen or twenty minutes . . . just as we have it without erasure or correction " (see Mary Day Lanier's accounts quoted in Starke, 407-408, and note 124, Letters of 1880). It is also incorporated in a surviving MS of " Sunrise " (*JT*) following line 57, with the marginal notation: " This little intercalary song to be in italics, or, perhaps better, in smaller print than the main text." (See facsimile facing p. 275, vol. X; *1884*, 245, says erroneously that it followed line 53.) One of three such songs, this is the only one that Lanier extracted for separate publication; he was paid $15.00 for it by the *Independent* (see W. H. Ward's letter of Dec. 24, 1880, and the note to " Sunrise," following). It has been set to music by various composers, notably George W. Chadwick and Francis Urban. According to *Luke* xxii:39 the olive grove in Gethsemane was the place where Christ was wont to go for prayer. For the place of this poem in Lanier's religion see the Introduction to the present volume.

## SUNRISE (62-67)

Written in Baltimore, Dec., 1880; revised, Jan., 1881.

Published posthumously in *Independent*, XXXIV, 1 (Dec. 14, 1882); reprinted with a few changes in spelling and punctuation in *1884*, 3, as I of " Hymns of the Marshes."

Text: MS *RL*, entitled " Hymns of the Marshes / I / Sunrise," signed " Sidney
Lanier / 435 N. Calvert St. / Baltimore, Md.," undated but clearly the final
version, both from the appearance of the MS and from the fact that it does
not contain " A Ballad of the Trees and Master." (A note in *1884*, 245, says
that the first copy and first revision of " Sunrise " included the " Ballad," which
was omitted from the final version. The present text is apparently the one
followed in *1884*, but with a few changes in punctuation and five errors in
reading the MS, as indicated in the collation, I, 323. The MS is here reproduced exactly, except for a few changes in mechanics, following *1884*: capitals
removed from *sleep*, ll. 11, 14; *silence's* for *silence'*, l. 67; hyphen for *build-fire*,
l. 128; capital for *Sun*, ll. 175, 181.) Two other MSS survive; for a full
collation of variants see pp. 323-325, vol. I.
    This poem was written when Lanier had a fever temperature of 104° (*1895*,
xviii). A note by *MDL* in H. W. Lanier, *Selections from Sidney Lanier* (New
York, 1916), 164, reads: " The lines of *Sunrise* were so silently traced that for suc-
cessive days I removed the little bedside desk and replaced in its sliding drawer
the pale-blue leaves faintly penciled, with no leisure for even mental conjecture
of them. . . . That hand 'too weak to sustain the effort of carrying food to
the lips,' I had propped to the level of the adjustable writing desk. After New
Year the perfect manuscript was put into my hand, and I was bidden to read
it." A letter from *MDL* to Charlotte Ware, Sept. 13, 1910, describing the
composition of " A Ballad of Trees and the Master," written shortly before
Dec. 2, 1880 (see note 124, Letters of 1880), says that the " Ballad " was
incorporated " a month later " in the first draft of " Sunrise "; but a letter to
Katherine Tyler, Feb. 23, 1923, states specifically that the latter was written in
" December, 1880 "—hence probably near the end of the month. A note in *1884*,
243, says that " Sunrise " was Lanier's " latest completed poem," and this is
in a general sense true; for it was written at the beginning of the final illness
that all but incapacitated him during the last eight months of his life. Some of
the brief untitled verses on pp. 208-210 of the Centennial edition may have been
written thereafter, however, and a number of the Poem Outlines definitely were.
A note to the " Ballad," *1884*, 245, says: " It was one of several interludes which
he at first designed, but, for some reason, afterwards abandoned." Lanier himself
extracted " A Ballad of Trees and the Master " (144) for separate publication;
*MDL* published a second posthumously, " Between Dawn and Sunrise " (142);
a third is now first published, " To the Sun " (143). Asterisks indicate their
position in the MS. Though Lanier did not live to publish " Sunrise " himself,
the MSS reveal his intention of making it the initial poem in his projected
volume, " Hymns of the Marshes." The general consensus of critical opinion
has ranked it, along with " The Marshes of Glynn," at the head of his poetry
(see Introduction).

## TYRANNY (67-68)

    Written in Prattville, Ala., Jan. 23, 1868 (see letter of Jan. 24); revised
in 1879.
    Published in *Round Table*, VII, 124 (Feb. 22, 1868), as " Spring and
Tyranny "; reprinted, with title and one word changed, in *1884*, 93-94.
    Text: *Clover* 65, early print corrected, as IV of " Street-Cries " (see p. 359,
below). *1884* is apparently based on this text, but *MDL* failed to substitute
*barren* for *sickly* (l. 16) and *in your natal* for *with your dainty* (l. 18). Three
MSS survive: *JT*, *CL*, and *Ledger* 262-263, all signed " S. L." and bearing the

early title; the last two are dated "Jan. 23, 1868." They show three minor variants in addition to those given above.

This is one of a group of poems dealing with the evils of Reconstruction (see Introduction). The attitude towards commerce and industrialism—Prattville had been a prosperous manufacturing town—is markedly different from Lanier's later tirades against Trade (see especially "The Symphony").

## THE RAVEN DAYS (68-69)

Written in Prattville, Ala., Feb. 25, 1868 (as dated on a surviving MS).

Published in *Scott's Monthly*, VI, 873 (Dec., 1868); reprinted without change in *Banner of the South*, I, 2 (Jan. 30, 1869), and *New Eclectic*, IV, 248 (Feb., 1869); and with three changes in *1884*, 213.

Text: *Scott's Monthly*. Two MSS survive, one of which contains 28 rejected lines; for a full collation see p. 288, above.

This is one of a group of poems dealing with the evils of Reconstruction (see Introduction).

## LIFE AND SONG (69)

Probably written at Scott's Mills, near Macon, Ga., summer of 1868 (from evidence of publication date and the relationship of the poem to the facts of Lanier's life at this period): revised in 1879.

Published in *Round Table*, VIII, 157 (Sept. 5, 1868); reprinted without change in *Scott's Monthly*, VI, 718 (Oct., 1868); and in *New Eclectic*, III, 250 (Oct., 1868); revised version in *1884*, 94-95.

Text: *Clover 66, Round Table* print revised and numbered V of "Street-Cries" (the text followed in *1884*). "Life" and "Song" have been capitalized, l. 11. One MS survives; for a full collation of variants see p. 289, vol. I.

Written at a time when untoward circumstances were turning Lanier aside from an incipient career as author, this poem may have found its germ in Milton's "he who would not be frustate of his hope to write well hereafter in laudable things, ought himself to be a true poem" ("Apology for Smectymnuus," *Works*, III, 303, Columbia Edition). Ironically, it was his first success, a favorite with anthologists, and widely copied at the time of its publication; in addition to the reprintings given above, may be cited the Atlanta *Constitution* and an unidentified Montgomery newspaper (clipping dated Sept. 13, 1868, *JT*, with an editorial note replying to an inquiry in the former as to the identity of the author).

## THAR'S MORE IN THE MAN THAN THAR IS IN THE LAND (70-71)

Written in Macon, 1869-1871 (from the evidence of publication and the date in *1884*, "Macon, Georgia, 1869").

Published in the Macon *Telegraph and Messenger*, Feb. 7, 1871 (clipping in *CL*), with headnote indicating original publication; reprinted without change in *Southern Farm and Home*, II, 253 (May, 1871), and in *1884*, 172-174. (Apparently copied in newspapers throughout the South; reprinted in a version without the dialect in the Toledo, Ohio, *Blade*, May 18, 1871, and elsewhere, and in one unidentified newspaper with illustrations, entitled " Jones "—see facsimile, I, 337.)

Text: *Telegraph and Messenger* (with correction of misprints in punctuation, ll. 42-43, and *waggin* for *wagin,* following *1884* and the magazine printing of " Jones's Private Argument "). One MS survives; for a full collation of variants see p. 290, vol. I.

In spite of the statement in *1884*, vii, that it was published in a " Georgia Daily, 1869," no evidence has been found of publication earlier than 1871, and the earliest reference to it is in a letter of Mar. 11 (?) 1871—both being suggestive of recent composition. (It is dated " 1871 " in *MDL's* handwriting in a MS list of poems, *CL*.) This letter and note 17, Letters of 1871, tell of reprintings in Georgia and Virginia newspapers; and an unidentified clipping from a Galveston, Texas, newspaper (*CL*) reprints the poem with the following editorial note: " This is the sort of doggerel with which the Georgia news-papers persuade their people to cease emigrating and stay at home. There is not a word of truth in the story. Had there been time for the five years to elapse, poetic truth would have made Jones rich." Though no conclusive evidence has been discovered for Lanier's authorship of the version without dialect, it is quite likely that he published it so in the *Telegraph and Messenger* (no file for this period discovered); for the reprint in the Toledo *Blade* credits that newspaper as its source. It also seems probable that the version with illustrations, signed " O. J. Hopkins &c Toledo O.," appeared in the *Blade* (probably the weekly edition, no file of which has been discovered); for the advertisements verso, dated May 27, 1871, are from Summit City, Mich., and Ft. Wayne, Ind.—neighboring cities to Toledo—and the editor of the *Blade* at this time was " Petroleum V. Nasby " (David R. Locke), who would have sponsored both verse and drawings of this genre, nor would he have removed the dialect editorially.

In a reminiscent letter, Sept. 25, 1883, Robert S. Lanier recorded an anecdote of its composition, but unfortunately did not give the date: " While practicing law with us, a youngish fat well to do looking farmer came in the office . . . [and] told Sidney how, a year or two before, he had bought an adjoining worn out ' farm from a neighbor who took the purchase money & himself & family to newer lands in Texas, & how that, a few days before, this neighbor came back from Texas to his house while he was at breakfast without money, in rags—: came back to see this farm renewed, & *thrift* all around, &C, &C. Shortly after . . . Sidney turned to his desk and composed the poem, . . . that was then published in The Daily T & Mʳ. here & republished all over the country." Jones county is east of and adjoining Bibb County, in which Macon is located. Lanier was later to see and describe the " Cracker " emigrant on his way to Texas (letter of Nov. 22, 1872). For a discussion of his dialect poems, both their historical importance and their relationship to current economic problems in the South (treated in serious prose and poetry as well as humor-ous), see Introduction, vol. I.

LETTERS

# CHRONOLOGY

| | | |
|---|---|---|
| 1842 | Feb. 3 | Born, Macon, Ga. |
| 1860 | July 18 | Graduated with first honor, Oglethorpe University, near Milledgeville, Ga. Returned, Oct., as tutor. |
| 1861 | July 10 | Enlisted in Macon Volunteers, 2nd Battalion, Georgia Infantry, C.S.A. Stationed at Sewell's Point, near Norfolk, Va. |
| 1862 | Summer | Near Petersburg. First battles. Transferred to Signal Corps. |
| | Winter | Campaigns in North Carolina (Dec.–Feb.) |
| 1863 | Mar. | Furlough in Macon. Began friendship with Mary Day. |
| | May | Stationed at Fort Boykin, near Newport News, Va. |
| | Dec. | Began writing *Tiger-Lilies* (novel); also poems. |
| 1864 | Summer | Detailed as Signal Officer on a blockade runner. |
| | Nov. | Captured aboard *Lucy* and imprisoned at Point Lookout, Md. |
| 1865 | Feb. 15 | Released from prison. Reached Macon, c. Mar. 15, ill. |
| | July–Dec. | Writing poems and novel. Mobile Bay, Ala., for health. |
| 1866 | Jan. | Clerk, Exchange Hotel, Montgomery. Renewed literary activity. |
| 1867 | Sept. | Moved to Prattville, Ala., as principal of Academy. |
| | Nov.–Dec. | *Tiger-Lilies* published. Married Mary Day (Dec. 19). |
| 1868 | Jan. 17 | First hemorrhage and beginning of serious illness. |
| | May | Closed Academy because of health and financial depression. |
| | Dec. | Began study of law in father's office, Macon, Ga. |
| 1869 | July 7 | Admitted to Georgia Bar. Ill, at health resorts (Aug.–Nov.). |
| | Dec. | Began law practice in Macon. |
| 1870 | Summer | Ill, at health resorts; then New York, care of Dr. E. E. Marcy. |
| | Oct. | Returned to law practice. |
| 1871 | Winter | Ill. Began contributions to *Southern Magazine,* Baltimore. |
| | Mar.–Nov. | Health resorts; then New York, care of Dr. Marcy. |
| | Dec. | Returned to law practice in Macon. |
| 1872 | Winter | Ill. Returned to law practice in May. |
| | July–Oct. | Health resorts in Virginia and Georgia. |
| | Nov. | To San Antonio for health. |
| 1873 | Winter | In Texas until March. Renewed literary and musical activity. |
| | May–Nov. | Planning to give up law for literature and music. In New York. |
| | Dec.–Mar. | First flute in the Peabody Orchestra, Baltimore. Lived at 64 Center St. |
| 1874 | Winter | Began friendship with R. M. Johnston and Innes Randolph. |
| | Apr.–Aug. | Georgia, for health. Wrote "Corn," composed music. |
| | Sept.–Nov. | In New York, seeking career in the arts. |
| 1875 | Winter | Returned to Baltimore. Peabody Orchestra season (Jan.–Mar.). |
| | Feb. | "Corn" published in *Lippincott's.* Beginning of national reputation. Met Baltimore and Philadelphia *literati.* |
| | Spring | Ill. Wrote "The Symphony." Commissioned to write *Florida.* |
| | Apr.–July | In the South, collecting material for travel book. |
| | July–Nov. | In Philadelphia and New York, writing *Florida.* Met Bayard Taylor and New York *literati.* Boston, Longfellow and Lowell. |

| | | |
|---|---|---|
| | Dec. 4 | Peabody Orchestra season began, lasting until Mar. 18, 1876. |
| 1876 | Winter | Wrote "Cantata" for Centennial, and "Psalm of the West." |
| | May 10 | Attended performance of "Centennial Meditation of Columbia." |
| | July–Oct. | At farm, West Chester, Pa., with his family. Seriously ill. |
| | Nov.–Dec. | In Philadelphia with Peacocks. *Poems* published by Lippincott's (Nov. 12). Desperately ill. Left for Florida, Dec. 21. |
| 1877 | Winter | In Tampa, regaining health. Wrote numerous short poems. |
| | June–July | In Baltimore, Washington, and New York seeking employment. |
| | Aug.–Sept. | At farm near Chadds Ford, Pa., ill. Wrote short poems. |
| | Fall | Returned to Baltimore after absence of 18 months. Joined by family, at 55 Lexington St., then 33 Denmead St. |
| | Dec. 15 | Peabody Orchestra season began, lasting until Mar. 16, 1878. |
| 1878 | Feb. | Began teaching at R. M. Johnston's Pen Lucy School. |
| | Spring | Several poems published. Gave Bird lectures on literature. |
| | Summer | Wrote "The Marshes of Glynn" and "The Physics of Poetry" (first state of *The Science of English Verse*). |
| | Fall | Edited *The Boy's Froissart* (1879). Moved to 180 St. Paul St. |
| | Nov. 2 | "Shakespere Course" at Peabody Institute (until May 5, 1879). |
| | Dec. | "The Marshes of Glynn" published in *A Masque of Poets*. |
| 1879 | Jan. 25 | Peabody Orchestra season began (until May 3). Ill. |
| | May–June | Edited *The Boy's King Arthur* (1880). Business trip to New York and Boston. |
| | July–Sept. | Rockingham Springs, Va. Wrote *The Science of English Verse*. |
| | Sept. | Baltimore, 435 N. Calvert St. Teaching at private schools. |
| | Oct.–Dec. | Johns Hopkins lectures, "English Verse; Shakespere." |
| 1880 | Winter– Spring | Seriously ill. Peabody Orchestra season (Jan. 31–Apr. 23). Hopkins course on Chaucer and Shakespere (Feb. 8–Mar. 15). |
| | May 12 | *The Science of English Verse* published by Scribner's. |
| | May–June | Ill with fever. Wrote "The Cloud" and "The Crystal." |
| | July–Sept. | Seriously ill at West Chester, Pa. |
| | Fall | Returned to Baltimore. Edited *The Boy's Mabinogion* (1881). |
| | Dec. | Desperately ill. Wrote "A Ballad of Trees and the Master," "Sunrise," and minor Hymns of the Marshes. |
| 1881 | Jan. 26 | Hopkins lectures on "The English Novel" (until Apr. 15). |
| | Winter | Health and strength failing rapidly. Gave up Peabody Orchestra concerts. |
| | May 18 | To Asheville, N. C., with brother; joined by wife (May 25). Set up "Camp Robin," Richmond Hill, near Asheville (June 4). |
| | Summer | Edited *The Boy's Percy* (1882). Visited by father and brother. Moved camp to Lynn, on Mount Tryon (Aug. 4). |
| | Sept. 7 | Died, 10 A.M. |

N. B. In the notes to the letters that follow, numbers in parentheses after the titles of Lanier's poems and prose refer to volume and page in the Centennial Edition, I-VI. Letters, cited or quoted in the notes, may be found in the same edition, volumes VII-X. All manuscripts are in the Johns Hopkins Library, unless otherwise noted.

## To Robert S. Lanier

Boykin's Bluff, Va.
Dec$^{br}$ 7th ''/63

My Dear Father:

I have delayed writing you, in the hope that I might be able to send you a copy of the introductory chapter of " my novel ": [1] but I have not had time to write it, and so wait no longer –. After Christmas, I hope to give more attention to the Novel itself.

Our friends in Surrey, extended to us the most cordial welcome imaginable: they have given us several delightful parties: have insisted on frequent visitings: and our relations, up there did not permit us to withdraw our attention, even if we had wished to do so –. All this has occupied much time which I should otherwise have devoted to matters literary –.

In the long night-guards, however, which we have to stand here, my mind has ample scope to expand itself, and it does so, always, with reference to the novel –. I have found it somewhat difficult, amidst the multiplicity of scenes and incidents which would crowd upon me in fascinating succession, to concentrate my attention upon what, I suppose, should be the first aim of the novel writer, viz; the forming of the bare outline of a consistent plot –. I find, however, of late, that the plot, in spite of all this confusion, is taking the matter into its own hands, and is gradually *shaping* itself out into form and comeliness: I think one more guard-night will finish it: and hope to send

·

[1] Lanier enlisted in the Macon Volunteers, 2nd Battalion, Georgia Infantry, C.S.A., on July 10, 1861, and went immediately to Virginia. In 1862 he transferred to the Signal Corps and was stationed at Fort Boykin, near Newport News. Here began his friendship with Virginia Hankins, who lived at nearby Bacon's Castle.

By this time, and perhaps largely under the stimulus of literary discussion at Bacon's Castle, Lanier had begun the writing of *Tiger-Lilies*. The difficulty of literary composition in the midst of war, referred to in the third paragraph of this letter, is echoed in a phrase occurring at the end of Bk. I, Chap. III, in the MS. of *Tiger-Lilies* (Clifford A. Lanier Collection, Johns Hopkins University), but omitted in the print version: " and I, here in Virginia scribble, between guard-hours ."

92

it to you, together with the introductory chapter, in my next –. Meanwhile I write for you, a little piece which sang itself through me the other day, and which I have given to a female friend in Surrey –. She is a tolerably good judge: and she thinks it very beautiful –. It does not compliment *you,* however, as it did *her*: and so your judgment will probably be more vigorous –. There's more in it than you'll see at one reading –. . . .

Cliff and I are in excellent health and spirits –. We were some-what disgruntled by the news from Bragg: [2] but not knowing certainly the position of affairs there, and distrusting the Yankee reports, we cling to a hope that all is not irretrievably lost in that direction –.

Tell Mother the socks will be very acceptable: the *knife* particularly so –. I need one almost every moment –.

Present our loving regards to all our friends: and kiss Mother for us many times –.

Your affectionate Son,

S. C. L.

To ROBERT S. LANIER

[Ft. Boykin, Va.,] May 28th "/64

My Dear Pa:

After many long days of suspense and anxiety, we have just got your letter, written twenty days ago, (7th May)–. Having been sent before the commencement of Johnson's retreat,[3] it contained not a word of all that we wanted to hear concerning the state of things, at home, resulting from that singular movement –. What does Gen. J. intend to do? I know nothing of him, except what I could gather from his Peninsula campaign and his short administration in the Vicksburg region:– judging from *these,* it seems to me he is a sort of monomaniac on " abandoning " and " retreating "–.

---

[2] Gen. Braxton Bragg was defeated by Gen. U. S. Grant at Missionary Ridge on Nov. 25, 1863, thus losing Chattanooga and Tennessee generally to the Federal forces.

[3] Gen. Joseph E. Johnston began his retreat in north Georgia on May 13, 1864. He was removed from his command on July 18, six weeks before the fall of Atlanta, being replaced by Gen. J. B. Hood.

We hear that the enemy are in a few miles of Atlanta –: and fear you will suffer from raiding-parties –. Meantime, with the utmost anxiety, we await further news from you –.

Am very sorry you didn't receive our letters –. Have written you *four* in the last three weeks –. Doubtless your failure to get them was caused by the recent numerous tappings of the railroads, with which the Yankee Cavalry have been solacing themselves by way of sweet revenge for the shower of defeats which we have poured upon their armies since the opening of the Spring campaign –.

I fear that Major M.'s dispatch, (sent, undoubtedly, with the *best* of motives) overrated the action to which it referred, and magnified your fears as to our future security –.[4] I wrote you an account, somewhat in detail, of the Affair, a month ago: hope you have received it by this time –. I did *not* lose my flute, *nor* the Novel, having taken the precaution to secure them, together with one or two other of my treasured " movables and hereditaments " about my person, in my haversack –. We lost all our clothes, however: apropos of which: – a citizen, who was taken prisoner by the Yanks, on their march down the road, and who accompanied them to our camp, told us, (after he was released) that he heard the scoundrels remarking, as they rummaged our knapsacks &c, " Talk about ragged Rebels! The d – d Rebs have got better clothes than *we* have! " – – The compliment to our wardrobe, however, was but a poor compensation for the loss of it –. . . .

I have no news –. Our campaign progresses well: but I have a " heart for any fate "–. Have you ever realized how splendid is this truth, that, whereas it *is* possible to conquer and enslave a man's *body*, it is yet quite utterly *im*possible to subjugate his *soul?* and that consequently a true man is always, by a divine right, essentially *free,* since even when bound hand and foot he may always defy and shame his captors with an unconquerable

[4] On Apr. 28, 1864, Major J. F. Milligan had telegraphed R. S. Lanier from Petersburg: " Your sons are a credit to you & a pride to their state. In the action of the 14th inst, their gallantry was particularly conspicuous. Thank God they are well & hearty. Regards to your esteemed family " (Clifford A. Lanier Collection, Johns Hopkins University). The activities of April and May were caused by Gen. Butler's advance on Petersburg, which broke up the Confederate signal line, leaving Lanier's party of scouts cut off. These experiences form the background of the few actual war experiences related in *Tiger-Lilies* (V, 98-136).

heart? It's perfectly glorious! — Deal out a thousand kisses and loving embraces to our Mother and Sister: and send another thousand to the dear ones in Alabama —; from your and their

S. C. L.

## To Robert S. Lanier

Petersburg Va
August 2nd /64

My Dear Pa

I can scarcely express to you the relief which I experienced on receiving your letter yesterday, written July 25th. [5] It had been two month since I heard from you; your letter written on May 24th having reached me just two months after that date —. The papers of day before yesterday announced a Yankee Raiding-party at Clinton, Ga. moving on Macon; and I, not knowing what your capabilities for defence were, supposed that you would have the old tale repeated in which " our forces, consisting principally of Militia, made a gallant resistance, but were over-whelmed by superior numbers, and routed &c &c," and that our beautiful city would fall prey to the barbarians —. But we have, this morning, the cheering news that Genl Iverson has met the enemy near Clinton, defeating him and capturing several hundred of his men —. And so, with our letter from you informing us that you are comfortably situated with our letter from Sister, also recd yesterday, loudly praising the kind hospitalities of Aunt Mina, and with one from Mother full of all love and holy invocations, we rest content, and for the first time in two long months allow ourselves to think with satisfaction of the dear ones whom we long so much to see —.

[5] R. S. Lanier's letter of July 25, 1864, to " My dear Sons " refers to Sidney Lanier's letter of July 1 (lost). With his wife and daughter away from Macon, R. S. Lanier had moved out to Camp Cooper, where he was serving as adjutant to Major Rowland. He reported raids near Covington, Athens, Madison, Eatonton, and Milledgeville. And in his letter of Aug. 6 he gave a detailed account of the repulse of Gen. Stoneman's raid on Macon by militia under Gen. Alfred Iverson and of the victory at Clinton.

Cliff and I have been "rudely torn" from our pleasant abiding-place in Surrey, and will probably remain in Petersburg for some time –. We are here awaiting orders from the War Department to go aboard a Blockading Vessel from Wilmington to Nassau or Bermuda – [6] Meantime we are stationed at a place near Petersburg, immediately in rear of Gen[l] Beauregard's Hd'Qr's, being the terminal Post of a signal line which stretches along nearly the whole front of our army –.

It is not yet absolutely certain that we will be ordered to the blockades: but esteeming it highly probable, we are held in readiness to obey the orders promptly, should they come – It is described to me, by a friend of mine who has been engaged for some time as a signal man in the blockading business, as a most delightful and desirable position, since one is there surrounded by pleasant and agreeable gentlemen, lives well, has plenty of leisure to read, and frequent opportunities to visit friends for a week or two, besides being enabled to make advantageous purchases of useful articles in the cheap markets of Nassau and Bermuda.

Affairs are very quiet here along our lines, tho' it is rumored to-day that Grant is again moving forces to his left, threatening the Petersburg & Weldon R. R. The excitement consequent upon the recent springing of the Yankee mine has subsided; and, beyond a little picket firing and an occasional shell shrieking into the city, an air of Sabbath calm prevails –. I am strong in the hope that the campaign, and, with it, the war, is nearly over –. Grant's repeated failures, and the terrible slaughter of his men (we yesterday shovelled six hundred dead Yankees into their own mine, the grave which they had dug for us!) are already beginning to excite in the mind of our erratic enemy that distrust which has always been the inevitable prelude to a change of Commanders and the abandonment of a campaign –. Several staunch War-papers at the North have recently come out for peace on *any* terms: and I firmly believe that since the recent speech of M[r] Long at his reception in Ohio, the Peace-party, (and that, too, not the restoration-of-the-union peace party, but the On-any-terms-Peace-party) at the North has

---

[6] The official records of the U. S. War Department show that Lanier was detailed as a Signal Officer on a Blockade Runner, by order dated August 2, 1864.

ceased to be a phantom, has clothed itself with flesh and blood, has organized into bone and muscle, and has become an earnest and significant reality –.[7]

Yet, I rejoice in the Peace-party, not because of any results which I expect directly from its operations in favor of our independence, but simply because it is an infallible indication of a wide-spreading belief in the ability of the South to *win* its independence *by force of arms* –. The true and effective Peace-party is led, not by M[r] Long, but by Gen. Lee. This noble Fugleman, with his ragged constituency, who combine filth with heroism, in such a way as the world has not before seen, who vote by bullet and not by ballot, who thunder from the Earth-works and not from the Hustings; This innovating politician who discards bribery, who spreads not soft-soap, who pulls not the concealed wires, who confers no lucrative positions, who makes no shoddy contracts, who rejects all the old and well-established " mechanical applicances " of Party, that is the man, these are the voters, who are to give us peace and to establish our independence –. Nor have we long to wait, before the end comes –. The North believes that this is the closing struggle; nothing is more curious than to notice how, in all their utter-ances, this idea is unconsciously but plainly presupposed –. The campaign is nearly over; its last battles are to be fought in a few weeks at farthest –. The crisis is come –. The Western Continent is in labor; the awe and agony of child-birth are upon her –. But I believe that by the New Year, /65, the gigantic throes will cease, and it will be announced to the World-Family that another son is born into it –. May all kind Fairies and good Angels preside at the birth of him, and endow him with all manly virtues and graces; so that his career in life may be that of a star in heaven, which

> " Maketh not haste,
> Which taketh not rest,
> But ever fulfilleth
> Its God-given hest " ! – –

---

[7] The peace movement of 1864 gained such momentum that the northern Democrats wrote a " peace-plank " into their platform for the presidential cam-paign, but the re-election of Lincoln ended it. Alexander Long of Ohio was one of the delegates to the Republican National Convention in 1864.

So! I've written a regular " leader " for the morning-papers –. I assure you I didn't do it with malice – prepense; more by token, I don't often bother my head about the chances of military events –

Gen. Lee held service at his Hd Q'rs. about two hundred yards from our station, on last Sunday –. Gen. Pendleton preached; Gen A. P. Hill was present, and some other Officers –. The table, which held the simple paraphernalia of our worship, a Bible and a Prayer book, was placed under a noble tree; the sky was serene: the sunlight was warm and beautiful on the green grass; a shell shrieked occasionally; a bird flew into the tree over the Preacher's head and sat and sang; my dog Flag, trotted composedly around and through the assemblage, rubbing himself sometimes against Gen. Lee, anon against Gen. Hill –, and then seating himself in the circle to stare at everybody, this being the first time that Flag ever attended Divine Service; the Preacher preached peace on earth and good-will towards men, dressed in a uniform which was trimmed with blood-red; – all of which incongruous elements set me into a reverie upon the illimitable mystery of the World, the end of which has not yet come – . – Gen. Pendleton is a noble, dignified man of large stature, and reminds me forcibly of a picture of Oliver Cromwell which I have seen somewhere – Gen. Lee has the Commander in every lineament of his face, and motion of his body; his dignity is graceful and simple, and his firmness which declares itself at first glance to be impregnable, is relieved by the intelligence and charity which one discovers in his eyes presiding over it –.[8]

You complain of our having written you nothing of our situation in Surrey –. This was impossible; since it was of the greatest importance that our position should be kept secret, as well as our occupation; and all our letters were sent at imminent risk of being captured by the Yankees –.

Cliff and I have recovered from our chills and are now in first-rate health and spirits –. Should we receive the orders which we expect, we have strong hopes of seeing you in a month or so –; but otherwise, we will not apply for furlough until the campaign is over –.

[8] See Lanier's account of this service in his memorial address on the death of Lee in 1870 (V, 274).

I wrote Mamie Day at the same time I wrote you – Did she get my letter? Ask her to write me –.

I regret more than I can express, the news of John Lamar's death –.[9]  Poor Gussie will be inconsolable; she idolized him – If you should find an opportunity to assist them, do so, for my sake –

Regards to any friends who ask after us – Please inquire constantly after Sam Knox who is probably in Gen. Hood's Army –. You could not do too much in the way of befriending him, should he be wounded or otherwise needing assistance – [10]

Write me often –. Our communication will I hope continue uninterruped –.

With all love,

Your son,

Sid. Lanier

To Milton H. Northrup [11]

Exchange Hotel
Montgomery, Alabama
May 12th "66
*address so.*

My Dear Northrop:

So wild and high are the big war-waves dashing between '61 and '66, as between two Shores, – that, looking across their " rude imperious surge," I can scarcely discern any sight or sound of those old peaceful days that you and I passed on the ' Sacred soil ' of M[idway] – The sweet,

---

[9] In his letter of July 25, 1864, R. S. Lanier had written: " Poor John Hill Lamar was killed recently in Maryland. Willie Le-Conte got home yesterday wounded in the leg at Atlanta on last Saturday."

[10] In his letter of Aug. 6, 1864, R. S. Lanier wrote: " Sam Knox was at Mr. Gresham's—wounded—but has probably gone home."

[11] Previously published, with omissions, in *Lippincott's,* LXXV, 305-306 Mar., 1905), by M. H. Northrup, whose introductory note stated: " On the return of peace and the reëstablishment of postal relations throughout the South, while still ignorant of [Lanier's] fate, I ventured a letter to my friend of ante-bellum days. A prompt response followed, inaugurating a correspondence that continued at irregular intervals for years." Northrup had been a friend of Lanier's at Milledgeville, 1860-1861.

half-pastoral tones that *should* come from out that golden time, float to me mixed with battle-cries and groans — It was our glorious Spring: but, My God! the flowers of it send up sulphurous odors, and their petals are dabbled with blood.

These things being so, I thank you, more than I can well express, for your kind letter. It comes to me, like a welcome sail, from that Old World to this New one, through the war-Storm. It takes away the sulphur and the blood-flecks, and drowns out the harsh noises of battle. The two margins of the great gulf which has divided you from me seem approaching each other: I stretch out my hand across the narrowing fissure, to grasp yours on the other side.

And I wish, with all my heart, that you and I could spend this ineffable May Afternoon under that old oak at Whittaker's and " talk it all over "!

I am glad that you continue to be of the gay troubadour-craft of letters: and especially congratulate you upon occupying so complimentary a position in our guild, as that of Correspondent to the World, which, by the way, is the only N. Y. paper that I take.

You must know that Clifford and I lost all we had, and have been compelled to go to hard work for our living. We have, however, through kind friends, obtained positions with good salaries, so that we are free, at least, from the pressure of immediate want. In the moments that we can spare from business we continue our studies, with even more ardor than while we had plenty of time to devote to them.

Cliff has finished a novel,[12] written entirely during intervals snatched from business: and I am working upon one which I hope to finish ere long. We also hope to get out a volume of poems in the fall, written by *both* of us, conjointly.

You will laugh at these ambitious schemes, when I tell you that we have not yet offered for print a single thing! But, we have no newspapers here with circulation enough to excite our ambition: and of course the Northern papers are beyond our reach. Our literary life, too, is a lonely and somewhat cheerless one; for beyond our father, a man of considerable literary acquirements and exquisite taste, we have not been able to find

[12] *Thorn-Fruit,* published by Blelock & Co., New York, 1867. Sidney Lanier did not finish his novel, *Tiger-Lilies,* until the spring of 1867.

a single individual who sympathized in such pursuits enough to warrant showing him our little productions. So scarce is " general cultivation " here! But we work on, and hope to become, at least, recognized as good orderly citizens in the fair realm of letters, yet.

There's so much to tell you, and so much to hear from you! Our adventures (I say our, for Cliff and I were by each other during all the war) would fill, and possibly *will* fill, a volume: and I do not doubt that yours will prove equally varied.

Let me have them; and if you will keep me posted as to your whereabouts, I'll keep up a talk with you.

I'm thirsty to know what is going on in the great Art-world up there: you have no idea how benighted we all are — I've only recently begun to get into the doings of literary men, through the Round Table,[13] which I've just commenced taking.

Write me soon: and believe that I am always

Y<sup>r</sup> Friend

Sidney Lanier

Clifford sends kind regards. Many of y'r old friends at the college were killed in battle. Will particularize some other time.

## TO MILTON H. NORTHRUP

Exchange Hotel,
Montgomery Alabama
June 11th "66

My Dear Northrop:

I have to thank you for your promptness in replying to my letter, as well as for your kind expressions in

---

[13] *The Round Table: A Saturday Review of Politics, Finance, Literature, Society, and Art* was published in New York from Dec. 19, 1863, until July 30, 1864; and from Sept. 2, 1865, until July 3, 1869. The editors, during the period in which Lanier not only subscribed but contributed to the *Round Table*, were Dorsey Gardner and Henry Sedley.

regard to its contents. Since I like *friendship* better than all things else in the world, I'm well content to believe that y'r complimentary terms originated in *that,* rather than in any merit of what was written.

I proceed to give you a very condensed " syllabus " of my war-experiences. In June, of '61, 1 enlisted as private in the 2nd Georgia Battalion of Infantry, then stationed amongst the marshes of Sewall's Point, Va, immediately opposite Ft. Monroe. Here we played " Marsh-Divers " and " Meadow-Crakes " for Six months, our principal duties being to picket the beach: and our pleasures and sweet rewards-of-toil consisting in Agues that played dice with our bones, and blue-mass pills that played the deuce with our livers.  Unless you 've had a real James River chill and fever, you'll utterly fail to appreciate the beauties of the Situation.

We were next ordered to Wilmington N. C., where we experienced a pleasant change in the Style of fever; indulging, for two or three months, in what are called the " dry shakes of the sand-hills," a sort of brilliant tremolo movement brilliantly executed, upon "that pan-pipe, man," by an invisible but very powerful performer.

We were then sent to Drury's Bluff: and, from there to the Chickahominy, participating in the famous Seven days battles around Richmond – Shortly afterward, my regiment went upon a special expedition down the South bank of the James, and, after a little gunboat-fight or two, was sent to Petersburg, to rest.  While in Camp there, I, with Cliff and two friends, obtained a transfer to Maj. Milligan's Signal Corps; and becoming soon proficient in the System, attracted the attention of the Com'd'g Off. who formed us into a mounted Field Squad and attached us to the Staff of Maj. Gen. French.

After various and sundry adventures, in that capacity, we were ordered to proceed to " The Rocks," a point on the James near its mouth, opposite Newport's News, where we remained about a year and a half, acting as scouts, and transmitting our information across a Signal line which extended up the river to Petersburg.  Our life, during this period was as full of romance as heart could desire.  We had a flute and a guitar, good horses, a beautiful country, splendid residences inhabited by friends who loved us, and plenty of hair-breadth 'scapes from the roving bands of Federals who were continually visiting that Debateable Land. I look back on that as the most delicious period of my life, in many respects: Cliff and I never cease to talk of the beautiful women, the serenades, the moon-light dashes on the beach of fair Burwell's Bay (just above Hampton Roads), and the spirited brushes of our little force with the enemy.

The advance of Gen. Butler upon Petersburg broke up the Signal line, but our party was ordered to remain, acting as scouts in the rear of Gen. B.'s army. By dint of much hiding in woods, and much hard running from lair to lair, we managed to hold our position and rendered some service, with information of the enemy's movement.

From here, My Bro. and I were called by an order from our Sec'y of War, instructing us to report for duty to Maj.-Gen. Whiting, at Wilmington. Arrived there, we were assigned to duty on Blockading Steamers, as Signal Officers; Clifford on the " Talisman," I on the " Lucy." Cliff made three delightful and adventurous trips: from Nassau to Wilmington: was wrecked, on the last voyage, and just saved his life, getting on a federal Schooner just in time to see his Steamer go down. He went then to Bermuda, and was on the point of sailing for Wilmington as Sig. Off. of the St'r Maude Campbell, when, hearing of the capture of Wil[ming]ton, he went to Havana, thence, after a pleasant time of a month with friends in Cuba, to Galveston Texas, whence he *walked* to *Macon, Ga*: arriving just in time to see our Mother die. I, meanwhile, ran the blockade of Wilmington, successfully, but was captured, in the gulf-stream, by the Federal cruiser Santiago de Cuba, carried to Norfolk, thence to Fortress Monroe, and Camp Hamilton, and at last to Point Lookout, where I spent four months in prison. Some gold, which a friend of mine had smuggled into the prison in his mouth, obtained the release of both of us. I made my way home, by a long and painful journey, and, immediately upon my arrival, losing the stimulus which had kept me going so long, fell dangerously ill and remained so for three months, – delirious part of the time. I had but begun to recover, when Gen. Wilson entered and occupied the city (Macon, Ga.). Then Cliff came; then we buried our Mother; – who had been keeping herself alive for months by the strong conviction, which she expressed again and again, that God would bring both her boys to her, before she died.

Then peace came, and we looked about, over the blankest world you can imagine, for some employment – My Brother first came here, as book-keeper, of this hotel: I meanwhile spending the winter at Point Clear on Mobile Bay. In January last, I came here –.

And so, you have a very outlinish outline of my history.

Your letters do me more good than you imagine – Himmel! My dear Boy, you are all *so* alive, up there, and *we* are all *so* dead, down here! I begin to have serious thought of emigrating to y'r country, so that I may live, a little. There's not enough attrition of mind on mind, here, to bring out any sparks from a man.

I offer you my sincere congratulations upon the flattering proposition made to you by y'r friends in Syracuse –. From what I know of you, I should think that the life of a journalist would suit your temperament and talents exactly. Success to you, Monsieur le Feuilletoniste! And may the Devils be kind to you.

I won't weary you. Write me: and accept the constant regard of Y'r friend

Sidney Lanier

Cliff. sends kind regards.


To Robert S. Lanier [14]

Exchange Hotel
Montgomery Ala
July 13th "/66

My Dear Father:
                    The notes from you & Uncle Clifford are rec<sup>d</sup> and " digested."

As far as regards your (and his) suggestion in regard to *the propriety of expressing individual opinions of the Author in other ways besides the utterances* of the characters in the book, –

---

[14] Lanier had sent the MS of part of his novel, *Tiger-Lilies,* to his father and his uncle, Clifford Anderson, for criticism. Their suggestions are sufficiently implied in his comments on their letters.

I think perhaps you have failed to appreciate the distinctive feature of the *Novel,* as contrasted with the *Drama.* The difference between these two great methods of delineating events is, simply and only, that the Novel permits its Author to explain, by his *own mouth,* the " situation ": whereas, in the Drama, this must be done by the characters. But even a written Drama *tends* towards the Novel: for it has *stage-directions:* and a Novel is nothing more than a *Drama with the stage-directions indefinitely amplified and extended.* And if the Author of such a Drama choose to insert, in his stage-directions, his individual opinions as to the best positions &c upon the Stage (which, in the Novel, is the World, & men & women the players), these opinions are regarded as the advice of one who, writing for the stage, may be rightly supposed to know more of it than common readers and common players. And this natural view of the question is enforced by Authorities and precedents without number. The epigrammatic apophthegms of Victor Hugo; the polished man-of-the-world's advice of Bulwer; the erratic " Extra-leaves " of Jean Paul: the shallow but good-natured moralizings of G. P. R. James: the shrewd old-man's talks of Thackeray: the vigorous sermonizings of M^rs Browning, – all these attest the legality of the expression, by the Novel-writer, of his own opinions in terms as such, outside of that indirect utterance of them which appears in the " poetical justice " of the Denouements.

The " error in fact " to which Uncle C. alludes can surely be nothing more than some obscurity in my assignment of the *time when* the war-feeling overspread the country. It is stated that " in the early Spring of 1861," – this war-wind began to blow &c: will not this do very well, as pointing to the 12th of April, of that year, when the Sumpter gun was fired, which set the whole country in a blaze?

I believe I must agree with you both, as to the propriety of mentioning living persons by name – I was dubious about the good taste of it, at first: but the temptation was strong to hit 'em a lick as I passed by.[15]

---

[15] The surviving MS of *Tiger-Lilies* mentions several living persons by name, omitted in the print. For an account of this and a history of the composition of the novel—mentioned in the following paragraph—see the introduction to *Tiger-Lilies* (V, vii-viii, xxxv-xxxvi).

I begin to see the end of the novel. The story assumes a far
soberer tone, as it progresses: and I have, in the last part,
adopted almost exclusively the *dramatic,* rather than the descriptive, style, which reigns in the earlier portions, interspersed with
much *high talk.* Inded, the book, which I commenced to write
in 1863 and have touched at intervals until now, represents in
its change of style almost precisely the change of tone which
has gradually been taking place in *me,* all the time. So much
so that it has become highly interesting to *me*: I seem to see
portions of my old self, otherwise forgotten, here preserved.
If the book should possess no other merit, it will perhaps be
valuable, to others even, on this very account: being the genuine
and almost spontaneous utterance of a developing mind, which,
says Carlyle, would be interesting even if the mind were that
of a hod-carrier!

Cliff has only a few pages to write, to complete the revised
copy of his book. We think, now, that we will publish in the
same volume under one title.

We get on quietly – Aunt Jane has just returned from the
Point. Grand Pa & Ma are spending a day or two with us.

We echo your wish that we could be together this summer
but I don't see the chance for it, unless *you can come* here.
Can't you?

Our love and kisses to Sister. How I long to fold her up,
once!

The family unites in love to you all. Our congratulations to
Uncle C. on the accession to the future army of the country.[16]

                                                              Sid.


## To Mary Day [17]

                                                 Prattville Ala
                                                 Oct. 24th 1867.
Sweet Wife-To-Be:

        Tonight I violently laid hands upon and seized unto my
own behoof and use, three good hours of time the which hours
I had previously bargained, conveyed and covenanted unto the

---

[16] A son had been born to the Clifford Andersons on July 4.

[17] In August 1867 Lanier became engaged to Mary Day, whom he had met in
Macon during a furlough, spring 1863. At the end of September 1867 he moved to
Prattville, Ala., as principal of the Academy there.

Prattville Debating Society, – the same being the hours from
7 A. M. up to this present hour of half-past ten: and I have
been endeavoring with my most lightning-like scratching of the
pen, to empty a drawer-full of letters which have remained
unanswered for a month past: and have just succeeded. During
these hours I have been saying to myself, as I would finish each
letter, – *one* closer to my Darling: and so here am I, my Sweet,
gazing into thine eyes, and calling out to my soul which is gone
down into the gray loveliness as into the sea. And yet, I must
first talk to thee anent a wedding thou and I wot of. To-wit:
I would, My Darling, that thou wouldst write me down, in fair
black and white, good and true answers to these following
interrogatories, namely:

1. Precisely what day is this wedding hereinbefore alluded
   to, – to come off?
2. Precisely what *hour* is this same wedding to be celebrated
   and sanctioned by the priest?
3. Precisely who are to be the attendants, – the bottle-holders
   and sponge-holders, as it were, – of this wedding?
4. Precisely at what time should the cards of this same wedding
   be issued, and would My Lady Queen prefer the same to be
   engraved in N. Y. or N. O?
5. Precisely whither is it my Liege's royal intention to order her
   journey: her relays of carriages, how will they travel: her suites
   of apartments, where: her ovations, her illuminations, her
   rejoicings, – along what route of the land will these be?

Anent this last question, Dear Wife-I-yearn-for, let me say
for thy consideration, and sole free decision: that of course the
N. O. trip is *now* not feasible.[18] – As for any other place to
which we might journey, I know none that offers enough
pleasure to make it worth the fatigue of thy dainty limbs in
getting there. Moreover, I have thought that what money we
might spend in making any trip, would, if worked by thy
brain and thy deft fingers, put many a sweet comfort in our
home, and make it as nice a home for thine and my first year
as thou or I could wish. Our dining-room and one of our bed-
rooms want curtains and a carpet: and a thousand little orna-
ments which would last us some years might be bought for
that which would otherwise endure for only a few days. As

[18] Because of the yellow fever in New Orleans and because of the death of
Mr. Shannon and Gertrude Lanier Shannon's departure from that city.

for the *pleasure* of the trip, there *thou* must decide: I have no pleasure but in thee, with thee, *here.* I am happy as any king, and care for naught else of place or travel. My idea is, to bring thee immediately, or the morning after the wedding, to our loved ones in Montgomery, where thou and I will be petted and loved, by friends and kindred, until my work commences again. Thou lovest me too well not to speak me thy true mind: I have spoken thee mine: write: thou art my Queen.

Thou wilt like to know somewhat of household matters. Thou shalt know it. I have a Man-servant, the best I have ever seen: large, good-looking, respectful, smart, and quiet. I have no trouble whatever; he works all day long, at every thing he can find to do. Our cook is a woman of the severest dignity. Her habits of life are Spartan in their simplicity and stern self-denial. For instance, altho' it is well-known she has more good clo'es than any colored woman in the country, she yet dresses in a short homespun dress, – being set, by nature, upon " remarkable long and narrer " pedestals–, and disdains stockings averring that they are in de way anyhow. She possesses, however, the loveliest traits of character: among which I may mention a son, 14 years of age, which I don't pay any hire for him, but which he knows all about a horse, and runs errands, and makes fires, and acts as my body-servant. To give you an idea of my cook's economical ideas: I had thought of putting out the washing, fearing it would be too much for her, besides cooking: and had sent for a laundress to come and see me.

Enter Laundress, accompanied by Cook. My cook is a very sententious person. Laundress smiling; Cook severe.

" 'Oman come to see you, Mass Sid," says Cook.

" Yes, sir," says Laundress, all in a heap, " I'se splendid washer woman, bin livin' wid so and so five year, wash white, furnishes my own soap &c &c ad infinitum."

Cook listens, with thunder gathering on her brows. Laundress having finished, thunder peals.

" Mass Sid, you'se crazy. Let de 'oman go back home whar she cum fum! " and cook flounces out of the room, after ye manner of ye strong-minded.

I let de 'oman go back whar she cum fum, and find my washing well done.

We have War-fulls, beefsteak, butter, and good bread and coffee for breakfast: ham and salads (alias B. & G.),[19] okra, sweet potatoes, roast beef, butter-beans &c for dinner: tea, toast, cold round of beef, or broiled, with Worcester Sauce, for Supper. I am just importing some Buckwheat Cakes, Cheese, Mackerel, (I like 'em broiled, for breakfast) Codfish & Irish potatoes (fish-balls, you know) and maccaroni. My cow was to have been here yesterday, but ran away from her driver and got back home: will be over in a day or two. I have Cliff's horse, and will keep him until I start for Macon. We have the best garden-spot, so said, in the state: also a nice orchard of 3 or 4 acres, and stable-lot.

As for the neighbors: beyond kind greetings on the street, I have had no time to cultivate any of them. I prefer *not* to do so, even if I *had* time: since I wish to be alone with thee in all my spare moments.

I have five music-scholars, piano: teach them between school-hours. I am getting up a concert, proceeds to build a school-gymnasium. I play the cabinet-organ (Mason & Hamlin's) at Pres. church Sundays. Saturdays, run all over the country collecting monthly bills. Nights examine text-books, correct compositions, make out reports, post up books, reorganize school-exercises continually changed by new scholars & classes, speak at debating Society, play flute, piano, guitar & fiddle for visitors, attend to household business, and dream of thee, my Sweet, My Well-Beloved, My Blessing, My Rest, My

One.

78 Scholars today.


## To Milton H. Northrup [20]

Macon, Ga.  Dec. 16th 1867.

My Dear Milton:

Your answer to my Norfolk letter, of which you advise me in y'r last, has never reached me: yet, if I had

---

[19] Probably " Bacon and Greens."

[20] Northrup had moved to Washington, D.C., as correspondent of the New York *Express*.

Lanier went to Macon for the Christmas holidays. He and Mary Day were married there on December 19, and returned to Prattville at the end of the month. *Tiger-Lilies*, published by Hurd & Houghton at Lanier's expense, was on sale in Macon early in December.

had the remotest idea where to address you, I should have exhibited the magnanimity which illuminates *y'r* conduct,—and sh'd certainly have written you again.

It is charming that you should enter life at Washington under such agreeable auspices, and I share y'r pleasure, believing that you will extract the honey, and not be poisoned by the darker juices,—of that Weed they call Society, there.

Indeed, indeed, y'r trip-to-Europe invitation finds me all *thirsty* to go with you: but alas, how little do you know of our wretched poverties and distresses here, – that you ask me such a thing! My Dear Boy, some members of my family, who used to roll in wealth, are, every day, with their own hands, ploughing the little patch of ground which the war has left them, while their wives do the cooking and washing. This, in itself, I confess I do not regret: being now a confirmed lunatic on the "dignity of labor" &c: yet it spoils our dreams of Germany, ruthlessly.[21] I've been presiding over eighty-six scholars, in a large Academy at Prattville, Ala., having two assistants under me: 'tis terrible work, and the labor difficulties, with the recent poor price of cotton, conspire to make the pay very slim. I think y'r people can have no idea of the slow terrors with which this winter has invested our life in the South. Some time I'm going to give you a few simple details, which you must publish in your paper.

Tiger Lilies is just out, and has succeeded finely in Macon. I have seen some highly complimentary criticisms in a few N. Y. papers on the book: tho' they mistake the whole plan of the book, and what was written in illustration of a very elaborate and deliberate theory of mine about plots of novels, has been mistaken for the "carelessness of a dreamy" (N. Y. Evening-Mail) writer. I would I knew some channel thro' which to put forth this same theory.

What a horribly jejune and altogether pointless affair is the "Southern Society," of Baltimore! My name was published as a contributor: but I shall certainly send nothing to such a set of asses.

Do write me what you think of Tiger Lilies. H & H. don't treat me well, and advertise very slimly: indeed, I have as yet

---

[21] At Oglethorpe, 1860-1861, Lanier and Northrup had planned to study at Heidelberg.

seen *no* advertisement of *theirs*.   The book would sell, if properly advertised: a firm took hold of it *here,* and have already disposed of a large number of copies. — Mine have not arrived: when they come, will send you one. — I have hope of getting you something to do, for " the Telegraph," of this place, one of the largest and heaviest papers of Georgia.

Write me.  I have scratched off this, in a great haste, freezing in a hotel reading-room, where a big fire is snapping and (as is the Southern custom) all the doors and windows are open.

Yr Friend

Sidney Lanier.

A letter addressed here will always find me.


## To Jane Lanier Watt

Prattville, Ala. Jan'y 12th 1868.

My Darling Auntie:

We half-way hoped that you would drop in on us yesterday, or today: we think you're very mean because you didn't, and we're going to punish you by writing to you.

Our little town was the scene of some excitement yesterday, — tho' we hope that the agitation is now entirely abated.   The Radicals, in pursuance of their keeping-the-steam-up policy, must needs hold a meeting in the streets of the town, and make speeches to a crowd of foolish negroes who, as is their usual custom, were armed with all manner of muskets, shot-guns, pistols, bludgeons &c &c.   During the speaking, one of the negroes became intoxicated with whiskey and patriotism and proceeded to vent his high-wrought soul by firing his pistol in the air and giving utterance to sundry threats against the white race in general.   His conduct became so outrageous that a member of the town council, passing-by, ordered him to cease on penalty of arrest and lock-up.   The refractory ward imme- diately presented his pistol at the Councilman and swore to shoot him if he advanced, while a large crowd of armed negroes gathered around to support their friend.  The Councilman, (A brave fellow: Geo. Smith, of the Sash & Blind Factory, here) immediately walked up to him; the negro fired and missed; Smith, tho' armed with a pistol, did not fire but jumped on him and wrested his pistol away. By this time, however, a dozen negroes had rushed upon Smith and thrown him to the ground; several whites on the street joined in the attempt to relieve Smith; pistols, double-barrels, knives, brickbats & bludgeons came into play; and the scene was altogether a lively one, until by some miraculous means the infuriated crowd was quieted. I hear of five wounded, – four negroes and one white, besides Smith who wonderfully escaped with a few bruises. Was in my house eating dinner, and knew nothing of the fray until I heard the shots, when, thinking we must all fight for it, I valiantly seized my pistol, made Maydie don her bonnet, and sat me down to await the enemy's charge.

Which your pickles are surely the best pickles! And don't I eat a whole one every day, bird-seeds and all? And don't we bless you for 'em from the bottom of our – gastronomical apparat*uses* ?

Sandy, the wagon-driver goes to town tomorrow: please tell Cliff that he left the bundle of books at Watt & Beall's, and ask him to see that Bob. [Watt] puts 'em aboard the wagon. Sandy will call.

My school is smaller than last year. The people come to me almost with tears in their eyes, and represent their fearful impoverishment which prevents them from sending children to school. I have so far only sixty-five scholars: and will have to discharge one of my assistants.

Love to everybody. Receive a hundred kisses, Darling Auntie, from

Your loving

Sid & Mamie.

TO ROBERT S. LANIER

Prattville, Ala.
Jan'y 21st 1868.

My Dear Father:

Y'r kind letter announcing for<sup>d</sup>ing of H. & H.'s draft was rec<sup>d</sup>, and I read with great pleasure y'r encouraging account of y'r business.

A telegram from H. & H. dated Jan. 9th, but delayed in transit here, announced that one hundred & seventy two copies only of Tiger-Lilies remained on hand, and asked if they should issue a second edition. This is very cheering, and gives me some ground of hope that I may in time realize some small profit on the book. I did not reply to the telegram, as I had previously written them, (thro' you), inquiring terms upon which they would reprint.

The draft on J. F. D. L.[22] was remainder of am't agreed upon between myself and him, sometime ago, and went towards the last payment due H & H, whom I still owe $200.

On Friday morning last I was attacked with a hemorrhage of the lungs, which lasted, tho' *not* copious, for fifteen or twenty minutes. I went up to school and taught till twelve, when, finding myself somewhat weakened, I returned home. Have not been to the schoolhouse since, (this is Tuesday!) finding much fatigue in using my voice, together with general weakness: but am improving daily, and will resume school duties, nothing interfering, by first of next week. Cannot at all account for the attack: had been in most vigorous health all the time previous; was suffering from slight cold when I retired night before: woke up at usual hour, and found my mouth full of blood. I have no pain, beyond a slight oppression about the chest: and no cough. Had not intended to tell you of it at all: but May, with her great eyes dilating serious, thought " it wouldn't be loving, not to tell you: " and so I yielded. I hope you will not be anxious: since I feel that I shall entirely recover.

I begin to entertain serious doubts of the safety of remaining out of the city. There are strong indications here of much bad feeling between whites and blacks, especially those engaged in the late row at this place: and I have fears, which are shared by Mr Pratt [23] and many citizens here, that some indiscretion of the more thoughtless among the whites may plunge us into bloodshed. The whites have no organization at all, and the affair would be a mere butchery: in addition to the fact that it might come when we were unprepared for it. The Stanton imbroglio may precipitate matters. Give me y'r views.

Clifford & Willie spent last Saturday night and Sunday with us.

---

[22] J. F. D. Lanier was a wealthy New York cousin.
[23] Daniel Pratt, founder of Prattville.

We had a glorious reunion, and all wished for you.  May sends many kisses.  Love to Uncle C & fam.

Sid.

Don't forget to send the Eclectic you spoke of.  I'm casting about for a plot.  Cliff is at work on a very good thing,  Have no criticisms of Thorn-Fruit appeared in Macon papers.[24]

## To Milton H. Northrup [25]

Macon, Ga
March 15th 1869.

My Dear Milton:

I have been y'r debtor for some months, for y'r very kind and interesting – not to say, *tantalizing* – letter, written from Naples: and – aside from the fact that, in *epistolary* debts, I rarely pay more than Twenty-five cents in the Dollar: – I should have answered y'r letter long ago, but have waited to receive some intimation from you that you had returned to this Home of the Brave &c.

Y'r " promotion," My Dear Boy, gives me sincere pleasure.  You'll be Duke of Albany, yet, I hope.  I fancy y'r position, as Agent of the Associated Press, must be one which would entitle you to a vast deal of consideration from those whom, by a twirl of y'r pen, you can present in a very ridiculous or very sublime light, in all the morning-papers, as happens to strike y'r lordly humor.  If you're like our Georgia man who has been doing the Georgia Legislature by Telegraph, you can wield more power by a " heading " than a Frenchman did with an epigram in the days of the Revolution.  Use your lightning fairly.  My Fine Ariel: do your spiriting gently, and let not harm come to

---

[24] In his reply of Jan. 26, R. S. Lanier wrote: " Sent Cliff to-day a pleasant notice of his book in [the Macon] ' Telegraph.' . . . I have sent you ' Southern Society's' criticism of ' Tigers.' . . .

" As to your second edition: I am thinking what to say about it.  It strikes me as a hard bargain that a whole first edition should be exhausted & you get not a dollar for it.  At all events I say if a second edition is to be published it must not be done *now* at your risk– & I say further, never hereafter put a line of yours in press where *you* have to *risk*."

[25] Lanier had closed the Prattville Academy in May 1868 because of financial difficulties and illness.  After six months spent in recovering his health, he began the study of law in December.

the patriots that sacrifice even their souls in making the Laws of the Country.

With a most monstrous yawn and gulp I swallowed my envy, when I heard of y'r projected tour to the great old Lands, and genuinely rejoiced in the pleasure wh. I knew must be in store for you. As for *my* sweet old dreams of studying in Germany,[26] *eheu!* here is come a wife, and By'r Lady! a boy, a most rare-lung'd, imperious, world-grasping, blue-eyed, kingly Mannikin; and the same must have his tiring-woman or nurse, mark you, and his laces and embroideries and small carriage, being now half a year old: so that, what with mine ancient Money-Cor-morants, the Butcher & the Baker & the Tailor, my substance is like to be so pecked up that I must stick fast in Georgia, unless litigation, and my reputation, should take a simultaneous start and both grow outrageously. For, you must know, These Southern Colleges are all so poor that they hold out absolutely no inducement in the way of support to a Professor: and so last January I suddenly came to the conclusion that I wanted to make some money for my wife and my baby, and incontinently betook me to studying Law: wherein I am now well advanced, and, D. V. will be admitted to the Bar in May next. My advan-tages are good: since my Father & Uncle (Firm of Lanier & Anderson) are among the oldest lawyers in the City and have a large practice, into which I shall be quickly inducted.

I have not however ceased my devotion to letters, wh. I love better than all things in my heart of hearts: and have now in the hands of the Lit. Bureau in N. Y. a vol. of Essays, I'm (or rather have been) busy too on a long poem, yclept " the Jacquerie," on which I had bestowed more real *work* than on any of the frothy things which I have hitherto sent out; tho' this is now necessarily suspended until the summer shall give me a little rest from the office business with wh. I have to support myself while I am studying law.[27]

[26] In his letter of Oct. 30, 1868, from Naples, Northrup had given an account of his European travels with a reference to " Heidelberg where I spent two glorious days . . . & where I did not forget that *you* would have been, had not war darkened our land."

[27] The volume of essays here referred to never materialized. Of the poem, Lanier had written his brother Clifford on November 4, 1868: "It is to be a novel in verse, with several lyric poems introduced by the action. The plot is founded on what was called 'the Jacquerie,' a very remarkable popular insurrection wh. happened in France about the year 1359, in the height of Chivalry." He worked on it sporadically for many years, but never finished it.

I shall be delighted, Dear, to see you in Macon, and can promise you a view of a beautiful City, some pleasant rides amid green leaves, some good music, and a hearty welcome. . . .

And so, having drawn all this upon y'rself, believe, My Dear Milton, that I am always

Your Friend

Sidney Lanier.

## To Paul H. Hayne [28]

Macon, Ga. April 13th 1870

My Dear Mr. Hayne:

Watching, night and day, for two weeks past, by the bed-side of a sick friend, I have had no spiritual energy to escape out of certain gloomy ideas which always possess me when I am in the immediate presence of physical ailment: – and I did not care to write you that sort of letter wh. one is apt to send, under such circumstances, since I gather from yr. letters that you have enough and to spare of these dismal down-weighings of the flesh's ponderous cancer upon suffering and thoughtful souls.

I am glad, therefore, that I waited until this divine day. If the year were an Orchestra, today would be the Flute-tone in it. A serene Hope, just on the very verge of realizing itself: a tender loneliness, – what some German calls *Waldeinsamkeit*, wood-loneliness, – the ineffable withdrawal-feeling that comes over one when he hides himself in among the trees, and knows himself shut in by their purity, as by a fragile yet impregnable wall, from the suspicions and the trade-regulations of men: and an inward thrill, in the air, or in the sunshine, one knows not which, half like the thrill of the passion of love, and half like the thrill of the passion of friendship; – these, which make up the office of the flute-voice, in those poems which the old masters wrote for the Orchestra, also prevail throughout today.

[28] The correspondence with Hayne, the Charleston poet (1830-1886) now living near Augusta, Ga., began in the summer of 1868 and continued until Lanier's death. Though they never met, he was one of Lanier's very few literary friends.

Do you like, – as I do – on such a day to go out into the sunlight and *stop thinking,* – lie fallow, like a field, and absorb those certain liberal *potentialities* which will, in after days, re-appear, duly formulated, duly grown, duly perfected, as poems? I have a curiosity to know if to you, as to me, there come such as this day: – a day exquisitely satisfying with all the fullnesses of the Spring, and filling you as full of nameless tremors as a girl on a wedding-morn; and yet, withal, a day which utterly denies you the gift of speech, which puts its finger on the lip of your inspiration, which inexorably enforces upon your soul a silence that you infinitely long to break, a day, in short, which takes absolute possession of you and says to you, in tones which command obedience, *today you must forego expression and all outcome, you must remain a fallow field, for the sun and wind to fertilize, nor shall any corn or flowers sprout into visible green and red until tomorrow,* – mandates, further, that you have learned after a little experience not only not to fight against, but to love and revere as the wise communication of the Unseen Powers. ——

Have you seen Browning's "The Ring and The Book"? I am confident that, at the birth of this man, among all the good fairies who showered him with magnificent endowments, one bad one – as in the old tale – crept in by stealth and gave him a constitutional twist i' the neck, whereby his windpipe became, and has ever since remained, a marvellous tortuous passage. Out of this glottis-labyrinth his words won't, and can't, come straight. A hitch and a sharp crook in every sentence bring you up with a shock. But what a shock it is! Did you ever see a picture of a lasso, in the act of being flung? In a thousand coils and turns, inextricably crooked and involved and whirled, yet, if you mark the noose at the end, you see that t is directly in front of the bison's head, there, and is bound to catch him! That is the way Robert Browning catches you. The first sixty or seventy pages of "The Ring and the Book" are altogether the most doleful reading, in point either of idea or of music, in the English language; and yet the monologue of Guiseppe Caponsacchi, that of Pompilia Comparini, and the two of Guido Francheschini, are unapproachable, in their kind, by any living or dead poet, *me judice.* Here Browning's jerkiness comes in with inimitable effect. You get lightning-glimpses, – and, as one naturally expects from lightning, zig-

zag glimpses – into the intense night of the passion of these
souls. It is entirely wonderful and without precedent. The
fitful play of Guido's lust, and scorn, and hate, and cowardice,
closes with a master-stroke:

> " . . . Christ! Maria! God! –
> *Pompilia, will you let them murder me?* "

Pompilia, mark you, is
dead, by Guido's own hand; deliberately stabbed, because he
hated her purity, wh. all along he has reviled and mocked with
the Devil's own malignant ingenuity of sarcasm. —

You spoke of a project you wished to tell me. Let me hear it.
Yr. plans are always of interest to me. Can I help you? I've
not put pen to paper, in the literary way, in a long time. How
I thirst to do so, how I long to sing a thousand various songs
that oppress me, unsung, – is inexpressible. Yet, the mere work
that brings bread gives me no time. I know not after all, if
this is a sorrowful thing. Nobody likes my poems except two
or three friends, – who are themselves poets, and can supply
themselves!

Strictly upon Scriptural principle, I've written you (as you
see) almost entirely about *myself*. This is doing unto you, as
I would you shd. do unto me. Go, and do likewise. Write me
about yourself.

Your Friend

Sidney Lanier

## To Paul H. Hayne [29]

New York, Aug. 9th 1870

My Dear Mr. Hayne:

Y'r. letter, containing the poem, reached
me at Lookout Mountain, Tennessee, where I had been spending
some weeks.

---

[29] After delivering a public address in Macon, late spring 1870, Lanier suffered
severe hemorrhage from the lungs, and was forced to spend the next six months
at watering places and in New York trying to regain his health. For the two years
following he alternated between attempts to practice law and disabling attacks of
illness.

I received it at night, about midnight. Some friends, — one of whom was Mr. Jefferson Davis—were sitting in the porch of my cottage, and I could not resist the temptation to read the poem aloud to them. So, – while my fair wife held the candle and shaded it with rounded white hand from the mountain-breeze, I read: and I feel very confident you would have been gratified with the sentiments of approval which followed, in hearty sympathy with the piece. I like it better than anything you have written: it has in it the *magnetism* wh. distinguishes genuine poetry from culture-poetry. Write me some more like this, good Friend!

I am travelling for my health. If you know what this phrase means, you know to what a melancholy state I am come. It wd. seem that the foul fiend, Consumption, hath me on the hip. Against him, I still fight: but God knows the event thereof. I had started for Minnesota: but I find the journey so disagreeable that, after resting here a day or two, I'm going back to Orange C. H. Va. where I have a friend living among the Sweet mountains, with whom I shall stay some weeks: and where, an thou hast any bowels of compassion left in thy Soul's abdomen, thou wilt write me, " care Charles Taliaferro, Esq."

I do no work at all. I am too ill. This is Apollyon's unkindest cut of all. In this he hath wounded my sword-arm. Well, well. And so, write me, dear Mr. Hayne, and believe that I always enjoy heartily your cheering words, and that I am always Your Friend

                                        Sidney Lanier

## To Paul H. Hayne

                                   Macon, Ga. April 17th 1872

My Dear Mr Hayne,

                        It would seem that Fate does not desire me to write a review of " Legends & Lyrics," — just as the old hag did not desire me to negotiate yr. poems you sent me in New York; for now—as then—I had written the first page of a review, when I was stricken down with illness, from which I am just beginning to crawl forth. The review of " L. & L."

was particularly near my heart: for I was keenly desirous of pointing out, and dwelling upon, a certain rare and lovely feature in your writings, wh., in these days, gives me a world of pleasure. I mean the entire *absence,* in every thing you write, of *Trade* in any of its forms. Utterly *uncommercial*: that is glorious, my dear Friend, and that is the spirit of your writings.

Trade, Trade, Trade: pah, are we not all sick? A man cannot walk down a green alley of the woods, in these days, without unawares getting his mouth and nose and eyes covered with some web or other that Trade has stretched across, to catch some gain or other. 'Tis an old spider that has crawled all over our modern life, and covered it with a flimsy web that conceals the Realities. Our religions, our politics, our social life, our charities, our literature, nay, by Heavens, our music and our loves almost, are all meshed in unsubstantial conceal-ments and filthy garnitures by it.

But your poems are not. Here the brooks wimple down the burn in order to be beautiful, and not in order to make money by turning mill-wheels: and the trees wave, and the birds sing, and sweet human emotions come into the woods and blend therewith: and no money-changers sit in the still leafy temples.

It is not necessary for me to explain, to *you,* what I mean by these hasty metaphors. You know what the commercial spirit is: you remember that Trade killed Chivalry and now sits in the throne. It was Trade that hatched the Jacquerie in the 14th Century: it was Trade that hatched John Brown, and broke the saintly heart of Robert Lee, in the 19th.

As soon as I get so that after my day's work, — which is continuous and exhausting every day — I can think at all, I propose to write my review. I read aloud to my wife, t'other night, the last strophe of the poem " To Sleep ": and we agreed — and my wife, mark you, hath an ear in her soul, and a soul in her ear, of the delicatest apprehension in the world! — that there is not a sweeter piece of melody in the language.

Let me know what you are doing; and believe me

                         Your Friend

                              Sidney Lanier

## To Mary Day Lanier

[Alleghany Springs, Va.,] July 12 th 1872

How necessary it it, Dear Comrade, that one should occasionally place oneself in the midst of those more striking forms of nature in which God has indulged His fantasy !

It is very true that the flat land, the bare hillside, the muddy stream, comes also directly from the Creative Hand: but these do not bring one into the sweetness of the heartier moods of God, – in the midst of them it is as if one were transacting the *business* of life with God: whereas, when one has but to lift one's eyes in order to receive the exquisite shocks of thrilling form and color and motion that leap invisibly from mountains and grass and streams, then one feels as if one had surprised the Father in His tender, sportive and loving moments.

To a soul, then, weak with the long flesh-fight, and filled with a sluggish languor by those wearisome disappointments which arise from the constant contemplation of men's weaknesses and from the constant back-thrusting of one's consicousness of impotence to strengthen them, – thou, with thy nimble fancy, canst imagine, what etherial and yet indestructible essences of new dignity, of new strength, of new patience, of new serenity, of new hope, new faith and new love, do continually flash out of the gorges, the mountains and the streams, into the heart, and charge it, as the lightnings charge the earth, with subtle and heavenly fires.

A bewildering sorcery seems to spread itself over even those things which are commonplace. The songs and cries of birds acquire a strange sound to me: I cannot understand the little spontaneous tongues, the quivering throats, the open beaks, the small bright eyes that gleam with unknown emotions, the nimble capricious heads that twist this way and that with such *bizarre* unreasonableness.

Nor do I fathom this long unceasing monotone of the little shallow river that sings yonder over the rocks in its bosom as a mother crooning over her children: it is but one word that the stream utters: but, as when we speak a well-known word over and over again until it comes to have a frightful mystery

in it, so this familiar stream-sound fills me with indescribable
wonder.

Nor do I comprehend the eloquence of the mountains, which
comes in a strange *patois* of two tongues: for the mountains
speak at once the languages of repose and of convulsion,— two
languages which have naught in common.

Wondering, therefore, from day to night, with a good wonder
which directs attention not to one's ignorance but to God's
wisdom: stricken, but not exhausted, by continual tranquil
surprises: surrounded by a world of enchantments which, so
far from being illusive, are the most substantial of realities: —
thou knowest that nature is kind to me.

— Indeed, O My Sweet, O My Wife, my heart would utterly
break, here, for lack of thee ,— were I not so " in-the-spirit "
that I can hear *thy* heart beating, across all the miles betwixt
us: and, with that sweetest rhythm pulsating softly in my soul,
I can lull for a little time the overmastering desire that thy
true eyes might look on this beauty at the same-time with mine.
Somehow, I do not doubt they *will* do so, some day: and this
faith, too, gives me a little patience. . . .

Breath upward some faint exhalations from thy flowers, that
they may float on and wreathe about thy

Lover.

### To Mary Day Lanier [30]

" Menger Hotel."<br>
San Antonio, Texas.<br>
Nov. 25th 1872

With many fair expressions, I parted from the Dane at Austin,
and took stage yesterday at 8 ½, A. M. for this place. We
arrived last night at 12 ½: being a steady ride, through the
great round waves of the " rolling prairie " of sixteen almost
unbroken hours. But we had a queer stage-load of nine pas-

---

[30] By November 1872 the state of Lanier's health was so desperate that he was
sent to spend the winter in Texas, in the vain hope that this climate would be
beneficial to his consumption. (See Lanier's essays on Texas, VI, 187–246.)

sengers: a milliner, of Michigan: an army officer, from away
out on the frontier: a miner from Chico, California: a substantial burgher from Indiana: and a much-travelled lady who
is at present combining the important avocations of landlady
and Milliner at San Marcos: and what with gathering a whole
hive-full of honey for future use from these most diverse
flowers, all in the summer atmosphere of a long dream of you,
I whiled away the time marvellous smoothly, and am not nearly
so tired today as I have the right to be.

San Antonio is charming. The hotel at wh. I am stopping is
of stone, with a fine paved court in the rear, after the manner
of the Cuban hotels, and fair broad pavement in front where
we sit in arm-chairs and look out upon the Alamo plaza. A
few yards off is the Alamo: and I walked over just now,
and stood in the angle of the wall where Crockett made his
desperate stand and where he was slain. 'Tis a quaint old
building of a bluish-gray stone, with carven pillars at the
entrance, and niches on each side for saints to stand in.

As I strolled down the main street this afternoon, I found
myself in midst of a most *bizarre* exhibition of such sights and
sounds as might be supposed to arise from the rushing conflux
of Americans, Mexicans, Germans, Frenchmen, Swedes, Nor-
wegians, Italians, and negroes: but things are more decently
done, life is less crude, civilization is less new, than at Austin,
and this variety, which was there grotesque, is here picturesque.
Presently, I stood, before I knew it, on a bridge over the San
Antonio River which flows directly through the City: and my
surprised eyes ran with delight along the lovely windings of
the green translucent stream, flowing beneath long sprays of
weeping willows and playing unceasingly with the swaying
stems of the water-grasses. Many enclosures of dwelling-houses
run down to the stream, on each side, and afford ample field
for pretty summer houses and lawns. I found also some
churches which, as compared with anything else in Texas, are
simply magnificent: indeed there is nothing in Macon which
can at all compare with the new Episcopal Church now being
built here, or with the Catholic Cathedral.

This morning after a lazy and long-drawn breakfast, I
sauntered out on the pavement, sat me down, – and began to
dream away in the balmy summer air, thinking what an accom-

plished flâneur I would soon be, in such a languishing company of breezes as played softly about. Presently I had occasion to go indoors for a few moments: and when I returned, to my astonishment the air was cutting, the breeze whistled shrilly, I laughed involuntarily at the absurdity of my ten minutes by-gone dream of summer, and incontinently stepped off, in anything but the sauntering pace of the flâneur, for my overcoat.

It was the beginning of a " Norther," which has continued all day: tho' it is, I believe, a mild species of that fierce genus, and I have found no difficulty in keeping warm.

I called on Col. Withers today, and was received with the greatest cordiality. He was at Richmond during the war, being Asst. Adjt. Gen. of the Confederate States: was an officer of the old army: and is now conducting the San Antonio National Bank, upon a career of great prosperity as I am informed.

On the whole, San Antonio is the only spot in Texas which has not greatly disappointed me: and I think I shall spend a few days, here. 'Tis a place of eighteen thousand inhabitants: and is full of life and activity. Address your letters to me at " The Menger Hotel, San Antonio, Texas." If I should leave, they will be forwarded. Tell your father I have met here a young Mr. Frazier, grandson of the partner in the old house of Frazier Trenholm & Co. of Charleston. He is book-keeper in the bank of which I spoke, and seems to be a pleasant young gentleman.

Distribute, I pray you, a host of kisses for me, betwix't my father and yours, my dear Sissa, and my little men. I dare not enlarge upon loving messages to them all, tonight: for I feel myself upon the very imminent brink of a deep sea of home-sickness, into which I must not plunge. Know that I am in better condition than I have been in two months past: and have drawn some delightful free breaths that give me great buoyancy, and a thankful soul to God.

S. L.

### To Mary Day Lanier

San Antonio, Texas
Jany 30th 1873

Last night at eight O'clock came Mr. *Scheidemantel,* a genuine lover of music and fine pianist, to take me to the *Maenner-chor,* which meets every Wednesday night for practice. Quickly we came to a hall, one end of which was occupied by a minute stage, with appurtenances, and a piano : and in the middle thereof, a long table at which each singer sat down as he came in. Presently, seventeen Germans were seated at the singing-table, long-necked bottles of Rhine Wine were opened and tasted, great pipes and segars were all a-fire, the leader, Herr *Thielepape* (pron. nearly *Teelypapper*) – an old man with long white beard and moustache, formerly Mayor of the City – rapped his tuning-fork vigorously, gave the chords by rapid arpeggios of his voice, (a wonderful wild high tenor such as thou wouldst dream that the old Welsh harpers had, wherewith to sing songs that would cut against the fierce sea-blasts) and off they all swung into such a noble, noble old German full-voiced *lied,* that imperious tears rushed into my eyes, I could scarce restrain myself from running and kissing each one in turn and from howling dolefully the while. And so, O my Heart,– I all the time worshipping thee with these great chords and calling upon thee to listen and to love with me –, we drove through the evening until twelve O'clock, absorbing enormous quantities of Rhine Wine and beer whereof I imbibed my full share. After the second song, I was called on to play – and lifted my poor old flute in air with tumultuous beating heart for I had no confidence either in that or in myself. But, du Himmel ! Thou shouldst have heard mine old love warble herself forth. To my utter astonishment, I was perfect master of the instrument. Is not this most strange? Thou knowest I had never learned it: and thou rememberest what a poor muddle I made at Marietta in playing difficult passages: and I *certainly* have not practiced : and yet there I commanded and the blessed notes obeyed me, and when I had finished, amid a storm of applause, Herr Thielepape arose and ran to me and grasped my hand and declared that he hat never heert de flude accompany itself pefore ! I played once more during the evening: and ended with even more rapturous bravos than before. Mr. Scheide-mantel grasping my hand this time and thanking me very earnestly.

My heart, which was hurt greatly when I went in to the music-room, came forth from the holy bath of Concords greatly refreshed, strengthened and quieted, and so remaineth today. I also feel better today than in a long time before. Moreover

I am still master of the flute, and she hath given forth to me today such tones as I have never heard from a flute before.

For these things, I humbly thank God! . . .

I will not write thee further today. Thou art my dear Sweet, and I am thy faithful humble

**Lover.**

### To Clifford A. Lanier

San Antonio, Texas
Feb. 8th 1873

My Dear Clifford: Your letter came to me this morning, and was as a fair invocation to some good saint in the beginning of the day. I ought indeed to have written you, ere now, – if for no other purpose, at least, to tell you why I *can't* write much. I have been working on a quite elaborate Magazine Article upon " San Antonio de Bexar," wh. has required a good deal of reading and of pottering about in search of information; besides this, I've sent some letters to the World,[31] and have been engaged in the troublesome task of collecting material for more: besides this I have been putting some fire under one or two other pots wh. I don't intend to say anything about until I see that they are coming to a boil: and then, you know, I send some little adoring breath to my worshipful sweet Mary every day, and a letter reporting progress to father about twice a week, in addition to an unconscionable amount of fortuitous correspondence wh. *will* drop along somehow spite of all I can do; – and, to make matters worse, my hurt lung has begun to protest very loudly during the last three or four weeks against my writing at all, and now spites my heedlessness of its earlier protestations by giving me so much pain in my right arm as to make me incapable of writing more than a little at a time. I particularly regret this, for the reason that it seems to me I was never in my life so full of all manner of poems and books nor so confident of being able to succeed in this way of life.

I've had, too, for a month past, a good deal of trouble with my disease, and an amount of my time wh. seems simply

---

[31] In addition to writing pot-boilers for newspapers and magazines, Lanier was turning again to poetry, especially his ambitious long poem "The Jacquerie."

astonishing until one actually goes through it – has been spent in various ways and means of repelling and fortifying against these attacks.

All of wh. is said, not as one complaining, – for with much suffering I grow firm and clear in the faith that God understands His world and that all things (including my little hurts) do fit into some wise administration whose polity is deeper than death wherebeyond man sees not – but only to let you understand how joyfully I wd. keep myself in full and frequent communication with you, if I *cd.* . . . .

I think to return by the first of April, perhaps earlier. I am, in the whole, disappointed in the *winter*-climate here; though I doubt not the fall-climate, whose dying days so delighted me when I first came – is very fine. Again, I cannot go out on the plains to rough it, without either subjecting myself to the danger of murder by Indians – a danger altogether greater than I had ever supposed before I came here – or else attaching myself to some party whose movements are uncertain and who might keep me out a great deal too long. Moreover, I want to go to Denver, Colorado: wh. from all accounts has a far finer climate (finer for *me*, I like *cold*) than this, and wh. is in the great line of Western advancement. San Antonio, I think, is soon to be a dead place, in all business. Its previous prosperity has been mostly due to the want of railroads: and as soon as some projects now under weigh are completed, it will collapse like a sucked orange.

Please find herein Invoice I Lot Kisses, Extra Family; wh., when they arrive, distribute among all those dear ones that need a love-reminder from

Your

S. L.

### To Paul H. Hayne

Marietta, Ga. May 26th 1873

My Dear Mr. Hayne:

The gracious odor of yr. " violets " [32] has reached into my soul, and I have been loth to send them

---

[32] In his letter of May 2, 1873, Hayne had sent Lanier a MS poem with this title.

back to you. Stanza No. III is unalloyedly delicious: and the
closing line, —" Breathing of heart-break and sad death of
love," — is simply ravishing. This sings itself over and over
in my heart: and this; –

> " Some with raised brows, and eyes of constancy
> Fixed with fond meanings on a goal above."

What a tender music these two lines make! Are you, by the
way, a musician? Strange, that I have never before asked this
question, — when so much of my own life consists of music.
I don't know that I've ever told you, that whatever turn I have
for Art, is purely musical; poetry being, with me, a mere tangent
into which I shoot sometimes. I could play passably on several
instruments before I could write legibly: and since, then, the
very deepest of my life has been filled with music, which I have
studied and cultivated far more than poetry. I only mention
this in order that you may understand the delight your poetry
gives me. It is so rarely *musical,* so melodiously pure and
silvery in flow: it occupies in poetry the place of Mendellsohn
in music, or of Franz Abt, or of Schubert. It is, in this respect
simply unique in modern poetry: Wm Morris comes nearest
to it, but Morris lives too closely within hearing of Tennyson
to write unbroken music: for Tennyson (let me not blaspheme
against the Gods!) is not a musical tho' in other respects
(particularly in that of phrase-making) a very wonderful writer.
While at Alleghany Springs last summer I loaned to Miss Julia
Foster, of Augusta, my copy of yr. " Legends & Lyrics," on
condition she should return it. I've written her since about it
but my letter probably failed to reach her, as I knew not her
address save that she lived in Augusta. Having a copy from
you, I didn't want to lose it: and if you have another by you
I wd. be glad if you wd. straightway write yr. name therein
and mail to me.

I do not know the man Williams, you mention. I have been
greatly amused at some strictures upon you made by certain
Knights of Mrs. Westmoreland, in condign punishment for yr
critique on Mrs. W.'s. book. I have not read that production
but from all I can hear, 'tis a most villainous poor pitiful piece
of work; and, so far from endeavoring to serve the South by
blindly plastering it with absurd praises, I think all true
patriots ought to unite in redeeming the land from the impu

tation that such books are regarded as casting honor upon the section. God forbid we should really be brought so low as that we must perforce brag of such works as " Clifford Troupe " and " Heart Hungry ": and God be merciful to that man (he is an Atlanta Editor) who boasted that sixteen thousand of these books had been sold in the South!

This last damning fact (if it be a fact, — and I sh'd not wonder) ought to have been concealed at the risk of life, limb and fortune.

I'm glad to hear you're going to travel; but you are starting too soon.[33] I hope to get to New York City about the 1st of July. If you should be there any time between that and the middle of October, let me know, by a note addressed to care of " Winslow, Lanier & Co. 27 Pine St. N. Y." — an address which will always reach me.

I return yr. " Violets " : and I hope that when you go to Heaven you'll be wafted there on the sighs of just such another bunch!

Yr. Friend

Sidney Lanier

To Mary Day Lanier[34]

Baltimore, Sep. 19th 1873

So ! At last I have a little moment to draw breath in, and to speak a word to my dear Heart.

In the dead waste and middle of the night, I arrived at Enfield [N. C.] (where I had concluded was my best chance to find a conveyance to reach Ginna) got off the train – which was behind time – in a monstrous hurry, at a lonesome depot, saw the baggage-man throw off my valise, caught hold of one end of my trunk while the train was at smart speed starting off, ran

---

[33] In his letter of May 2 Hayne had written that he was leaving about the middle of the month on a trip to Philadelphia, New York, and Boston.

[34] The first half of this letter describes Lanier's visit to Virginia Hankins ("Ginna"), his wartime sweetheart in Virginia. He had tried several times to visit her at the family home, Bacon's Castle, now sold. Their first reunion since the Civil War took place in North Carolina, where she was teaching school.

with it till I got a good grip, then fearlessly bade the baggage-
man to cast loose, – which he did, and my poor trunk bumped
on the earth with fearsome thud; – but Providence watched
over me, and it fell in the sand.   I got quarters, stuck my feet
in my blanket, pulled up a great quantity of cover over me, and
dug myself a deep place in my feather-bed—so bitter-cold was
the night—and fell off into a good sleep.   Next morning, I
fared forth toward Scotland Neck, in a spring-wagon drawn by
a good horse, and driven by an old gentleman – a Native –
with whom I held much high converse upon agricultural matter
until we reached our destination.   I dined, sent a note to Ginna
who replied in a most sweetly-startled fashion, and at half-past
four jumped in a buggy and drove to her home.   The day was
so beautiful that we could not stay in doors, so into the buggy
again, and away through the lovely woods and past the charming
residences.   Here live seven Smiths, all brothers, all rich, all
in the houses of their ancestors, all well-educated, tasty people
in just such a cluster of elegant country homes as I don't think
is elsewhere to be found in the South.   They have their own
Episcopal Church, – a lovely brick edifice, beautiful with vines
outside, and with a fine organ inside.   Returning from our drive
they press me to stay, so my traps are brought out from the
hotel, and I take up my quarters at Ginna's, – one of the Smith's
where she is a guest.   Everybody seems as kindly and genial as
can be: next day Miss Adelaide Smith volunteers to teach
Ginna's School, so that the latter may be with me : which is
done, and Ginna and I, soon after breakfast, take to our buggy
again and fare forth into the woods, where, arriving at a pretty
spot, I stop the horse and stretch myself back in the buggy-seat
with my feet comfortably on the dash-board, what time Ginna
reads me passages here and there from her book.   After much
quarrelling and disputing, she finishes and we drive home: then
the flute comes out, Ginna sings, and I play seconds, (with a
good piano, too) : then dinner, rest, and in the late afternoon
we walk to the Church, climb the fence, Ginna vaulting there
over like a young fawn, wander about, then sit on an iron
garden-seat in the enclosure and watch the sun go down.   Home
to supper: then the flute, voice and piano, Blackbirds,[35] much

[35] A musical composition by Lanier, probably the one written in Texas and
first called *Field-larks and Black-birds*.

talk &c, and the night closes. Next morning, they have out the old family carriage, and Ginna, with young Smith, drives down with me to the village, where I embark in the hack to return to Enfield. As we shake hands, Ginna says, – with all manner of wondrous lights shinging through her brown eyes – "Write and tell May that your coming has been like the Skies to me, and I shall never know how to thank her for sending you," together with other like messages.

Meantime I have had the most monstrous sore-throat that was ever concocted, the pain almost driving me mad, and now as we go back towards Enfield it becomes ravenous and gnaws me like a vulture. I go bravely to work, however, get some Iodine & Glycerine mixed, make a probang out of my tooth-brush, and, what with this and Brown's Trochees, when I awoke on the Steamer yesterday morning, I found myself much better, and am quite free from soreness this morning.

Altogether the visit to Ginna was simply delicious, and I think she enjoyed it keenly. Her lot is in a sweet place and I am rejoiced to think of her lonesome life being brightened by so many friends, who all seem to be exceedingly fond of her.

Arriving here yesterday about nine, I bathed, & dressed leisurely, and finally despatched a note to Mr. Wysham,[36] about one. He came in three minutes after he received my note, but I was at dinner. As I came out from dinner, and sauntered to the desk for a tooth pick, he came up, grasped my hand, we had a word or two, made an appointment for four O'clock, and off he dashed on business. At four he came, took me to his house, where I found a charming residence, but dismantled, (his family not yet having returned), carried me straightway into his library, – both talking all the time – bustled about, and finally got us both fairly down to a duett of Kuhlau's. We had but begun it, however, when arrived Mr. Winterbotham, a fine young pianist, whom he had invited to play our accompani-ments, and so we adjourned to the piano in the drawing-room. – a fine Weber. Then we had Bach's sonatas (Fl. & P.), a duo (2 Flutes) from Rigoletto, with Piano accompaniment, (mag-

[36] Lanier's new friend Henry C. Wysham was at this time playing the flute in the Peabody Institute Concerts. In a letter of Sept. 25, Mary Day Lanier reported to R. S. Lanier: "This gentleman is– according to Sidney– 'a keen and faithful man of business'– a lawyer in active practice."

nificent, and unlike any duo I have ever heard before) then I played the Swamp-Robin [37] with much applause (though fearfully done, my mouth being dry as powder with excitement, and I couldn't get any tone at all), then Kuhlau's grand duo, (2 Fl. & P.). Then he took me to tea, and we started afterwards to Dr. [J. J.] Chisholm's, whose daughter plays much with Wysham. On the way we pass a house where some one is playing the piano. "Stop" says W: peers in through the windows, clutches me, and we go in just for a lark. Mr. [B. F.] Horrwitz, Mrs. Horrwitz, (she is playing) Mr. [James?] Gibson, the latter an accomplished old N. Y. beau: to these we enter, fall a-talking, crack a thousand jokes on the flutes, (which we secretly left in the hall) (and some of the same jokes would not at all do to repeat, though the lady got off the worst one): but presently Mr. Horrwitz goes smelling round, finds the flutes, brings them in in great triumph and noise, and we fall to playing all manner of improvised duetts. Presently they insist on *me*, and I play "Blackbirds," with stunning effect. Then we play Scotch airs for old Mr. Gibson, some other people drop in, play, play, play: then we seize our flutes, and dash off to Dr. Chisholm's; where, on entering, I am presented to four ladies, one of whom seizes my hand at hearing my name, and declares that I must pardon her for that Mrs. Eason of Charleston is one of her dearest friends and she has heard her speak of me so often &c &c. This is pleasant. Then we fall to: Wysham plays some wonderful things of De Jong's; I play our Fürstenau, & Briccialdi's Nocturne, Miss Chisholm rendering a lovely accompaniment at sight. Then Wysham plays The Kaleidoscöp, and more De Jong: then we take some two-part songs, (Virginia Gabriel's songs, unique and lovely) which bring down the house: then some sacred music, – two Fl. & P. – : then with a grand flourish from Lucia, 2 Fl. & P. we leave; W. takes me to the Allston Club (an Art Club) [38] registers me, we sit a moment, I take

---

[37] A musical composition by Lanier, no copy of which has survived. It was apparently first composed as early as 1867 (see VII, 392 n.) but was quite possibly revised during the recent summer in Marietta (see Lanier's letter to his brother, July 21, 1873, above, referring to his "Woods-translations on the flute").

[38] The Allston Association was a club founded in 1858-1859 to sponsor American artists, named in honor of the painter Washington Allston. From 1870 to 1875 it was amalgamated with the Wednesday Club, an organization of musical and dramatic amateurs, also dating from 1858. At the time of Lanier's letter, 1873, the club rooms were on St. Paul Street above Monument. Two

some whiskey; and then we part, for Wysham is an early bird, and a regular withal, always retiring at half-past ten.

Thus we have had a six hours' stretch of it.

Wysham declares himself utterly astonished at my playing, in view of my facilities, and declares that my powers are simply without limit, needing only the restraint of a good musical associate, and a little practice.

He plays very beautifully, and is my superior in technique, I judge: tho' of course, I have been playing pieces I never heard, and that too under dreadfully frightening circumstances, so that I cannot say how our sight-reading would compare. He recognizes the peculiar quality of my nature-pieces: " there is, (says he) a ' natural magic,' as you call it, in your music such as I have never heard from any one else." [39] He has true ideas of expression, and is greatly pleased with mine. All his expressions go to show that he is greatly impressed with my playing.

Dr. Browne has just called, and has taken up my balance of available time (in a vastly pleasant way, indeed): and so I must now close. I am well. Tonight I am to take tea at Dr. Chisholm's and we are to give a grand musical entertainment (Wysham and I, Miss Chisholm, Mrs. [Fred M.] Colston, Mr. Winterbotham) afterwards. W. calls for me at five: which will be, now, very soon after I get my dinner. W. had a lovely bouquet for me yesterday, arranged by himself. We are like two young lovers.

Embrace thy father – and my sons, for thy

Husband.


## To Robert S. Lanier

New York, Sep. 24th 1873

My dear Father:

I arrived here last night from Baltimore. I had stopped there – expecting to stay only a couple of days – to see

---

guest invitations extending the privileges of the Allston Association to Lanier for thirty-day periods have survived, dated Sept. 18 and Dec. 24, 1873 (Charles D. Lanier Collection, Johns Hopkins University). Lanier was later to become a member of the Wednesday Club.

[39] In a letter to his brother Clifford, Sept. 27, 1873 (here omitted), Lanier declared: " [The] ' natural magic ' of my compositions . . . is all that I now pretend to as distinguishing them from others."

my friend Wysham.   Having once seen him, however, I found
him a soul so congenial that it was quite impossible to leave
him so soon, and I stayed five days, during which he devoted
himself to my pleasure, and to my profit, with a whole-souled
friendliness I can never forget. Wysham is a lawyer, in full
practice, but is also renowned as being one of the finest Amateur
Böhm-Flute players in the world. He was pleased, beyond my
utmost hopes, with my playing.

On the last day of my stay, he had Mr. Hamerick,[40] – who is
director of the Peabody Academy of Music in Baltimore, and
one of the most accomplished composers and *Maestros* in the
world – at his house, to meet me and hear me play.   Immediately after the first piece I played alone, Mr. Hamerick
informed me that he was endeavoring to induce the Trustees
of the Peabody Academy to supply him with funds for the
formation of a large Orchestra; and he forthwith offered me
the position of first flute, therein, in the event of his success,
at the same time expressing himself in the most marked manner,
both upon the style of my composition, and my playing, (it was
one of my own pieces that I had performed.)   This position
would give, *per se,* $120 a month: and five scholars (Wysham
declared he would guarantee *twenty,* but five would be all I wd.
care for) would increase this amount to $200 a month.  Thus
I cd. live, and at the same time have a good part of every day
to write my books and work for the position I desire in the
world of letters: adding to these advantages, the further one
of having daily access to large libraries, the deprivation of
which I have so keenly felt heretofore.

Altogether, this plan offers so many advantages that I think
it would be my duty to accept the place, and I eagerly await
the result of Mr. Hamerick's negotiations now pending with
the Trustees. Mr. Hamerick also gave me a strong letter to
Theodore Thomas: but I am here too late to use it, as Thomas
starts today (I am told) on his usual winter tour.[41]  Indeed,
I would not care to go with him: for I do not desire — it wd.

[40] Asger Hamerik (1843-1923), Danish composer. From 1871 to 1898 he was
director of the Peabody Institute in Baltimore, and conductor of its orchestra.

[41] Theodore Thomas (1835-1905), a German musician, who had come to
America at the age of ten. In 1862 he had organized in New York his own
symphony orchestra, whose concerts Lanier had attended. Later he became the
conductor of the New York Philharmonic Society.

be folly for me to attempt — to travel in this cold North during the winter.

Thus, you have my plan, so far as it is matured, and I sincerely hope it will meet your approval.

As to the Florida project you mention: — much reflection convinces me beyond doubt that this kind of writing is not my forte, 2nd that it does not pay, 3rd that there is no *career* in it at all, for one spends one's time writing that which people throw away as soon as read, — and it is my desire to write something that my boys may hear of, in the future.[42]

As for the Lecture project, it is quite impossible, for the same reason that it was impossible for me to continue practicing law, *viz.* that I cannot *speak* in a crowded room. I find that playing the flute is highly beneficial; while loud speaking is injurious. Finally, as for the loping horse and the out-door work; — while I am deeply grateful to you for the offer and for the spirit which prompts it — yet there are many reasons against it. For instance, (to adduce only one, of many) I am now thirty-one years old: I am determined to win myself some sort of place in men's regard: how *could* I do that, in attending to the " out-door work " of the Office? Again, my attending to the out-door work &c would not at all increase your income: and that is not large enough for us both. In short, I believe that you will readily agree with me, upon reflection, that my views are well-considered, and that the Baltimore plan is, in view of all the elements of my situation, the best. If that *fails,* I do not know what I shall do; but propose to stay in New York about a month in order to see if any other more feasible projects may not result. I have some valuable letters which I shall take occasion to present at an early day, and these will put me in the way of many things, I hope.

I have written you thus fully, because I observe from the tone of your letter that you are a little inclined to think I ought to have unfolded myself more fully to you before. But pray do not believe me in fault; my silence has only been due to my reluctance to announce plans which were before so apparently chimerical, — for I never could have reasonably dreamed of

[42] The " Florida project " and the " Lecture project " (mentioned in this and the following paragraph) were apparently discussed in a letter from R. S. Lanier that has not survived; neither of them materialized.

making so fine a figure, with my poor untaught music and
playing, before those who have been accustomed to hear the
finest music in the world, and it did really seem, even to me,
highly chimerical for me to attempt to shine in music, under
such circumstances: yet my dependent condition made it my
duty to try that, for it seemed my last resort in order to be a
self-sustaining man while I write my books. . . .

   With a great deal of love, for yourself, Mama and Pringle,
I am

Your Son

Sidney  Lanier

To Mary Day Lanier

[Brooklyn] Nov. 16th 1873

*"*

―――――――――――――――――

*"*

As for money, there hath been nothing but disappointment after
disappointment, it hath seemed to me as if God had turned
over my plans for the nonce to the Devil and this latter had
amused himself with me in an inexhaustible round of frolic-
some malignities and thwartings.  The hopes, the fears, the
angers, the humiliations, the agonies, the intangible insults
which I could not resent, the quite tangible failures which I
could not prevent,– how can I bear to tell thee of these ?  I
cannot.  I simply hint that they have been, – because thou art
my dear, dear Wife. and thou hast the right to my whole life.
Moreover I wd. not have thee believe that the small disjointed
scrawls that have latterly come from me to thee, were due to
any ordinary fatigue – I had not written Harry Wysham a
scratch in two weeks.  I did not even know that half so much
time had passed.  I enclose his letter wh. awoke me to that
melancholy fact.  Thou wilt see that the Orchestra is to be
formed: but to last only four months, – and each player to get
only $60 a month.  Yet I am going, without hesitation: for (1st)
this will occupy but a little time, and 2nd, I can largely supplement the poor pay with a pupil or two and in other ways, and

3rd it will give me a foothold which I can likely step from to something better, – for the Peabody Academy is a literary as well as musical institution, – and they don't know all my accomplishments yet ! There's a brag: – but thou hast a lover's soul, and I will not scratch it out.

— Until, therefore, I can get there (to Baltimore) and go to work, and see my probable income, I can not write more definitely in this regard. Thou great trusting Heart, with how many cruel *indefinitudes* hast thou been compelled to tantalize the cravings of thine eagerness! . . .

"
" ————I have had some pleasant musical successes. I played on Wednesday night at a concert in Brooklyn, before some 800 people, and made some stir, particularly in the papers, – notices whereof I send thee herein.[43] Of course, the talk in the notices about a *debut,* the *debutant,* &c. is simply absurd: 'twas no *debut* at all, I only played for the fun of it and by way of feeling the pulse of these audiences in a quiet way (for these little concerts are not ordinarily heard of at all in the newspapers) before venturing to prescribe for the big music-sick patient of New York. When I am ready to come out, which will be after I practice four months in Baltimore – I shall make my debut under the auspices of the Philharmonic, or of Theo. Thomas, – or not at all. Meantime, these notices will amuse thee. They are considered wonderfully flattering. There are so many aspiring musicians here, who work for years and years, and are never heard of at all.

[43] Five clippings from New York newspapers of Nov. 13, 1873, noticing this concert survive in the Charles D. Lanier Collection, Johns Hopkins University. They are labelled by Lanier: the New York *Commercial Advertiser, Sun, Evening Mail,* and *Times,* and the *Brooklyn Eagle.* They speak of him as " a flutist of remarkable skill and purity of style," " an admirable artist . . . thoroughly conversant with his instrument," " a performer of fine taste and culture," and " a Southern gentleman, whose name is known to some of our readers as the author of a pleasant, wild story of love and war in the South." According to the New York *Times*: " The most interesting incident was the début of . . . Mr. Sidney Lanier. . . . In the second part of the program the débutant was down for a composition of his own, which he names ' Blackbirds.' It is a poetic fantasie upon the strain of the Southern blackbird, which it transforms into wild, sweet music, and, as a composition it is of classic purity, and decided originality."

There also survive in the Charles D. Lanier Collection an unidentified clipping indicating that the notice in the New York *Times* was reprinted in a Baltimore newspaper, announcing that Lanier had been engaged by Hamerik for the Peabody Orchestra, and a program of the concert.

Perhaps the most complete triumph I have had was on last
Sunday evening, being over one Miss Alice Fletcher, – who is,
by the way, a person much in the Arististic world, and is
secretary of *Sorosis*, though certainly as unmasculine and as
sweetly feminine and Truely womanly as one could desire. [44]
She is, I am told, the intimate friend of Janauschek, – and has
travelled much abroad. I wish I could spread before thee all
the scene, which was very fine. But I cannot, for very weariness
of my miserable right arm. Suffice it, that when I had played
Blackbirds, and the Swamp-Robin, before her and an audience
of some half-dozen more of cultivated people, the house rose
at me: Miss Fletcher declared that nothing like it existed out
of Wagner: that I was not only the founder of a School of
music, but the founder of American music: that hitherto all
American compositions had been only German music done
over, but that these were at once American, un-German, classic,
passionate, poetic, and beautiful: that I belonged to the
Advance-Guard, which must expect to struggle but which could
not fail to succeed, – with a hundred other things, finally closing
with a fervent expression of good wishes in which all the
company joined with such unanimity and fervor that I was in
a state of embarrassment wh. thou mayst imagine ! I wrote
her a note next day, desiring to make some more articulate
response than blushes, to her recognition: and I have a lovely
note from her in reply which *thou* shalt have in a day or two. [45]
— On Wednesday I played flute trios with Mr Pasquale and
Mr. Yzquierdo. We sat down to a bound volume of Kuhlau's
trios at three O'clock, and played without leaving our seats
until five. They gave me first flute. Dear Wife, dear Wife,
how I craved thee, how I agonized for thee, as we breathed
these miraculous harmonies and unearthly-dainty melodies !
I had taken Mr. McDonald there, with me. He could scarcely

---

[44] Alice Cunningham Fletcher (1838-1923), ethnologist and pioneer writer
on Indian music. " Sorosis " was a woman's club founded in New York in 1868,
the first of any significance in America.

The allusion in the following sentence to Janauschek, the actress, was probably
prompted by the fact that Mary Day Lanier had seen her in a performance of
*Deborah* in Macon the previous winter (see her letter to Lanier, Feb. 3, 1873).

[45] Alice Fletcher's reply (Nov. 14, 1873) to Lanier's letter is reproduced in
*Letters* (New York, 1899), pp. 79-80, note. She wrote in part: " Your flute
gave me that for which I had ceased to hope, true American Music, and awakened
within my heart a feeling of patriotism that I never knew before."

contain himself, – newspaper hack as he is ! – and his great eyes got as deep as the sea,– and nigh as moist.   Think, – Mr. Yzquierdo, who has been playing in N. Y. for years among the very best professional flutists, and who is certainly the best reader I ever saw, – says *I* am the best *he* ever saw, – I, who surely as thou knowest have scarcely read a half-dozen new pieces in any year of my musical life, – before this last month or so !   How splendid it is:   I could never tell thee how I enjoy such things: for it is not I, but always *thy* husband,– in whom I have much interest.

——    And now, enough, this time.   I shall dream of thee, shall kneel to thee, shall retrace thy features on my heart, shall fancy the waving of thy garments, shall light my soul's darkness with the gray glory of thine eyes from afar and feed my Sense's hunger with the red sweetness of thy distant lips, shall love thee, shall bless thee, shall pray for thee and to thee, shall utterly adore thee, – all this day, being for this holy length of time nothing more, nor less, nor other, than

Thy
Lover.

### Robert S. Lanier

Baltimore, Md. Nov. 29th 1873.

My dear Father:

I have given your last letter the fullest and most careful consideration.   After doing so: I feel sure that Macon is not the place for me.   If you could taste the delicious crystalline air and the champagne breeze that I've just been rushing about in, – I am equally sure that, in point of climate, you would agree with me that my chance for life is ten times as great here, as in Macon.

Then, as to business.   Why should I, — nay, how *can* I —, settle myself down to be a third-rate struggling lawyer for the balance of my little life,— as long as there is a certainty, almost absolute, that I can do some other things so much better?   Several persons, from whose judgment in such matters there can be no appeal, have told me, for instance, that I am the

greatest flute-player in the world: and several others, of equally
authoritative judgment, have given me almost equal encouragement to work with my pen. (Of course, I protest against the
necessity which makes me write such things, about myself: —
I only do so, because I so appreciate the love and tenderness
which prompt you to desire me with you, that I will make the
fullest explanation possible of my course, out of reciprocal
honor and respect for the motives which lead you to think
differently from me.) My dear father, think how, for twenty
years, through poverty, through pain, through weariness,
through sickness, through the uncongenial atmospheres of a
farcical college and of a bare army and then of an exacting
business-life, through all the discouragements of being born
on the wrong side of Mason-and-Dickson's line and of being
wholly unacquainted with literary people and literary ways, —
I say, think how, in spite of all these depressing circumstances
and of a thousand more wh. I could enumerate, these two
figures of music and of poetry have steadily kept in my heart,
so that I could not banish them! Does it not seem to you, as
to me, that I begin to have the right to enroll myself among
the devotees of these two sublime arts, after having followed
them so long and so humbly and through so much bitterness?
If I could only make you see all this, as clearly as I *now* feel it,
now when I have actually engaged in this service!

The object of my visit to New York was to see at once, by
using the severest tests, — that is, by measuring strength with
the best artists there — whether there was any hope for me to
excel greatly, either as musician or writer; and secondly, to
arrange matters so that in case the Baltimore project failed,
I could get some engagement in New York, immediately.

The Baltimore Orchestra is now *un fait accompli,* and having
been offered, entirely without solicitation either by myself or
my friends, the place of First Flute in it, I have accepted it.
Mary will tell you the details of the engagement, wh. I have
written her. It is the very best place I cd. have found, just at
present, occupying but little time, and thus giving me a splendid
opportunity to write and study. As for the climate, I have no
fears whatever. It is better than that of New York: and I have
continued to prosper, physically, even in the New York climate.
In spite of a wretched cold, such as would have laid me up for

months at Macon, my appetite has continued good, my strength
has constantly increased, and the old dyspepsias that used to
drag me down are wholly unknown. I am full of energy, full
of unwritten music, full of unrhymed poetry, and I look forward to a winter crowded with vigorous work and profitable
study.[46]


To Mary Day Lanier

Baltimore, Dec. 21st 1873

Last night, we gave a magnificent concert. The house was
crowded. Read the enclosed *Carte,* showing the fare we spread
before the people. O my God, how I did sigh and long for
thee, dear Heartsease: had I thee, the music wd. have been
complete, life wd. have been utterly full, my heart wd. have
bathed itself in a sublime sea of passionate content.

The Orchestra was inspired. The *Symphonie Fantastique* –
as difficult and trying a piece of Orchestration as was ever
written – was played to a marvel. Dost thou not remember
that I once put *thee* into music? So, in this *Symphonie,* every
movement centreth about a lovely melody, repeated in all
manner of times and guises, wh. representeth the Beloved of
the opium-eating musician.

—— I will make a *Symphonie* with thee for its melodic cynosure
some day, wh. shall be more lovely than Berlioz', because thou
art more lovely than any one that Berlioz cd. have known.

— Then the " Hunt of Henry IV," O my Sweet-Heart ! It
openeth with a grave and courteous invitation, as of a cavalier
riding by some dainty lady, through the green aisles of the deep
woods, to the hunt: a lovely, romantic melody, the first violins
discoursing the man's words, the first flute replying for the lady.
Presently, a Fanfare: a sweet horn replies out of the far woods:
then the meeting of the gay cavaliers: then the start, the dogs
are unleashed, one hound gives tongue, another joins, the stag
is seen, hey, gentlemen! away they all fly through the sweet
leaves, by the great oaks and beeches, all a-dash among the

[46] The MS is not signed and the end of the letter is probably missing.

brambles, till presently Bang! goeth a pistol, (it was my veritable old revolver, loaded with blank cartridge for the occasion, — the revolver that hath lain so many nights under my head and (God hold my heart together!) *thine*, – fired by *Tympani*, (as we call him,) the same being a nervous little Frenchman who playeth our drums), and then the stag dieth, in a celestial concord of flutes, oboes and violins. O how far off my soul was, in this thrilling moment! It was in a rare sweet glen, in Tennessee, the Sun was rising over a wilderness of mountains, I was standing (how well I remember the spot!) alone, in the dewy grass, wild with rapture and with expectation, yonder came gracefully walking a lovely fawn, I looked into its liquid eyes, hesitated, prayed, gulped a sigh, then, – overcome with the savage hunter's instinct, – fired, the fawn leaped convulsively a few yards, I ran to it, found it lying on its side, and received into my agonized and remorseful heart the melting reproaches of its most tender, dying gaze. — But luckily I had not the right to linger over this sad scene: the conductor's *baton* shook away the dying pause, on all sides shouts and fanfares and gallopings " to the death," to which the first flute had to reply in time, recalled me to my work, and I came through brilliantly.

— The Chopin Rondo, Concerto for Piano and Orchestra, I cannot begin to describe to thee. It nearly killed me, with longing for thee: – for thou wdst. have understood it, as I did, thou wdst. have recognized the wondrous delicate, yet intense, thoughts which pervade it, the " Zäl " as Liszt calleth it. Herein the flute hath some lovely replies and dialogues with the piano, in solo; and the horns are exquisitely brought forth. – The songs were not particularly ·fine, tho' very enjoyable, The Masoniello overture thou hast of course heard before. It was played very brilliantly.

—— Today Wysham and I played a beautiful *Adagio Patetico* during the *Offertorium* at St. Paul's: – the largest church in the city. We had an Organ accompaniment, played by a glorious organist: and as the two spirituelle silver-tones went stealing and swelling through the great groined arches of the enormous church, I thought I had never heard flute-notes so worthily employed before. The people were greatly pleased: and Wysham was delighted. . . .

– Now God fill thy heart with the exquisite satisfactions thou hast poured into mine, prayeth thy

Lover——

## To Paul H. Hayne

Macon, Ga. May 23rd 1874.

My dear Mr. Hayne:

Your letter gave me sincere pleasure; and I would have sent you some expression of my gratification at hearing from you by a much earlier mail than this, had it not been for my Arabian eccentricities and unreliablenesses of movement, which have kept me on the wing for a month past. I am now in Macon, and shall remain here for three or four weeks, – then Northward again. I am truly rejoiced to see, by occasional evidences in the Magazines, that you are again active in that delicious business of Creation. . . .

The Review of your " Legends & Lyrics " was sent to Lippincotts', and declined. I afterwards mentioned to Browne that I had written it (tho' I did not offer it to him in terms): who told me that a review of the book had already appeared in the Southern Mag. So my piece lies bleeding, and I don't know what to do with it.

Tell me what you are doing.

In answer to your kind enquiries as to myself: I spent my winter in Baltimore, pursuing Music and meditating my " Jacquerie." I was *Flauto Primo* of the Peabody Symphony Orchestra, and God only could express the delight and exultatation with which I helped to perform the great works brought out by that organization during the winter. Of course this was a queer place for me: aside from the complete *bouleversement* of going from the Court-house to the footlights, I was a raw player and a provincial withal, without practice, and guiltless of instruction – for I never had a teacher. To go, under these circumstances, among old professional musicians, and assume a leading part, in a large Orchestra which was organized expressly to play the most difficult works of the great masters, – was, (now that it's all over) a piece of temerity that I do not remember ever to have equalled before.    But I trusted in Love, pure and simple:  and was not disappointed, for, as if by miracle, difficulties and discouragements melted away before the fire of a passion for music which grows ever stronger within my heart, – and I came out with results more gratifying than it is becoming in me to specify.    'Tis quite settled that I cannot practice law: either writing or speaking appears to produce small hæmorrhages which completely sap my strength:  and I am going in a few weeks to New York, – without knowing what on earth I am to do there – armed only with a Silver Bœhm flute, and some dozen of steel pens.

Happy man, – you who have your cabin in among the hills and trees.    You who can sit still and work at Home, – pray a short prayer once in a while for one as homeless as the ghost of Judas Iscariot.

Write me straightway: and write, as to one who is always

Your faithful friend

Sidney Lanier

## To Clifford A. Lanier

Macon, Ga, May 28th 1874

My dear Clifford:

. . . .

I came back here from Baltimore, at the close of the musical season, with the idea that my health was sufficiently restored to permit my resumption of my old place in the firm, which had been kept open for me.    A few days of law-work and of this dreadful climate have demonstrated the absolute impossibility of my being a lawyer, with the most mournful decisiveness.    The strength I had built up by a year of laborious and careful and expensive nursing and travelling, has been swept away in a few days by this overpowering and (to *me*) poisonous atmosphere.

In short, I am again all afloat, and must mature some plan by which to get back to the Northern air, which seems the only one where life is possible.

— I've shed all the tears about it that I'm going to;– and am now vigorously engaged in pumping myself full of music and poetry, with which I propose to water the dry world.  I suppose it may now be finally said, that God has cut me off inexorably from any other life than this.  So, St. Cecilia to the rescue ! – and I hope God will like my music.

— I think, now, to carry my wife and chicks to a certain farm-house about ten miles from Griffin, where board is cheap, and where there is great store of eggs, chickens and milk, – there to finish my Jacquerie and a lot of music wh. I have nearly ready for the press: then to New York – in a couple of months from now – to seek flute-engagements for the winter.

. . .

I hope soon to polish up de ole blind darkey.[47]
Write me.

Yr. Bro.

S. L.

To Robert S. Lanier

*195 Dean St.*
Brooklyn, N. Y.
Sep. 8th 1874.

My dear Father:

Your kind letter, annexed to Aunt Jane's is here.  I'm glad she is coming on, tho' I fear I shall not have time to escort her about, as much as I cd. wish.  However, I believe she is pretty independent, in the matter of beaus, and understands New York well enough to keep out of the labyrinths.

I am trying to find a publisher for some music which I have written: flute-and-piano pieces, and songs.  I also am endeavoring to find the most advantageous form in which to issue my poem " Corn," just written.  This last has received great com-

---

[47] This reference makes it clear that Clifford Lanier's poem mentioned in Sidney's letter of May 11 as needing revision was " The Power of Prayer " (I, 215).  Though conceived and first drafted by Clifford, it was so completely revised by Sidney (see his letter of Aug. 7, below) that it came to be considered their joint composition and was later published as such in *Scribner's*, May, 1875.

mendation from many sources. I am now gravitating towards the idea of getting it printed in book-form, – though it wd. not occupy more than fifteen or twenty pages–, with three or four illustrations of the principal topics in the poem, towit, 1st a man walking meditatively through a fine old Georgia forest of oaks and beeches, towards his corn-field, just beyond

> " The zig-zag wandering fence
> Where lissome Sassafras and brambles dense
> Contest with stolid vehemence
> The march of culture, – setting limb and thorn
> Like pikes against the army of the Corn."

— 2nd a magnificient big stalk of Corn
> " That stands
> Advanced beyond the foremost of his bands
> And waves his blades upon the very edge
> And hottest thicket of the battling hedge."

3rd    An old red hill of Georgia, deserted by its non-corn-planting tenant who has fled Westward,
> " That bares to heaven its piteous, agèd crest
> And seamy breast,
> By restless-hearted Children left to lie
> Untended there beneath the heedless sky,
> As barbarous folk expose their old to die.

> . . .                A gashed and hairy Lear
> Whom the divine Cordelia of the year
> – E'en pitying Spring – will vainly strive to cheer,
> – King, yet too poor for any man to own,
> Discrowned, undaughtered and alone ":

– and 4th,    this same hill under the culture of some better man and sounder system, for (so the poem ends)
> . . . " Old Hill, old hill,
> For all thy low estate
> Thou still art rich and great
> Beyond all cotton-blinded estimate,
> And long I marvel through the August morn
> What largesse rich, of oil and wine and corn
> Thou bearest on thy vasty sides forlorn.

To render to some future bolder heart
That manfully shall take thy part
With antique sinew and with modern art,
          And tend thee
          And defend thee!" [48]

— I sent the poem to Col. Barnett, who suggested this method
of publication, averring that he thought it wd. pay, by a large
circulation through the South. Dr. Holland wanted to print
it in Scribner's Magazine (of wh. he is editor) but it was too
long. I will see the publishers in a day or two. . . .

Your Son

S. L.

## To Mary Day Lanier

[Brooklyn,] Sep. 13th 1874.

Last night I won great favor in the eyes of Mr. Cortada, – a
noble musician, Pianist of the Oratorio Society of New York
and of the Handel & Haydn Society of Brooklyn. We played
a Sonata of Kücken, one of Kuhlau, Tercschak's *Babillard*, &
Fürstenau's Nocturne, together. He declareth that I can do
great things with a little study: and volunteereth to introduce
me to Dr. Dammrosch, (under whom he saith I must study),
who is Conductor of both the above-mentioned Societies. [49] He
also volunteereth to endeavor to get me the place of Professor
of the Flute at the Brooklyn Conservatory of Music. God
speed him.

I have sent the poem to Geo. McDonald & Co. Publishers,

[48] The passages here quoted are from an early version of "Corn" (I, 34, note).
In answer to his father's enthusiastic reply Lanier wrote on Sept. 17, 1874 (here
omitted): "I send a copy of 'Corn': it is the one that I sent for Mr. Hayne to
read and the pencil-comments are his."

[49] Leopold Damrosch (1832-1885), violinist, composer, and conductor. A
friend of Liszt and von Bülow, he had already made his reputation in Europe
with the orchestra at Breslau, when he was invited to conduct the Arion Society
Orchestra in New York, 1871. Here he introduced the newer German school
of composers, Wagner and Schumann as well as Liszt. In 1873 he founded the
New York Oratorio Society; in 1878, the New York Symphony Society.

of Chicago, with my plan for publishing same in book-form,
illustrated, – wh. I think wd. be vastly popular in the South.
This was Col. Barnett's suggestion: – he thought it wd. be a
pecuniary success.

I have writ thee of Latham's proposition.

I am to see Heuser again about the songs, and the " Gnat-
dance " [" Danse des Moucherons "]; when I hope to bring him
to better terms.

I have written to The Atlanta Herald, the Savannah Musical
Magazine, the Baltimore Gazette, the " Musical Eclectic " of
Atlanta, the Montgomery Advertiser & Mail, – to know if they
desire a N. Y. correspondent, either specially *quoad* Music, or
generally.   The two last have replied, declining– I have not
heard from the others.

I have sent the Article " Peace " (Eddy & Charley) to
" Southe[r]n Mag: " – it is accepted.[50]  I have sketched a lot
of articles on The Curiosities of Music, – in which I mean to
lead up, by degrees, to my theory of barbaric music, and of
those queer tunes wh. thou wert to copy for me from the
Pirate's (and Abe's) " Sacred Harp ": – wh. said articles I mean
to offer, by letter, tomorrow, to Dwight's Journal of Music.   I
remember that the editor of this Journal wrote me for my autograph just after " Tiger-Lilies " came forth.

I have also sketched a series of articles in the style of Isaac
Bickerstaff, (Addison) on certain phases of modern life, –
which I will offer, – as soon as I finish the first one for a sample
– to " the Nation ".[51]   I am also arranging a programme and
some music for a series of " Soft-Tone concerts " wh. I wish
to organize in N. Y.; giving Beethoven's great Octett for
Oboes, Clarionets & Flutes, some quartets & trios for flutes,
solos on Bass-flute & Concert-flute, &c.[52]

---

[50] This essay had apparently been composed four years previously.

[51] Three surviving MS fragments (Charles D. Lanier Collection, Johns Hopkins
University) seem to answer to this description: (1.) "Tatler, No. 268," 6 pp.;
(2.) " The Tatler, No. —," 3 pp.; (3.) " Mr. Querry," 4 pp.

[52] These " Soft-Tone concerts " never materialized.  But a number of fragmentary bits of music survive in MS in Lanier's copy books (Charles D. Lanier
Collection, Johns Hopkins University) which were apparently sketched for this
purpose: (1.) " Mem. Soft-Tone Concerts. / ' Lâ Rève ' for four flutes: air &
fantasy "; (2.) " Mem. for trio. Fl. B. F. & 'Cello "; (3.) " Bass Flute (To
tickle the ears of the groundlings) "; (4.)  " Mem. Quartette "; (5.) " Mem.
for Trio: Song "; (6.) " Mem. Concert-flute "; (7.) " Mem. for long flute."

I am also superintending, by daily visits to Badger's, the experiment of the long flute, wh. is now nearly done.

—— Here, then, Dear Heart, thou hast (as thou requestedst in thy last) pretty nearly all the plans and hopes wh. now occupy my time. I know thou wilt breathe thy soft wifely prayers that they may finally come to some accomplishment. If they do not, – then I am content, for I will have done all that I possibly cd.: more than this, God will not require. Of course some of these plans must needs involve much preliminary failure, trial, patience, and hard work. But I am growing used to these: and they season a man.[53]

And, then, – most blessed of sweet consolations ! I undergo all *for thee*, who art my Darling, and my One-Love, and my Silver Star, and my Perfect Sweet, and my Heart-Of-a-Rose; for thee whom I love each day with new and finer love, as if I were each day born into a larger heaven, a stronger

lover


## To Mary Day Lanier

### [Brooklyn,] Oct. 23rd 1874.

My poor Heart. . . .

I pray thee do not be sorrowful on account of *me*, in the matter of the disappointments which thy wifely heart hath divined. It is true, they have come; but they have been of great value to me. I will make to thee a little confession of faith; telling thee, My dearer Self, in words, what I do not say to my not-so-dear self, except in more modest feelings.

Know then that disappointments were inevitable, and will still come until I have fought the battle which every great Artist has had to fight since time began. This, – dimly felt while I was doubtful of my own vocation and powers –, is clear as the sun to me, now that I *know*, through the fieriest tests of life, that I am, in soul, and shall be, in life and in utterance, a great poet. The philosophy of my disappoint-

---

[53] Except for the publication of "Peace" in the *Southern Magazine* for October 1874, none of the projects mentioned in this letter ever materialized.

ments is:  that there is here so much *cleverness* standing betwixt
me and the public.  The "Readers" of the publishing-houses,
the editors of the magazines, are quick to discover cleverness in
writing, for it is an article in which they have dealt all their
lives, they know it as well as Mr. Stewart [54] knows silk from
woollen.  But works of Art are quite out of their line (as they
would say, in their abominable trade-dialect), they are incredu-
lous of genius, the keenest of them can recall bitter mistakes
in this behalf.  Dost thou remember "The Galaxy" and Walt
Whitman?  Or — for further example — read in the November Scribner's wh. I will send thee, the poem "Mildred in the
Library", from Dr. Holland's (the editor's) new book.  This
poem is merely a clever piece of joinery; it is put together, as is
the whole book from which it is taken.  But its author believes
it to be a great work: and he is one of the very best of the
Magazine-editors, besides being, as I gather from some little
personal interviews I have had with him, a man of unusual
generosity, warmth of heart, and goodness.  Now, as I said,
there is absolutely no method by which an Artist can get to the
people, save through these men: except by money, which I
have not: and therefore I know, and am adequately prepared
for, all the disappointments that await—not *me*, but thee,
dear, loving Heart, in my behalf.  If I were like Bret Harte, or
Mark Twain, and the others of this class of wonderfully clever
writers, my path would be easy: but what would I give for
such success?  I can not dream any fate more terrible to me,
than to have climbed to their niche, – the ledge where Lowell,
and Holmes, and that ilk, rest – and to find *that* my highest
and ultimatum.  If I had such success in my hand, I would
throw it out of the window, and live a quiet life.  And I am
sure, withal, that none of these writers has had a warmer
admirer, or a keener enjoyer, than me. . . .

I pray thee burn this.  It is meant for thine eye alone: and
is writ, for thy comfort, by thy

true-lover.

---

[54] The proprietor of a large department store in New York.

## To Mary Day Lanier

[Brooklyn,] Oct. 29th 1874.

Today I played for the great Dr. Dammrosch: – and won him. I sang the Wind-Song to him. When I finished he came and shook my hand, and said it was done like an Artist: that it was wonderful, in view of my education: and that he was greatly astonished and pleased with the poetry of the piece and the enthusiasm of its rendering. He then closed the door on his next pupil, and kept him waiting in the front parlor a half hour, while giving me a long talk. I had told him that I wished to pursue music. He said: " Do you know what that means? It means a great deal of work, it means a thousand sacrifices. It is very hazardous."

I replied, I knew all that: but it was not a matter of mere preference, it was a spiritual necessity, I must be a musician, I could not help it.

This seemed to please him: and he went on to speak as no other musician here *cd.* speak, of many things. He is the only poet among the craft here: and is a thoroughly cultivated man, in all particulars. He offered to do all that he could, in my behalf: and was altogether the gentleman and the wise artist.

Thou wilt share with me the pleasure I take in thinking that I have never yet failed to win favor with an artist. Although I am far more independent of praise than formerly, and can do without it perfectly well: yet, when it comes, I keenly enjoy it: particularly from one who is the friend of Liszt, of Von Bulow, and of Wagner.

Moreover I played abominably: being both tired, weakened by the warm weather, and excited.

I am pleased that Hammerik shd. have so cordially invited me back to my old place: and anticipate a winter in Baltimore full of substantial work. I find I need Thorough-Bass sorely: and am studying it with might and main. . . .

May God be in thy dreams this night like a generous sun in a blue heaven, — prayeth thy

lover.

## To Logan E. Bleckley [55]

195 Dean St.
Brooklyn, N. Y.
Nov. 15th 1874.

My dear Sir:

I did not know any method of showing you my thorough appreciation of your criticism on my " Corn " better than sending you a printed copy of the poem thoroughly amended & revised so as to avoid nearly all the flaws which you found in it; & I delayed answering your kind & valued letter in the hope of being able to do so.

But things go slowly here in Babylon, – with all the hurry & bustle: & I have not yet made such arrangements for publication as I wish.

My idea is first to get it printed in a magazine of influence, & then to issue it in the form of a small book.  I have your cry of jubilation,[56] & it makes my heart light up all manner of torches.    The War is over.

What a fight it has been!  We had to grip religious fanaticism & frantic patriotism for four years & rascality for ten.

If there are any other three Devils that are harder to wrestle with than these, they have not yet made their appearance in terrene history.    I have been wondering where we are going to get a *Great* Man that will be tall enough to see — over the whole country, & to direct that vast un-doing of things which has got to be accomplished in a few years.

It is a situation in which mere cleverness will not begin to work. The horizon of cleverness is too limited, it does not embrace

[55] Logan E. Bleckley ( 1827-1907 ) became associate justice of the Supreme Court of Georgia in 1875; his distinguished career culminated in a long term as Chief Justice. He was noted for his unconventional personality, an engaging literary style, and the unusual quality of his judicial decisions. Lanier met him in the summer of 1874 and on Oct. 9 sent him a copy of "Corn" with a request for criticism. Bleckley sent a detailed response on Oct. 14.

[56] Bleckley's letter here referred to has not been found.  Apparently, from the echoes in Lanier's letter, it reflected the growing optimism in the South that Reconstruction was coming to an end.  Popular risings had added Arkansas and Alabama to the southern states in which the Democrats had ousted the carpetbag governments and regained control during 1874.

enough of the heart of man, to enable a merely clever politician – such as those in which we abound — to lead matters
properly in this juncture.  The vast generosities which whirl a
small revenge out of the way as the winds whirl a leaf; the
awful integrities which will pay a debt twice rather than allow
the faintest flicker of suspicion about it; the splendid indigna-
tions which are also tender compassions, & which will in one
moment be hurling the money-changers out of The Temple, &
in the next be preaching Love to them from the steps of it:—
where are we to find these?  It is time for a man to arise, who
is a man.

If you write me in the next three weeks — & I am sure you
*would* if you knew what a genuine pleasure your letters are to
me —  direct to me at Macon.

After that I shall be in Baltimore, where I am again invited
to play first flute in the orchestra of the Peabody Conservatory
of Music; I shall spend the rest of the winter there.

Your encouraging words give me at once strength & pleasure.
I hope hard, & work hard to do something worthy of them
some day.

My head & my heart are both so full of poems which the
dreadful struggle for bread does not give me time to put on
paper, — that I am often driven to headache & heartache
purely for want of an hour or two to hold a pen.  I manage to
get a little time tho' to work on what is to be my first *Magnum
Opus*, — a long poem, founded on that strange uprising in the
middle of the 14th Century in France, called " The Jacquerie."
It was the first time that the big hungers of *the People* appear
in our modern civilization: & it is full of significance.

The peasants learned — from the merchant-potentates of
Flanders – that a man who could not be a lord by birth, might
be one by wealth: & so Trade arose & overthrew Chivalry.
Trade has now had possession of the civilized world for four
hundred years; it controls all things, it interprets the Bible, it
guides our national & almost all our individual life with its
maxims; & its oppressions upon the moral existence of man
have come to be ten thousand times more grievous than the
worst tyrannies of the Feudal System ever were.  Thus in the
reversals of time, it is *now* the *gentleman* who must arise &
overthrow Trade.  That chivalry which every man has, in some

degree, in his heart; which does not depend upon birth but which is a revelation from God of justice, of fair dealings, of scorn of mean advantage; which contemns the selling of stock which one *knows* is going to fall, to a man who *believes* it is going to rise, as much as it would contemn any other form of rascality or of injustice, or of meanness;– it is this which must in these latter days organize its insurrections & burn up every one of the cunning moral castles from which Trade sends out its forays upon the conscience of modern Society. — This is about the plan which is to run through my book: though I conceal it under the form of a pure novel.[57]

I must beg you to pardon such a long sermon: it is not writ with malice prepense only you seem to be an earnest man, & I know so few of them to whom one can talk of such things.

Your friend

Sidney Lanier.

Hon. L. E. Bleckley
Atlanta, Ga.

To Gibson Peacock [58]

64 Centre St.<br>Baltimore, Md.<br>Jany 26th, 1875.

My dear Sir:

A very lovely friend of mine,–Mrs. Fannie West-moreland—has been so gracious as to transmit to me, through my wife, your first comments on my poem " Corn " in Lippin-cott's, which I had not seen before. The slip appears to be cut from the " Bulletin " of 16th, or 17th.

---

[57] " The Jacquerie," which Lanier described elsewhere as a novel in verse, was never completed (I, 171).

[58] Gibson Peacock, editor of the Philadelphia *Evening Bulletin,* was an uncle of Mrs. Westmoreland, who was a friend of the Laniers in Brunswick, Ga. His critique of "Corn" said that it was "the best magazine poem we have seen for years . . . , full of the marks of poetic genius and poetic art. The opening passage recalls Keats at his best; but the later ones show a more virile but not less poetical strength, with an American fibre in it that makes it all the better" (*Evening Bulletin,* Jan. 15, 1875).

I cannot resist the impulse which urges me to send you my grateful acknowledgments of the poetic insight, the heartiness and the boldness which display themselves in this *critique*. I thank you for it, as for a poet's criticism upon a poet.

Permit me to say that I am particularly touched by the courageous independence of your review. In the very short time that I have been in the hands of the critics, nothing has amazed me more than the timid solicitudes with which they rarify, in one line, any enthusiasm they may have condensed in another,— a process curiously analogous to those irregular condensations and rarefactions of air which physicists have shown to be the conditions for producing an indeterminate sound. Many of my critics have seemed—if I may change the figure—to be forever conciliating the yet-unrisen ghosts of possible mistakes. From these you separate yourself *toto cælo*: and I am thoroughly sure that your method is not only far more worthy the dignity of the critical office, but also far more helpful to the young artist, by its bold sweeping-away of those sorrowful uncertain mists that arise at times out of the waste bitterness of poverty and obscurity.

— Perhaps here is more feeling than is quite delicate in a communication to one not an old personal friend: but I do not hesitate upon propriety if only I may convey to you some idea of the admiration with which I regard your manly position in my behalf, and of the earnestness with which I shall always consider myself

Your obliged and faithful friend,

Sidney Lanier

## To Mary Day Lanier

[Baltimore,] Mch. 24th 1875.

Small favors thankfully received.

Here hath come a letter from one A. Pope, the same being a high functionary in the net-work of railroads running (happy roads !) towards thee, towit, the " Great Atlantic Coast Line

&c&c&c ", asking me to call on a certain day at the Office of
said Roads in Baltimore: and I have called: and he wisheth
me to write, – By Homer and Lucretius, By Dan Chaucer and
John Keats and Will Shakespeare, — he wisheth me to write
a — . a — — — — (Choke, choke, choke) a – ch —. (gulp, gulp,
gulp) a Guide book To Florida Travellers.   He proposeth, By
Pegasus, to pay my hotel-bills and travelling expenses, and to
give me One hundred and twenty five dollars a month – By
Crœsus, in addition thereto: and I am to take from April to
the last of June for the work.[59]   I am to do Norfolk, Richmond, Petersburg, Wilmington, Raleigh, Charlotte, Columbia,
Augusta, Charleston, Savannah, Jacksonville, St. Augustine,
and Florida generally:  I am to relate their histories, recount
their products, immortalize their great men, describe their
topographies, and depict their " points of interest ": and am–,
according to the instructions of my patron and Mæcænas, to
get up a Guide-book, which shall at once be a literary attrac-
tion and a statistical thesaurus.   I owe all these honors to my
Mæcænas' having read " Corn ".

Well, Apollo was a swineherd:  By Gog and Magog, shall I
twist my nose at bread and meat?

My frame of mind is, as thou perceivest, expletive.   In fact,
I have accepted the offer.

Mr. Pope goes to New York to see the publishers:  and will
return early next week, to make the final arrangements.

Dear Heart, dear Love, dear Wife, if nothing go wrong, I
shall see thee within three weeks from this time:  it may be
earlier.   For this grace, Laus Deo, ten thousand times : and I
will arise and play me a heart's-relief on my piano.

I wrote Mrs. Bostwick.

Mayst thou sleep and dream that thy heart beats double, – prays
thy

lover.——

---

[59] *Florida* (VI, 3-183) was published in Nov., 1875, by J. B. Lippincott
& Co.   The work on this pot-boiler consumed nearer six months than three.

## To Edward Spencer [60]

64 Centre St.
Baltimore, Md.
April 1st 1875.

Dear Mr. Spencer:

. . . .

——"—— From what I know of your writings, I can easily see how great must have been your temptations to " versatility ": and I thank you for the warning, in that behalf, though I obstinately refuse to see that your own example points your moral, for your success in so many fields is rather a seduction thereto than a repulsion therefrom. Fortunately for me, a decisive limitation of faculty has prevented me from the disasters which must have ensued if I had attempted to caper over such an enormous playground as you breathe yourself in. Things come to me mostly in one of two forms, – the poetic or the musical. I express myself with most freedom in the former *modus*: with most passionate delight in the latter. Indeed I ought to say that, *apud me*, music is, in my present stage of growth, rather a passion than a faculty: I am not its master, it is mine. It is only within a few months that I had the least glimpse of my own relation to Art. May I tell you how I got it? It was through a chagrin. I had sent " Corn " to the Atlantic Monthly. It went under exceptionally favorable auspices. Mr. Hurd (one of the owners of the Atlantic Monthly) had read the *ms.* and sent it himself to the editor, with his commendation. Mr. Howells wrote back, that " with every desire to like " the poem, he " did not find it successful," that readers would be mystified by it, that there was no " connection between the apostrophe in the beginning and the bit of narrative at the close," and that " neither was striking enough to stand alone ": – and declined to put it in the Magazine. He finished

[60] Edward Spencer (1834–1883) of Randallstown, Md., was an author and journalist. On Feb. 22, 1875, he wrote Lanier of the pleasure he had found in reading "Corn," which had been reprinted in the Baltimore *Bulletin*.
Charlotte Cushman, mentioned at the end of this letter, was a celebrated actress. Lanier met her in January 1875 and enjoyed a warm friendship with her during the last year of her life.

by coolly asking Mr. Hurd to show the letter to me: – which
Mr. H. had done, through the mail.

—      I took the letter to my room, – it was a high room, in
Brooklyn, N. Y. from whose window I could see many things –
and there, during a day whose intensity was of that sort that
one only attempts to communicate to one's God, I led myself
to an infinite height above myself and meditated: and when
evening came I found myself full of the ineffable contents of
certainty and of perfect knowledge and of decision.   I had
become aware,– not by reasoning, I could only reason about it
afterwards, I know not what the process was – that my business
in life was to make poems.   Since then it has not occurred to
me to doubt about my sort of work.   Why should one disquiet
oneself with asking whether one is to sing solos, or to come
on only in the concerted parts?  God must have His chorus.

—      I please myself with believing you will be glad to know
that the martydom which has preceded the heaven of so many
finer singers than I am, is not likely to be mine.   " Corn " has
met with a recognition all over the country far beyond my
utmost hope, I am still all in a smile at having been sent for
the other day, by Miss Charlotte Cushman, who kept me
a-blush for an hour with big generous praises, enough to make
a man a pious and humble workman for the balance of his life

So !   I have told you what I have not dared to speak of, to
any man.   In so doing, my desire was to show you how sensible
I am of your goodness in writing me as you have, and how
glad I will be to call myself

Your friend

Sidney Lanier.

To Gibson Peacock

Philadelphia, Pa.
July 31st 1875.

If you have ever watched a shuttle, my dear friend, being
violently knocked backward and forward in a loom — never
settled for a second at this end before it is rudely smacked back

to the other— you will possess a very fair idea of the nature of my recent travels.

I do not know how many times I have been from North to South in the last six weeks: the negotiations about the Florida book, and the collection of additional material for it, have required my presence at widely-separated points often: and as my employer is himself always on the wing, I have sometimes had to make a long chase in order to come up with him. I believe my wanderings are now ended, however, for a time; and, as the very first of the many blessings which this cessation of travel will bring to a tired soul, I count this opportunity to send a line which will carry my love to you and to your *other* you.

Lippincott has made what seems to be a very fair proposition to print the Florida book, taking an interest in it which I think practically amounts to about one-half. I am going to add to it, by way of appendix, a complete Guide-book to Florida: and as this feature ought of itself to secure some sale among the fifteen or twenty thousand annual visitors, I am induced to hope that my employer may be reimbursed for his entire outlay, – though I keep in mind, what they all tell me, that the publication of any book is a mere lottery, and baffles all prophecy as to its success. Two chapters of the book, one on " *St. Augustine In April* ", and one on " *The Oclawaha River* ", are to appear in the Magazine, October and November numbers. . . .

Many thanks for Mr. Taylor's letter.[61] I do hope I may be able to see him during this next month. Do you think a letter from me would reach him at " Mattapoisett "? For his estimate of my " Symphony " seems to me so full and generous, that I think I will not resist the temptation to anticipate his letter to me. I will write also to Mr. Calvert tomorrow: his

---

[61] On May 21 Peacock had sent a copy of Lanier's poem, "The Symphony," to Bayard Taylor, an established poet and man of letters. Taylor's reply, June 3, said in part: "I hail in the author a new, rightfully anointed poet, in whom are the elements of a great success. . . . He has an unusual instinct of rhythm; but, what is best and most encouraging, it rests on a rich basis of underlying ideas."

"The Symphony" appeared in the June issue of *Lippincott's;* its publication prompted George H. Calvert's article on Lanier in the *Golden Age,* June 12, 1875.

The sonnets mentioned in the next paragraph were entitled "Acknowledgement" (see I, 56–58).

insight into a poet's internal working—as developed in his kind notice of me in the *Golden Age*—is at once wonderful and delightful.

The next number of Lippincott's will contain four sonnets of mine, in the Shakespearian meter. I sincerely hope they are going to please you. You will be glad to know that "the Symphony" meets with continuing favor in various parts of the land.

My month in Brooklyn will be full of the very hardest work. I will be employed in finishing and revising the Florida book, many of the points in which demand very careful examination. In August my railroad engagement terminates. . . .

Your faithful friend
Sidney Lanier

## To Bayard Taylor

195 Dean St.
Brooklyn, N. Y.
Aug. 7th 1875.

My dear Sir:
When a man, determined to know as well what is under as what is above, has made his plunge down to the bottom of the great Sea Doubtful of poetic endeavor, and has looked not only upon the enchanted caverns there but upon the dead bodies also: there comes a moment as his head re-emerges above the surface, when his eyes are a-blink with salt water and tears, when the horizon is a round blur, and when he wastes strength that might be applied to swimming, in resolutely defying what seems to be the gray sky overhead.

In such a moment, a friendly word — and all the more if it be a friendly word from a strong swimmer whom one perceives far ahead advancing calmly and swiftly — brings with it a pleasure so large and grave that , as voluble thanks are impossible, so a simple and sincere acknowledgement is inevitable.

I did not know that my friend Mr Peacock had sent you my " Symphony " until I received his letter enclosing yours in reference to that poem: your praise came to me therefore with the added charm of surprise. You are quite right in supposing the *Makamât* of Hariri of Basrah to be unknown to me. How earnestly I wish that they might be less so, by virtue of some account of them from your own lips! I could never describe to you what a mere drought and famine my life has been, as regards that multitude of matters which I fancy one absorbs when one is in an atmosphere of art, or when one is in con-versational relation with men of letters, with travellers, with persons who have either seen, or written, or done large things. Perhaps you know that with us of the younger generation in the South since the War, pretty much the whole of life has been merely not-dying.

I will be in Brooklyn about a month, and if you should come to New York in that time I beg you will send me a line to above address telling me where I can find you, – and *when*, so that I may not miss you.

I remember how Thomas Carlyle has declared a man will be strengthened in his opinion when he finds it shared by another mortal: – and so enclose a slip which a friend has just sent me, from the Boston Transcript, containing some pleasant words about my poems by Mr. Calvert.

Pray believe that I shall always hold myself, and always rejoice to be held by you, as

Your friend

Sidney Lanier.

To Mary Day Lanier

Westminster Hotel, N. Y.<br>Oct. 4th 1875.

. . . .

——————— Saturday night was to me an Arabian Night. My good Caliph Haroun Al Raschid Taylor took me to the Century Club and there for the first time in my life I had the delight of meeting and of conversing with thoughtful men and artists of many sorts. I wish I might tell thee the keen pleasure of it all.

I had also in the course of the evening some special indi‑
vidual warmths of greeting from here and there a man to
whom my little ventures had come to port, which were ver
charming.　Among others I was presented to David Hunting
ton, whose picture of Miranda inspired the poem that wa
printed in the Evening Post.[62]　He had seen the poem ther
when it first appeared, and had preserved it and spoken spe
cially to Mr. Bryant about it.　He was very gracious in warr
expressions of his sense of the compliment to his picture, an
of his appreciation of the poem which he said had completel
caught his idea of the Miranda creation, and had pleased Mr
Bryant as well as himself.

I was pleased more than all with a hearty and wholly un
expected offer of assistance from Mr. Stedmen,[63] who late i
the evening came to me and after many pleasant things abou
myself informed me that Scribner's would probably have som
book‑reviewing to do, that I was the man to do it, and that if
would consent he would see the editors and endeavor to mak
the arrangement.　Of course I consented.

In the course of the evening I met Gov. Tilden, Whitelaw
Reid (with whom I was greatly struck), Stoddard, Ward (th
Sculptor), Charlton Lewis, Holt, Putnam,[64] and many other
I found Ward a splendid fellow: and had a pleasant talk wit
Stoddard.

---

[62] Lanier's poem entitled "On Huntingdon's 'Miranda'" (I, 32) had been pub
lished in the New York *Evening Post,* Mar. 6, 1874.

[63] Edmund Clarence Stedman (poet, 1833–1908). It was probably wit
Stedman's and Taylor's kindnesses in mind that Lanier wrote to his father o
Oct. 9, 1875 (Here omitted): "I am sure you would be gratified if you coul
know all the pleasant things which my very meagre poetic accomplishment ha
brought me, here.　I have only to get something large before the public, i
order to take, before it, the pleasant position which I seem to have won amon
the literary men here.　I was really touched by some offers of assistance whic
were made to me at the Century Club the other night, where I was carried by m
constant friend Mr. Taylor: offers so warm, and so wholly unsought an
unexpected, could not have come from any source but hearty appreciation."

[64] Samuel J. Tilden (1814-1886), Democratic Governor of New York, 187‑
1876; Whitelaw Reid (1837-1912), editor of the New York *Tribune* sinc
1872; Richard Henry Stoddard (1825-1903), poet; John Quincy Adams War
(1830-1910); Charlton Thomas Lewis (1834-1904), lawyer and classicist; an
probably the publishers, George Haven Putnam (1844-1930) and Henry Ho
(1840-1926).

Yesterday morning my dear old Mr. Calvert [65] called, on
his return from Washington; and presently took me out for a
long drive in the Park, after which I dined with him and Mrs.
Calvert — a charming little old lady with profuse tight curls
of gray hair in front on each side of her face, and with manners and speech like thy father's when he is happy. Moreover
we dined at the Everett House; I had a sense of thee, all about:
constantly wondering whether mayhap thou hadst sate in the
very spot I was sitting and other the like particulars, whereby
I fear I was *distrait* enough. But the dear little gentle lady
talked evenly along: and we had a smoke, graciously allowed
by her, in their parlor after dinner: and then the good gentleman (he is over seventy three) must see me home, so out with
me into the night: and arrived at my house, he comes up to my
room, and we discuss many matters and I read him a poem or
two, writ on Saturday: and finally he sighs and declares he
*must* go: and I walk back to the Everett House with him:
where, arriving, in midst of some interesting talk or other, he
vows I shall not return alone to my lodgings and actually walks
all the way back with me, and after standing in the office a
little while to finish our talk, finally gets him home to Mrs.
Calvert.

Mr. Kirk has given me a job, of four ten-page articles on
India to be richly illustrated from French plates sent over by
J. B. Lippincott from Europe. I will have about $300 for the
four papers: the first one to come out in January next. He
has also engaged me to write the Centennial Poem, for the
July Magazine of 1876, which he proposes to illustrate, —
and for which I shall charge him a round sum. The whole
idea of the poem has come to me in a whirlwind of glory, and
I am thirsty for the time to arrive when I can sit daily by thee
and write it.[66] . . .

                                        lover.

[65] George H. Calvert (see note 61, above).
[66] "The Psalm of the West (I, 62–82). *Lippincott's* paid Lanier $300 for it.

## To Paul H. Hayne

Philadelphia, Pa.
Oct. 16th 1875.

My dear Mr. Hayne:

Your note – which has followed me about and finally reached me here – gave me a great deal of pleasure and I hasten to assure you that I have for months only been putting off from day to day the actual committal to paper of the letter which has been lying really written within me. This " putting off " has been due, not to laziness, but to its opposite. I believe I wrote you sometime ago that I had been employed to make a book on Florida. I commenced the travels preparatory thereto in April last: the thing immediately began to ramify and expand, until I quickly found I was in for a long and very difficult job: so long, and so difficult, that, after working day and night for the last three months on the materials I had previously collected, I have just finished the book, and am now up to my ears in proof-sheets and wood-cuts which the publishers are rushing through in order to publish at the earliest possible moment, the book having several features designed to meet the wants of the winter-visitors to Florida. It is in truth only a kind of spiritualized guide-book.

– This it is which has prevented me from writing you. With a nervous employer and a pushing publisher behind me, I have had to work from ten to fourteen hours a day; and the confinement to the desk brought on my old hæmorrhages about a month ago which quite threatened for a time to suspend my work forever on *this* side of River.

I'm thus minute in detailing the reasons for my failure to write you, because all along through these last three or four months when gratifying things have been happening to me in connection with my little artistic efforts, I have had constantly in mind the kindly help and encouragement which your cheering words used to bring me when I was even more obscure than I am now. Even in my insignificant experience I have seen so much of the hue-and-cry sort of criticism – that which waits until it finds how the big-mouth'd dogs are running and then squeaks in chorus without the least knowledge of, or regard for, the game or the course of the hunt – that I have learned to set a high value on genuine and independent judgments. These *you* gave me, and I will always be grateful to you for them.[67] . . . I will be glad to hear from you, and of you; being always

sincerely yours

Sidney Lanier

To Bayard Taylor[68]

Macon, Ga.<br>November 24, 1875.

My dear Mr. Taylor:

Poets understand everything: I doubt not you well know a certain sort of happiness which at the same time locks up expression and enlarges fancy, and you will therefore easily comprehend how it is that thirty days have passed

---

[67] In his reply, Oct. 23, 1875, Hayne expressed himself as deeply touched by this testimonial given in " the bright morning of your fame," so different from the way most men repudiate their old associations " the moment they begin to rise in the world." He added: " With *pride* no less than *pleasure*, I hail your really brilliant success in Literature. Some fools in this quarter of the world have thought proper to express *surprise*, at your waking up one morning (after the publication of ' Corn ') and ' finding yourself famous.' . . . They can't understand that *Lanier*, being a Georgian, *has*, or *could* have any *real* claim to artistic distinction! " He concluded by saying that he wanted Lanier to do for him what he had done for Henry Timrod— edit his literary remains after his death so that his memory " would not wholly die out." (But Hayne outlived Lanier by five years.)

No letters from Lanier to Hayne for the next five years have been found. But seven surviving letters from Hayne show that Lanier continued to write him, though at longer intervals, and that he sent him copies of his *Florida* and *Poems* (1877).

[68] On Nov. 13 Lanier had joined his wife in Macon. It was then decided that he would take his oldest son Charles to Baltimore with him for the winter, and that his wife would accept Clifford Lanier's invitation to come with the other children to Montgomery, Ala., for the winter.

without any message from me to you, although there has been no one of them during which you were not constantly in my mind.  This happiness of which I speak – which freezes one's pen and tongue while it melts one's heart – means in the present instance that I have been at home for ten days past, joyfully reunited with the other – and far sweeter – Moiety of me.  My three young men – one of seven, one of five and one of two years – keep me in an endless labyrinth of surprises and delights:  nothing could be more keen, more fresh, more breezy, than the meeting together of their little immense loves with the juicy selfishness and honest animalisms of the dear young cubs.  What a prodigious Candor they practise!  They're as little ashamed of being beasts as they are proud of being gods:  they accept themselves at the hands of their Creator with perfect unreserve:  pug nose or Greek, blue eyes or gray, beasthood or godhood – it's all one to them.  What's the good of metaphysical moping as long as Papa's at home and you've got a Mama to kiss and a new ball from now till dinner and *then* apples!

This is their philosophy:  it is really a perfect scheme of life, and contains all the essential terms of religion, while – as for philosophy – it is perfectly clear upon points which have remained obscure from Plato down to George Lewes.[69]

How I wish my lovely two-year-old boy – my royal Hal – could look you in the eyes for once, and put his arms deliberately round your neck and give you one of his fervent kisses!  Fancy that your big Lars was also a baby, and also a poet; and you'll have a whiff of it.

Your letters came to me while I was with Miss Cushman, and were the means of procuring for me two delightful afternoons with Mr. Lowell and Mr. Longfellow.  I was sorry to miss Mr. Aldrich.  I wrote him a little note, to find out when he would be in town.  He replied that he could not come until after I had left Boston, but added that he would be in New York during the winter, " when perhaps Mr. Taylor would be good enough – he is good enough for anything – to bring us together."

[69] Lanier had apparently been reading recently George Henry's Lewes's *Problems of Life and Mind*, which he refers to in *Florida* (VI, 52).

I'm sure you'll care to know that I had a charming visit to Miss Cushman, and that each day was crowded with pleasant things which she and her numerous friends had prepared for me.

I leave Macon for Baltimore on Friday next. My address there will be 64 Centre St., and I will hope to hear from you very soon after my arrival. I resume my old place as first flute of the Peabody Orchestra, which lasts until March; though hoping all the time still to find some opportunity for getting my longed-for chair of The Physics and Metaphysics of Music established in some college or other.

My pretty Comrade here begs that she may be allowed to join me in grateful and affectionate messages to you, — for she knows in detail all your thoughtful kindliness in my behalf. Pray let me not quite drop out of the recollection of Mrs. Taylor and of your daughter.

Your friend,<br>Sidney Lanier.

## To Mary Day Lanier

B&deg;<br>Jany. 8th 1876

Well then : God be praised that giveth us the victory. I have late this afternoon finished my third India paper, which was a great labor and strain: and tonight we have played a divine Concert of Scandinavian music whereof I enclose herein the programme; and my heart is so full of this heavenly melody that I cannot find me any rest till I have in some wise enlarged me by the addition of thee .

Moreover I have a charming piece of news which — although thou are not yet to communicate it to any one except Clifford — I cannot keep from thee. The opening ceremonies of the Centennial Exhibition will be very grand: and among other things there are to be sung by a full Chorus (and played by the orchestra, under Thomas' direction) a hymn, and a Cantata.

Gen. Hawley, Prest of the Centennial Commission, has written inviting me to write the latter (I mean the *poem*; Dudley Buck, of New York, is to write the music). Bayard Taylor is to write the hymn. This is very pleasing to me; for I am chosen as representative of our dear South; and the matter puts my name by the side of very delightful and honorable ones, besides bringing me in contact with many people I would desire to know.[70]

Mr. Buck has written me that he wants the poem by Jany. 15th: which, as I have not yet had the least time for it, gives me just seven days to write it in. I would much rather have had seven months: but God is great. Remember, thou and Cliff, that this is not yet to be spoken of, at all. . . .

But I must sleep. For the next seven days I am to be buried in my Cantata. God send that I shall find time to write thee: but an I do not, thou wilt think that I am underground forging gems to hang about the sweet neck of that Most Sweet to whom I am true

lover.

## To Bayard Taylor

66 Centre St.<br>Baltimore, Md,<br>Mch. 20th 1876.

*Bravissimo*, dear Mr. Taylor: why, this is the very Fitness of Things: the appointment matches, as a rhyme matches a rhyme: nothing can be more evident than that God has temporarily taken the direction of matters into His own hands. I think with all honesty, and apart from friendly preference, that you will do the Ode far better than either of the three other gentlemen could: and I send you my congratulations and fair wishes

---

[70] Lanier's Cantata, "The Centennial Meditation of Columbia" (I, 60–62), was set to music by Dudley Buck (1839–1909). Buck had just begun his long career as composer and conductor, having joined Theodore Thomas' Orchestra as assistant conductor in 1875. His greatest reputation came as a composer of religious music and concert cantatas—a reputation that was first established on a national basis by his Centennial Cantata.

with a certain sense of indignant triumph in the coming-to-pass of what ought to have been.[71]

I see, from what you say in reply to my letter on the Hymn, that my musical associations have put me under a certain general suspicion, with you, of a propensity to impart the principles of musical construction into poetry. But this was a principle far larger than any peculiar to music or to any one art. I am so much interested in it that I am going to beg you to let me plead the case with you a moment.

Permit me first to say that I came at it, not by any reasoning *prepense*, but by examination, afterwards, of wholly unconscious procedure. It revealed itself clearly to me in thinking about a little poem I wrote a few days ago. Perhaps I can best illustrate it by first quoting the poem, which is a pendant to a little song you have already seen, being No. II of " ROSE-MORALS " :

> Soul, get thee to the heart
> Of yonder tube-rose, hide thee there,
> There breathe the meditations of thine Art
> Suffused with prayer.
>
> ―――――――
>
> Of spirit grave, yet light,
> How fervent fragances uprise
> Pure-born from these most rich and yet most white
> Virginities !
>
> ―――――――
>
> Mulched with unsavory death,
> Grow, Soul, unto such white estate
> That art and virginal prayer shall be thy breath,
> Thy work, thy fate.

Now it seems to me – as a mere extended formulation of the thoroughly unconscious action of the mind in this poem – that every poem, from a Sonnet to Macbeth, has substantially these elements, – (1) a Hero, (2) a Plot, and (3) a Crisis: and that its perfection as a work of art will consist in the simplicity

―――――――

[71] In his letter of Mar. 17 Taylor said that he had been asked to write the Ode for the "grand national celebration of the 4th of July" instead of the Centennial Hymn for the opening ceremonies.

and the completeness with which the first is involved in the second and illustrated in the third.  In the case of a short poem the hero is the central Idea, whatever that may be: the plot is whatever is said about that idea, its details all converging, both in tone and in general direction, thereupon : and the crisis is the unity of impression sealed or confirmed or climax'd by the last connected sentence, or sentiment, or verse, of the poem.  Of course I mean that this is the most general expression of the artistic plan of a poem: it is the system of verses, which may be infinitely varied, but to which all variations may be finally referred.    I do not think that there is, as you feared, any *necessary* reason why a poem so constructed should present " a too-conscious air of design ":  that is a matter which will depend solely upon the genuineness of the inspiration and the consummate command of his resources by the artist.

Is not this frame-work essentially that of every work of any art ?  Does not every painting, every statue, every architectural design owe whatever it has of artistic perfection to the nearness with which it may approach the fundamental scheme of a Ruling Idea (or Hero), a Plot (or involution of the Ruling Idea in complexities related to or clustering about it), and a Denouement, or Impression-as-a-whole?

I don't mean this for a theory: I hate theories, I intend it only to be a convenient synthesis of a great number of small facts: and therefore I don't stickle at all for calling the elements of a work of art " Heroes ", or " Plots ", or " Crises ", and the like—, only using those terms as the shortest way of expressing my meaning.

Any way, fair fall the Ode.    I hope that God will let you into Heaven, with no limitations as to walking on the grass or picking the flowers, – till you've got all you want.

Mr. Buck has sent me a copy of the Piano-score of the Cantata, but I have not yet had time to examine it thoroughly. Anything will go well, though, with a large chorus to sing it and Thomas' Orchestra to play it.

If it will not trouble you I will be glad if you'll send me whatever announcement of your appointment shall be made.

Charley joins me in fair remembrances to you and the ladies of your house.

Write me soon, as to your always desirous

S. L.

## To Innes Randolph [72]

Exchange Hotel
Montgomery, Ala.
April 22nd 1876

Dear Innis:

Your notice is a work of art, for pure daintiness, penetration, and forbearance of such disagreement betwixt critic and artist as comes to no practical result. I like it better than anything which has been said of my poor little poem, and I thank you for it with all the more fervor because I see—now that I have had time to think a little, in this quiet land where all the home-people are in my favor from mere blind pride and where the dust of conflict has not yet appeared—how stern must be the fight with which I must hack some opening for that extension of poetic forms about which all my thoughts begin to cluster.

I think often, and with wonder, of the success with which you manage to keep your singular critical faculty upon the plane of pure Art in spite of the well-nigh paralyzing limitations which surround your work. I used sometimes to despair of ever seeing such a thing as a Southern Critic, particularly when I observed how completely our people were under the dominion of that provincial habit of thought which confounds the obligation of personal friendship with that of fidelity to the truths of Art. This feeling, at a time when the peculiar condition of our Southern Countrymen has caused the relation between Art and Criticism to assume a quite exceptional importance, gives me a keen interest in your critical career apart from any personal grounds, and I find myself all the time eagerly hoping for some enlargement of your utterances into a wider range. Mr. Hassard,[73] of THE TRIBUNE,

---

[72] This letter is here published for the first time, from the MS recently given to The Johns Hopkins University. Randolph had been a friend of Lanier's in Virginia during the Civil War. He moved to Baltimore in 1868 where he combined the practice of law with journalism. By 1874, when they renewed their friendship, Randolph was the music and drama critic of the Baltimore *Gazette*. The "notice" here referred to was a highly favorable critique of Lanier's "Cantata" (see notes 70 and 73).

[73] Early in the spring the text of Lanier's Cantata" had been released to the press for review, against his wishes. A storm of controversy ensued. Though a few critics defended the poem, the majority of newspapers over the country showered it with abuse, chiefly on the grounds of its obscurity. The two notices here referred to took a middle ground. When text and music were rendered by chorus and orchestra at the opening ceremonies of the Centennial Exhibition on May 10, Lanier's poem was vindicated (see note 75, below).

and the Musical Critic of THE ATLANTIC MONTHLY are the only two men besides yourself who show any approach to an understanding of that enormous breadth of culture which must be acquired by a musical critic before any weight can be attached to his judgments: and these two, unfortunately, always seem to me to exhibit rather (what some writer calls) *a languorous enjoyment of flavors* than any such big, frank, out-and-out acknowledgement of the paramount Gospel of Art as satisfies a man with a man's belly and a downright flat foot and a wife-and-children and a thousand dim yet gigantic hankerings after he doesn't know what. I well know how nearly irresistible is the tendency of a critic who is called upon to have opinions about everything to fall into this mere sippy daintiness of Stomach; but you appear to have a certain stalwart quality about you which secures you from that most insidious of all the artistic dyspepsias, and in this particular you strike me as clearly higher than any of your critical co-laborers in America. I pray that in full knowledge of the danger and of your own power you may remain so.

I'm sure you will care to know that I am being received with a perfect ovation in the South. Of course I understand that this is purely local pride, and not at all any guarantee of sympathy with artistic purposes: —and yet, to one who knows as clearly as I do the dreary struggle that lies ahead, it is very pleasant!

If you should come to Philadelphia (where I will be in a couple of weeks from now, for some time) pray communicate with me. Letters always reach me if addressed "care of Gibson Peacock, 1425 Walnut St. Philadelphia, Pa."

> Your friend,
>
> Sidney L.

## TO ROBERT S. LANIER

Philadelphia, May 12th 1876

My dear Father:

I have in vain tried to get time for even a note to you. I have found all manner of vexatious little matters revealed by the proof of my long poem, and these have required all the moments I could spare from what seemed pressing duty. I am still at work on the poem, but will finish tonight.[74]

You will have seen accounts of the great success with which the Exhibition opened, and I send you herewith Bayard Taylor's account in the TRIBUNE, and a more detailed notice of the Cantata performance in the Philadelphia PRESS.[75] I sat by Mr. Taylor during the ceremonies – both of us being a few feet from President Grant and the Central group which surrounded him. We had the best position of the whole multitude and often congratulated ourselves on the good fortune which caused us to meet on the platform and to witness this great scene in company. I wish I had time to give you some idea *how* great it was; probably nothing like it has ever been beheld or heard. The Cantata was sung with immense effect, and the great volume of tone from the chorus surprised and delighted the whole assemblage. The Bass Solo, commencing "Long as thine Art &c " was heard by at least twenty five thousand people, and was encored, – both of which circumstances are probably without parallel on an occasion of this kind. Mr. Taylor and I joined in the procession, after the final speech, and moved through the vast buildings in company with the *other* dignitaries, before the public was admitted.

At night I went to Mr. [George W.] Child's reception, where I was presented to the President, Secretary Fish and other eminent personages. I stood near Dom Pedro for some time, and studied his face while he was talking with my friend Mr. Peacock. I did not care to be presented to his majesty – though

[74] "The Psalm of the West," published in *Lippincott's*, July 1876.

[75] The grand opening ceremonies of the Centennial Exhibition on May 10, 1876, included the performance of Wagner's *Centennial Inaugural March*, Whittier's Hymn, and Lanier's Cantata– sung by a chorus of 800 voices and accompanied by an orchestra of 150 musicians. In his account of the occasion in the New York *Tribune*, May 11, 1876, Bayard Taylor declared: "I wish some of the critics who were made so unhappy by Mr. Lanier's cantata could have heard it sung to Mr. Dudley Buck's music. The words suffered ' a sea-change ' into another tongue; the stanzas relieved each other, and unexpected dramatic felicities were recognized by the mind through the ear. . . . It was original in the perfection of the execution no less than in the conception of both poet and composer. The effect upon the audience could not be mistaken." The Philadelphia *Press*, May 11, 1876, gave the full text of Lanier's Cantata, followed by a detailed analysis of the music. It spoke of " the multitude of eager listeners," the " well-trained chorus," and the admirable solo, concluding: " Protracted and most appreciative applause greeted this performance."

this was offered – for I saw that he was quite overrun with presentations, and knew that Mr. Peacock's conversation was in honor of his wife's old friendship with the emperor.[76]   Mr. and Mrs. Peacock called on him by appointment next day and had a charming visit.

Many of the papers have renewed the most bitter abuse and ridicule upon my poor little Cantata, and have displayed an amount of gratuitous cruelty and ignorant brutality of which I could never have dreamed.[77]   I am glad to know however that Gen. Hawley is pleased with the work.   He remarked to a friend some nights ago that he thought the papers had been very unfair to me about the poem and that he quite agreed in the view of it published in the TRIBUNE.

I am going to run over to New York in the morning. Expect to return Monday.   Received the letter forwarded by you.   After I get back will have more leisure to write.

Meantime, and always, God bless you, and all my dear ones. I write May a little note tonight.

Your son

S. L.

[76] Dom Pedro II, Emperor of Brazil.   Gibson Peacock's wife was the daughter of the Marquis de la Figanière, at one time Portuguese minister to the United States.

[77] According to the New York *Herald* of May 11, 1876: " Mr. Lanier is an intelligent poet and his verses have ideas and melody. But he seems to have made the common mistake of supposing that verse should be itself musical to be sung. Verse written for music should be simple, clear, direct and brief in its statements. . . . He has written a beautiful poem, but it is obscure to the eye and must be unintelligible to the ear. . . . The argument of the poem is not easily to be comprehended, and the language is harsh." Even more critical was the editorial in the New York *Times*, May 11, 1876. After a favorable review of Whittier's Hymn, came the following comment: " We wish we could say as much for Mr. Lanier's Contata. A more bewildering collection of rhymes we do not ever remember to have seen, or one more entirely at variance with the taste of the American people."

To Edward Spencer

West Chester, Pa.
Aug. 15th 1876

Dear Mr. Spencer:

A long illness has kept me from complying with your request until I fear the time is past when I can be of service to you. I am not sure, from your letter, whether it is the topography, or the personnel, of the club you want.[78] The former is simple. The club-building is on 15th St. between Irving Place and 4th Avenue, and looks as to its exterior like nothing but a plain brick dwelling-house. One enters and passes into a room on the right where one hangs one's hat on a peg, most likely alongside of hats that give one a sensation of awe – vast castors, much belled in the crown, with a certain look of the back-rooms of banks and trustee-meetings about them. Opposite this, across a passage, is the newspaper-room, where are files of all the papers. The passage gives presently into a stately room where are knots of gentlemen smoking and talking, the furniture being arranged for those indulgences, and the wine-room opening conveniently into the apartment. Your friend who carried you in asks you what you will take almost immediately; summons a colored waiter, delivers him your order (which if you are wise will be for brandy-and-soda, it being the best tipple of that nature I have ever seen), lights cigars, and points out to you the notabilities; calling them up if he knows them and introducing you in a very easy and informal way. On *my* first night I thus met Gov. Tilden, Mr. Dorsheimer, Whitelaw Reid, Ward (the Sculptor) Stedman, Stoddard, McDonough, and many others. One is likely to see young Austin Flint (a very fine-looking man), Draper, Gifford (the painter), Bayard Taylor, Conant (the sleek beast of Harper's Weekly) Bryant, and many others.[79] Without cere-

---

[78] Lanier's visits to the Century Club in New York, here described, were during the preceding October.

[79] Samuel J. Tilden (1814-1886), retiring governor of New York and Democratic candidate for the presidency; Wm. E. Dorsheimer (1832-1888), lieutenant-governor of New York, 1874-1878; Austin Flint (1836-1915), professor of physiology at the Bellevue Hospital Medical College; probably John W. Draper

mony you approach any of the groups formed: at the first lull
in the talk your friend introduces you round, the circle is opened
for you, you are asked to sit down and to have a cigar along
with whatever the people are drinking, – and then the conversation goes on, whatever you may have to say being listened to
with great politeness and respect – though among the familiars
one hears many sharp repartees and the utmost candor of disagreement though always in good taste and gentlemanly respect
for opposing opinion.   Presently folding-doors open (this is
on a Saturday night only) and a table is seen in the centre
of a large room, containing Oysters in various forms, salads,
crackers, sardines, lemons, &c; at one side of the room is another
large table which is a vast plateau of oysters on the half shell,
which you approach and prod up with silver oyster forks, being
very liberal previously with your lemon-juice and salt and
pepper.   This supper is free to all members and guests and is
served each Saturday night during the season.   Both this dining-
room and the room last mentioned have doors open into an
apartment as large as both of them which is hung with valuable
paintings many of them by members of the Club, and around
the base-board of which are shelves containing current numbers
of many reviews and magazines in several languages.   Here
one smokes and reads, or gazes at the pictures, or chats more
en duo with one's friend.   These comprise the lower rooms;
the story above has the rich hall of the Club, the library &c; I
explored it very hastily, and do not remember much of it, the
pleasant talk downstairs being very attractive to me during the
four or five visits I made.   Soon after my first visit – when I
was the guest of Bayard Taylor – a card was sent me, signed
by him, Stedman and Stoddard, inviting me to use the privileges
of the Club for thirty days.

   These items will probably furnish you with what you want.
If they do not, I will take great pleasure in supplementing them
as far as I am able.

   I hope your health is good.   Pray give my love to Dr. Browne
when you see him or write him.   I am here for the summer:

---

(1811-1882) or his son Henry Draper (1837-1882), both professors at the
University of the City of New York and pioneers in astronomical photography;
either Sanford R. Gifford (1823-1880) or Robert S. Gifford (1840-1905), both
landscape painters; S. S. Conant, editor of *Harper's Weekly*, 1869-1885.   The
others here mentioned are identified in note 64, above, except McDonough.

address simply, West Chester, Pa.   What's the novel you're writing?

Sincerely yours

Sidney Lanier.

TO BAYARD TAYLOR

1425 Walnut St.
Ph<sup>a</sup> Pa.
Nov. 24<sup>th</sup> 1876.

My dear M<sup>r</sup> Taylor:

      A peculiar affection of the side has almost incapacitated me for any use of the pen, temporarily; but I must send you a little note in order to share with you – for I would like you to have half of *all* my good things in this world – the pleasure which your generous notice in THE TRIBUNE [80] has given me.  I recognized it as yours at once; and I therefore did not stint myself in my enjoyment of its appreciative expressions any more than I would mar my smoking of your cigars, or my drinking of your wine, with *arrières pensées*, – for I knew that the one was as free as the other.

    I was particularly pleased with the light way in which you touched upon my faults; and I say this not hastily, but upon a principle to which I've given a good deal of meditation.   The more I think of it, the more I am convinced:  that every genuine artist may be safely trusted with his own defects.   I feel perfectly sure that there are stages of growth – particularly with

---

[80] A review of *Poems* (Philadelphia, 1877) in the New York *Tribune,* Nov. 21, 1876; reprinted in Bayard Taylor, *Critical Essays and Literary Notes* (New York, 1890), pp. 312-314.
Taylor said, in part: " Mr. Lanier's dainty little volume contains only ten poems, but they embody as much character and thought as are usually found in the first hundred of a new poet.  It is impossible to read them without feeling the presence of a clear individuality in song – a nature free, opulent, exquisitely impressible to a great range of influences, melodious, and daring almost to an arbitrary degree. . . .   In poetic aim, form, and choice of themes, Mr. Lanier has expressed himself so positively that he cannot be mistaken for any one else." After some praise of individual poems, he designated Lanier's chief faults as " redundancy " and " apparent *abandon* to the starts and bolts . . . of Fancy." In conclusion he said: " It is still too soon to decide whether Mr. Lanier's true course is to train or carefully prune this luxuriance.   Meanwhile we heartily give him welcome, and congratulate his native South on a new poet."

artists of very great sensibility who live remote from the business-life of men – in which one's habitual faults are already apt to be unhealthily exaggerated from within and the additional forcings of such a tendency from without, through perpetual reminders of shortcomings, becomes positively hurtful, by proud-fleshing the artistic conscience and making it unnaturally timid and irritable. In looking around at the publications of the younger American poets I am struck with the circumstance that none of them even *attempt* anything great. The morbid fear of doing something wrong or unpolished appears to have influenced their choice of subjects. Hence the endless multiplication of those little feeble magazine-lyrics which we all know; consisting of one minute idea, each, which is put in the last line of the fourth verse, the other three verses and three lines being mere sawdust and surplusage.

It seems to me to be a fact bearing directly upon all this, that if we inquire who are the poets that must be read with the greatest allowances, we find them to be precisely the greatest poets. What enormous artistic crimes do we have continually to pardon in Homer, Dante, Shakespeare! How often is the first utterly dull and long-winded, the second absurdly credulous and superstitious, the third over-done and fantastical! But we have long ago settled all this, we have forgiven them their sins, we have ceased to place emphasis upon the matters in which they displease us; and when we recall their works, our minds instinctively confine remembrance to their beauties only. And applying this principle to the great exemplars of the other arts besides poetry, I think we find no exception to the rule that as to the great artist, we always have to take him *cum onere.*

I have to send you my thanks very often: I hope they don't become monotonous to you. Your praise has really given me a great deal of genuine and fruitful pleasure. The truth is that, as for censure, I am overloaded with my own: but as for commendation, I am mainly in a state of famine; so that while I cannot, for very surfeit, profitably digest the former, I have such a stomach for the latter as would astonish gods and men.

. . .

Your faithful true friend

S. L.

## To Bayard Taylor [81]

1425 Walnut St.
Philadelphia, Pa.
Dec. 6th 1876

My dear Mr Taylor:

My physician has become alarmed at the gravity and persistence of my illness and orders me immediately to Florida, denouncing death unless a warm climate is speedily reached. He might as well talk to the stars whose light hasn't yet reached us, as try to persuade me that any conceivable combination of circumstances could induce me to die before I've written and published my fine additional volumes of poems; nevertheless it is decided that my wife is to leave here with me on Monday night next, for Florida, and I'm scratching this hasty note in the possibility that your nomadic habits might bring you to Philadelphia within that time simply to ask that you won't fail – if they *should* bring you here – to give me a final sight of you. I'm still at the Peacocks'.

I hope you didn't take cold at Greenwood the other day. My wife would join me in messages to you and Mrs. Taylor, but she ran over to New York this morning on a flying business-visit for a couple of days.

Many thanks for the Post notice.

Your friend

S. L.

[81] A week before, Lanier received an unexpected gift which caused him to change his plans. It was an envelope, postmarked " New York, Nov. 29, [1876,] 4:30 P. M.," addressed to him at 1425 Walnut St., Philadelphia, which has survived (Charles D. Lanier Collection, Johns Hopkins University) with the following annotation in Lanier's autograph: " In this envelope there came to me, on the morning of Nov. 30th 1876, a five hundred dollar bill, unaccompanied with any writing. I have never been able to obtain the slightest clue to the name of the sender. I was then ill at Mr. Peacock's and this money saved my life, by enabling me to go to Florida, where my physician had ordered me."
With the receipt of this money, which was probably the gift of Gibson Peacock (see Lanier's letter of Dec. 3, 1877, to him), Lanier abandoned his determination to return to Baltimore and resume his place in the Peabody Orchestra. Replying to a lost letter by Lanier, Asger Hamerik, conductor of the orchestra, wrote on Dec. 2, 1876: " How sorry I am that you are sick. What shall we do, and how get along without you?
" Indeed I am afraid to direct, without both seeing, hearing and feeling your flute on the wont place.

### To Gibson Peacock

Tampa, Fla.
Dec. 27th 1876.

My dear Friend:

On arriving here we find that your friendship has as usual anticipated us. May and I, strolling down to the Post Office to rent a box and not daring to think of letters, are told by the clerk that he thinks there is something for us,—and the something turns out to be your pleasant budget, which we incontinently open and devour, sitting down on the steps of the Post Office for that purpose, to the wonderment of the natives. Your news of our dear mannikins is the first we have had and is a fair gift for our Christmas. May calls out to me while I am writing this that *she* does not wonder, either, at Sidney's desire to kiss Mrs. Peacock, and that she would vastly like to do so at this moment, for her own private delectation.

The letters you sent were all pleasant, in one way or another. One is from H. M. Alden, Editor *Harper's Magazine*, enclosing check for fifteen dollars and accepting the poem (*The Waving of the Corn*) sent him by me through Bayard Taylor. Another is a very cordial letter from " Geo. C. Eggleston, Literary Editor *Evening Post*," making tender of brotherhood to me in a really affectionate way and declaring that " the keen delight with which he recently read my volume of poems sharpens the pang he feels in knowing that one in whose work he sees so rich a promise lies on a bed of illness."

The Postal Card is from Gilder, whom I had requested to make a slight addition to my article on *The Orchestra* in Scribner's.[82]

The fourth letter is as you guessed from Emma Stebbins, and I enclose it for you to read. It seems from the last portion of it that she has quite abandoned the idea of writing the life of Charlotte Cushman, substituting for that the project of merely printing a Memorial Volume.

---

" But I hope the sun shall improve you, and we will yet see you in Baltimore this season."

[82] Lanier's article, " The Orchestra of Today " (II, 291), had been accepted by R. W. Gilder on Nov. 6, 1876; he was paid $80.00 for it, but it was not published until Apr., 1880.

The *Bulletin* with the notice you mention has not yet arrived. I am very much pleased that the Psalm of the West has given Mrs. Champney a text to preach from. One begins to add to the intrinsic delight of prophet-hood the less lonesome joy of human helpfulness — when one finds the younger poets resting upon one for a support and buttress in this way.

You will be glad to know that we are situated much more comfortably than we could have hoped. Tampa is the most forlorn collection of little one story frame houses imaginable, and as May and I walked behind our Landlord who was piloting us to the "Orange Grove Hotel" our hearts fell nearer and nearer towards the sand through which we dragged. But presently we turned a corner and were agreeably surprised to find ourselves in front of a large three story house, with many odd nooks and corners, altogether clean and comfortable in appearance, and surrounded by orange-trees in full fruit. We have a large room in the second story, opening upon a generous balcony fifty feet long, into which stretch the liberal arms of a fine orange-tree holding out their fruitage to our very lips. In front is a sort of open plaza, containing a pretty group of gnarled live-oaks full of moss and mistletoe. They have found out my public character already: somebody who had traveled with me recognized me on the street yesterday and told mine host. He and his wife are all kindness, having taken a fancy, I imagine, to my sweet Angel May. They have just sent up a lovely bunch of roses and violets from the garden,— a sentimental attention which finds a pleasant parallel in the appearance of a servant at our door before breakfast to inquire whether we prefer our steak fried or broiled.

The weather is perfect summer, and I luxuriate in great draughts of balmy air uncontaminated with city-smokes and furnace-dusts. This has come not a moment too soon: for the exposures of the journey had left my poor lung in most piteous condition. I am now better, however: and May is in good case, except that the languid air takes the spring from her step, and inclines her much to laziness. She had a perfect democratic eye during the journey: the Doctor's tourniquet having pressed so hard that a space as large as a silver dollar under the eye showed first an inky black, then a brilliant purple, like the damaged optic of a prize fighter. It is now much decreased, and bids fair to disappear in a day or two.

We have three mails a week: two by stage from Gainesville (which is on the railroad from Fernandina to Cedar Keys) and one by steamer from Cedar Keys. Address me simply " Tampa, Fla." I have a box (No. 8:– I don't think there are more than twenty five or thirty in all) at the Post office, and the clerk knows me: — as in fact everybody else does, a stranger is a stranger in Tampa.

So: I must stop. Tell my dear Maria Peacock that we should never have gotten along without the blue blanket: and kiss her for me as for one who loved her very dearly even before he owed his life to her. May sends you a kiss, and so does

Your faithful

S. L.

To Bayard Taylor

Brunswick. Ga.<br>April 26th 1877.

Dear Mr Taylor:

Pray don't trouble to send THE BEE to HARPER'S. I haven't the least idea of letting you act as poem-broker for me any longer. I'm now getting well enough to write a little, and May (that's my wife) is becoming a capital secretary.

If you should not have sent off THE BEE before this reaches you, I'll trouble you to enclose it to me: I've kept no copy, and am not sure that I remember it exactly.

Have you happened to see the illustrations to an *extravaganza* of mine (a sort of story which one " makes up as he goes along ", to a lot of importunate youngsters) in the May number of ST. NICHOLAS? [83] They seem to me, who am but little of a critic however in such matters, to be very charming. Mrs. Dodge appears not to have received the proof-sheets, which I returned from Tampa, in time; for in them I carefully cor-

---

[83] " The Story of a Proverb " (VI, 324), for which Lanier had been paid $24.00 *ca.* Dec. 10, 1876. Mrs. M. M. Dodge, mentioned below, was the editor of *St. Nicholas Magazine.*

rected some very disagreeable repetitions, and faults of punctuation, which appear in the publication.

I believe there is a little scrap of a poem of mine in SCRIBNER'S for May;[84] but I haven't seen it.

I take real delight in thinking of you at Cedarcroft among the leaves. How fares my Master, the Chestnut-tree? If you only had there the infinite sweetness of Spring which is now in full leaf and overflowing song all about us here! I have at command a springy mare, with ankles like a Spanish girl's, upon whose back I go darting through the green overgrown woodpaths like a thrasher about his thicket. The whole air seems full of fecundity: as I ride, I'm like one of those insects that are fertilized on the wing, – every leaf that I brush against breeds a poem. God help the world, when this now-hatching brood of my Ephemeræ shall take flight and darken the air.

After the third of May, my address will be " Macon, Ga. "; we will spend a month there. As for further plans, – about which you kindly ask – they will depend entirely on my state of health at the end of May. I *hope* to be in New York during June: – but you will be informed of my motions. . . .

Your friend<br>S. L.

## To GIBSON PEACOCK [85]

Washington, D. C.<br>Sep. 27<sup>th</sup> 1877.

Dear Mr. Peacock:

Yours was forwarded to me here.

Just as I received your check, a severe pleuritic attack seized me and kept me in great pain for ten days. I then got up from bed to come here, in the desperate necessity to do what could

---

[84] "The Stirrup-Cup."

[85] Lanier had spent June and July in Baltimore, New York, and Philadelphia; August and September at a farm near Chadds Ford, Pa. His futile efforts to find employment and a steady income resulted in illness and despair. In this crisis he had borrowed $50 from Peacock.

be done.  Last Monday at daylight an exhausting hæmorrhage came, which has kept me confined to my room ever since.  In this enforced inactivity, I have had nothing to return to you. This morning a check comes from Lippincott for a little story I sent, and I enclose it, endorsed to your order.  Please let me know what your address will be, so that I may send the remaining twenty-five at the earliest possible moment.

There does not appear the least hope of success here.  Three months ago the order was given by Secretary Sherman that I should have the first vacancy; but the appointment-clerk, who received the order, is a singular person, and I am told there are rings within rings in the Department to such an extent that vacancies are filled by petty chiefs of division without even being reported at all to the proper officers.  You will scarcely believe that, in my overwhelming desire to get some routine labor by which I might be relieved from this exhausting magazine-work so as to apply my whole mind to my long poem on which I have been engaged, I have allowed a friend to make application to every department in Washington for even the humblest position—seventy-five dollars a month and the like— but without success.  I also made personal application to several people in Baltimore for similar employment, but fruitlessly.  Altogether it seems as if there wasn't any place for me in this world, and if it were not for May I should certainly quit it, in mortification at being so useless.[86]

I hope you will have a pleasant holiday.  Give my love to my dear Maria Peacock and say how glad I am to think of her long relief from the household and other cares which give her so much trouble.

Your friend,

S. L.

---

[86] Though it appears but little in surviving letters, Lanier's spirits seem to have reached a low ebb during the summer of 1877.  This is echoed in Paul Hayne's reply, July 19, 1877, to a lost letter apparently written by Lanier before leaving Macon in June: "The *whole tone* of your communication shows the natural, the *inevitable* despondency which comes of a diseased physical condition . . .; & *poverty* (accursed poverty!!) being added, as you remark, to physical weakness, *must* produce a general condition of things the reverse of agreeable. . . . Touching *literary* success, it is evident that you take too low a view of your own position, & prospects."

## To Richard M. Johnston [87]

55 Lexington Street,
Baltimore, Md.,
November 6, 1877.

My Dear Col. Johnston,

Mrs. Lanier's illness on Saturday devolved a great many domestic duties upon me, and rendered it quite impossible for me to make the preparations necessary for my visit to you on Sunday. This caused me a great deal of regret; a malign fate seems to have pursued all my recent efforts in your direction.

I have attentively examined your " Dukesborough Tale." [88] I wish very much that I could read it over aloud in your presence, so that I might call your attention to many verbal lapses which I find and which, I am sure, will hinder its way with the magazine editors. I will try to see you in a day or two, and do this. Again, ascending from merely verbal criticism to considerations of general treatment, I find that the action of the story does not move quite fast enough during the *first* twenty-five pages, and the *last* ten, to suit the impatience of the modern magazine man.

Aside from these two points, – and they can both be easily remedied, – the story strikes me as exquisitely funny, and your reproduction of the modes of thought and of speech among the rural Georgians is really wonderful. The peculiar turns and odd angles, described by the minds of these people in the

---

[87] Richard Malcolm Johnston (1822–1898) was a minor author who published several volumes of tales about his native Georgia. After the Civil War he moved to Maryland, where he established the Pen Lucy School; he had been a friend of Lanier since 1874. About the middle of October 1877 Lanier brought his wife and children to Baltimore; for the first few months they settled in an apartment on Lexington Street.

[88] " Mr. Neelus Peeler's Conditions," later collected in the third edition of Johnston's *Dukesborough Tales* (New York, 1883). Lanier is said to have negotiated its acceptance by R. W. Gilder, editor of *Scribner's* (where it was first published), and to have forwarded to Johnston the pay check—the first he had ever received for a story (see F. T. Long, " The Life of Richard Malcolm Johnston in Maryland, 1867-1898," *Maryland Historical Magazine*, XXXIV, 315-316, Dec., 1939).

course of ratiocination (Good Heavens, what would Sammy Wiggins think of such a sentence as this!), are presented here with a delicacy of art that gives me a great deal of enjoyment. The whole picture of old-time Georgia is admirable, and I find myself regretting that its *full* merit can be appreciated only by that limited number who, from personal experience, can compare it with the original. . . .

Your friend,<br>Sidney L.

To Gibson Peacock

33 Denmead St.[89]<br>Baltimore, Md.<br>Jany 6th 1878

My dear Mr. Gibson;

The painters, the whitewashers, the plumbers, the locksmiths, the carpenters, the gas-fitters, the stove-put-up-ers, the carmen, the piano-movers, the carpet layers,— all these have I seen, bargained with, reproached for bad jobs, and finally paid off: I have also coaxed my landlord into all manner of outlays for damp walls, cold bath-rooms, and other the like matters: I have furthermore bought at least three hundred and twenty seven household utensils which suddenly came to be absolutely necessary to our existence: I have moreover hired a colored gentle woman who is willing to wear out my carpets, burn out my range, freeze out my water-pipes, and be generally useful: I have also moved my family into our new home, have had a Xmas tree for the youngsters, have looked up a cheap school for Henry and Sidney,[90] have discharged my daily duties as first flute of the Peabody Orchestra, have written a couple of poems and part of an essay on " Beethoven and

[89] On Dec. 22, 1877, finding the dust and noise of downtown Baltimore intolerable, the Laniers had moved to the outskirts of the city (Denmead being the present 20th Street).

[90] Lanier's eldest son, Charles, had by this time been enrolled at R. M. Johnston's Pen Lucy School, at which Lanier himself began to teach about a month later.

Bismarck", have accomplished at least a hundred thousand miscellaneous necessary nothings,–and have not, in consequence of all the aforesaid, sent to you and my dear Maria the loving greetings whereof my heart has been full during the whole season. . . .

I confess I *am* a little nervous about the gas-bills, which must come in, in the course of time; and there are the water-rates; and several sorts of imposts and taxes; but then, the dignity of being liable for such things! is a very supporting consideration. No man is a Bohemian who has to pay water-rates and a street-tax. Every day when I sit down in my dining-room—*my* dining-room! I find the wish growing stronger that each poor soul in Baltimore, whether saint or sinner, could come and dine with me. How I would carve out the merry thoughts for the old hags! How I would stuff the big wall-eyed rascals till their rags ripped again! There was a knight of old times who built the dining-hall of his castle across the highway, so that every wayfarer must perforce pass through: there the traveller, rich or poor, found always a trencher and wherewithal to fill it. Three times a day, in my own chair at my own table, do I envy that knight and wish that I might do as he did. . . .

We all send you heartfelt wishes for the New Year. May you be as happy as you are dear to

Your faithful

S. L.

## To Clifford A. Lanier

33 Denmead St.

B° April 21st 1878.

My dearest Clifford:

I have been wanting to write you of many pleasant things which have happened to me recently, but the time has not presented itself when I could do so. I have never accomplished so much work in the same time, since I commenced to work at all: and have had the rare good fortune of seeing happy results flow almost immediately from every stroke.

About six weeks ago I was invited to deliver a course of lectures to a private party of ladies, in their own parlors, the class consisting of about a dozen members. The subjects were, for the first four lectures " The Science of Poetry," and for the last four " The Sonnet-makers of Queen Elizabeth's Time." The labor involved in preparing these was very great: but it was also very congenial, and I have therefore thriven on it. The lectures — or rather " morning-talks," for they are delivered each Saturday at half past twelve — have been delightfully received. After the first one the class increased to twenty members, and by the third had reached thirty-two. Here we had to stop, as a large number was inconvenient for a private parlor: but another class is now forming, and nearly complete. Each member pays five dollars for the course of eight lectures.

There seems every probability that these will lead to some larger experiments in the same field. President Gilman (of Johns Hopkins University) was at my third lecture, and came up at its close, in the most cordial way, with congratulations and an invitation to deliver it at the University. The project is now mooted of arranging a place in town for the special higher culture of women, where my lectures can be delivered to classes the year round, in conjunction with others on scientific subjects.

I send you a programme of the complimentary concert given me by the Peabody Orchestra and others at the close of the season. The affair was arranged without my knowledge, and was a very pleasant surprise to me. At one of the Peabody Concerts a few weeks ago I played a *Concerto* of Hartmann's (a Danish writer) for Violin and Orchestra, taking the violin-part with my flute. At its close the whole Orchestra applauded, and the leader stepped down and congratulated me. This, it seems, was the immediate occasion of the complimentary concert. The latter was well attended, and netted me, above all expenses, a hundred and sixty-four dollars.

I have tried to get a copy of the New York INDEPENDENT containing my poem " Clover " to send you, but have not succeeded. You will find a poem of mine called " The Dove " in SCRIBNER'S for May, just out. Have I sent you a sonnet of mine to Mrs. Auerbach, (a great pianist, living here) which appeared in the Baltimore GAZETTE?

Father will probably forward you an editorial from the N. Y. EVENING POST, containing some auguries of my future as poet which are at least pleasant indications.[91]

I'm glad you liked the sonnet on dreams:[92] you always hear the best that's in a poem, however. May and I wished for you the other night with more than usual intensity: a young professional " reader " of this City has been making a great success of your and my (but very little *my*) " Power of Prayer " before popular audiences, and having learned that I was one of the authors she very kindly proposed to come out to my house and recite it for me. You would be surprised to see what a wealth of dramatic capability there is in the thing: and the young lady did it very well, though I easily saw many points where it would have been possible to make the ideas more effective. . . .

God bless you all.

Your faithful

S. L.

---

[91] In a review of Edgar Fawcett's volume of poems, *Fantasy and Passion*, in the New York *Evening Post*, Apr. 1, 1878, the critic (probably Geo. C. Eggleston) said that of the very few younger men who seemed qualified to " maintain the poetic succession in this country when the masters who are growing old shall cease to sing . . . Mr. Sidney Lanier and Mr. Fawcett give the fairest promise of succeeding to the high places. Neither of them has won a first place as yet, of course, . . . but both have given proof of the possession of genuine genius — proof which is wanting in the case of nearly all the rest of our younger singers." The reviewer found them somewhat alike in fervor of imagination, luxuriance of fancy, and the apt use of figurative language, but otherwise they were different — especially in their faults: " Mr. Lanier has greater spontaneity — too great we sometimes think — and a stronger tendency to undertake large work . . . to chisel rough full-length figures out of blocks of stone. . . . [But he] mingles good work with rubbish most annoyingly sometimes . . . [and is] audacious and even lawless. . . . They have both made excellent beginnings. They may not win for themselves foremost places in the new generation, but thus far, without doubt, they are well in advance of their fellows in the race."

[92] " The Harlequin of Dreams " (I, 112), published in *Lippincott's*, Apr., 1878.

## To Walt Whitman

33 Denmead St.
Baltimore, Md.
May 5th 1878.

My dear Sir:

A short time ago while on a visit to New York I happened one evening to find your LEAVES OF GRASS in Mr. Bayard Taylor's library: and taking it with me to my room at the hotel I spent a night of glory and delight upon it. How it happened that I had never read this book before — — is a story not worth the telling; but, in sending the enclosed bill to purchase a copy (which please mail to the above address) I cannot resist the temptation to tender you also my grateful thanks for such large and substantial thoughts uttered in a time when there are, as you say in another connection, so many " little plentiful mannikins skipping about in collars and tailed coats." Although I entirely disagree with you in all points connected with artistic form, and in so much of the outcome of your doctrine as is involved in those poetic exposures of the person which your pages so unreservedly make, yet I feel sure that I understand you therein, and my dissent in these particulars becomes a very insignificant consideration in the presence of that unbounded delight which I take in the bigness and bravery of all your ways and thoughts. It is not known to me where I can find another modern song at once so large and so naive: and the time needs to be told few things so much as the absolute personality of the person, the sufficiency of the man's manhood *to* the man, which you have propounded in such strong and beautiful rhythms. I beg you to count me among your most earnest lovers, and to believe that it would make me very happy to be of the least humble service to you at any time

Sidney Lanier [93]

[93] Whitman's reply, on a postal card, May 27, 1878, read: " I have to-day sent by mail, same address as this card, my Volume *Leaves of Grass* — Please notify me (by postal card will do) soon as it reaches you safely. Walt Whitman."

To Robert S. Lanier

33 Denmead St.

B○ May 13th 1878.

My dearest Father:

I am not quite so pushed for time this week, my lectures being now over for the season; and I am trying to rest my pen-arm a little, which has had a severe race of it for the last two months.

The Lecture-Committee of The Peabody Institute met last Friday and resolved to tender me their lecture-hall for the season of 1878-9. I am to deliver a series of lectures, extending from the 1st November to 1st April, two each week, under the auspices of the Peabody. Prest. Gilman (of Johns Hopkins University) has in the very kindest manner— and at a good deal of personal trouble — arranged to cooperate with me in such a manner as to make my course a very attractive one. During the second half-year of the series, when the progress of my lectures will have brought me to Shakespere, we are to have a sort of Shakesperean Revival: parallel with my own treatment of Shakespere. Prof. Childs of Harvard (who had been engaged by the Johns Hopkins University for a special course) will deliver a series of ten readings from Macbeth; Prof. Gildersleeve, (Greek prof. in Johns Hopkins) will give two lectures on the relation between the Greek drama and Shakespere's: Mr. Royce (Fellow of Johns Hopkins) will give two lectures on Shakespere in Germany: and two other gentlemen from Johns Hopkins will contribute lectures on their own specialties converging upon the same theme.[94] We hope to wind up the whole with a beautiful spectacular exhibition representing an audience of Shakespere's times assembled on the stage while a play goes on.

It is proposed to sell a hundred subscription tickets to the whole course at twenty dollars each, and this is to be my remuneration.

[94] A MS outline of the original plan submitted to the Peabody Institute has survived. It called for an elaborate program of eighty lectures, half to be given by Lanier. The series as actually given was reduced to forty lectures in all. Though it brought Lanier no financial reward, it did enhance his reputation as a scholar and lecturer.

It would thus seem that my next year's work is thus most
delightfully mapped out.   My lectures are to consist of ten
introductory discourses on Literary Technic, thirty on the less-
known poetry of the Elizabeth Period, and ten on subjects connected with Shakespere — fifty in all.   These are studies which
I take such delight in pursuing that I can not well imagine a
pleasanter prospect for my next season in Baltimore.

Meantime: it is necessary for me to devote the entire summer
to the preparation of these lectures, and I am going to New
York day after tomorrow for the purpose of making such fiscal
arrangements as will enable me to do so.   The carrying through
of the whole project has been a matter of much work and
thought, and the action of the Trustees is regarded as a great
compliment to me. . . .

Your loving

S. L.

To Bayard Taylor [95]

180 St. Paul St.
Baltimore, Md.
Oct. 20th 1878.

My dearest Minister – always a minister of grace to me – , I
have long forborne to write you because I knew your whole
mind would be occupied with a thousand new cares and I could
not bear to add the burden of a letter thereto.   But you must
be getting easy in the new saddle by this: and somehow I feel
that I can't wait longer before sending you a little love-letter
that shall at least carry my longing over the big seas to you
Not long ago I was in New York for some days; but you were
in Germany; – and the city seemed depopulated.   There were
multitudes of what Walt Whitman calls

Little plentiful manikins
Skipping about in collars and tailed coats,

---

[95] Taylor had sailed in April 1878 as Minister to Germany. He died in Berlin,
Dec. 19, 1878, shortly after this letter reached him.

Lanier's new address was just a few blocks north of the Peabody Institute. He
had moved closer to the center of the city to find a cheaper house and to "avoid the
huge drain of car fare."

but my Man, my *hæleða leofost* (as it is in Beówulf), was wanting, and I wandered disconsolately towards 142 E. 18th St., – where I used so often and so ruthlessly to break in upon your labors – as if I could *wish* you back into your chair rolling out the prophecy of Deucalion. Even the Westminster Hotel had new proprietors and I felt a sense of intentional irony in its having changed from the European to the American plan, – as if for pure spite because you had left America and gone to Europe. My dear, when *are* you coming back?

A short time ago I found in a second-hand book-stall a copy of Sir Henry Wotton's works and letters printed in 1685, and bought it, – with about all the money I had; for a joke of old Sir Henry's on a minister carried my mind to you. Having been asked, (he narrates the story himself, being then on a ministerial journey through Germany) to write in an album, he chose to define a Minister, and said: *a Minister is a man sent to lie abroad for the good of his country.*

I have seen your Deucalion announced, but nothing more. Indeed I have been so buried in study for the past six months that I know not news nor gossip of any kind. Such days and nights of glory as I have had! I have been studying Early English, Middle English, and Elizabethan poetry, from Beówulf to Ben Jonson: and the world seems twice as large. I enclose a programme of lectures I am to give before a class of subscribers at the Peabody Institute this winter from which you will see the drift of my work.

You will also care to know that SCRIBNER'S has accepted three papers of mine on " The Physics of Poetry ", in which I have succeeded in developing a complete system of prosody for all languages from the physical constitution of sound. It has given me indescribable pleasure to be able, through the principles therein announced, to put formal poetry on a scientific basis which renders all its processes perfectly secure.[96]

---

[96] Lanier's essays on "The Physics of Poetry" grew into *The Science of English Verse,* and their publication was cancelled in favor of the book.
   Of "The Marshes of Glynn," mentioned in the next paragraph, Lanier wrote to his father, July 13, 1878: "I have just sent off three poems, hot from the mint. One of these—called "The Marshes of Glynn," and descriptive of the great salt-marshes on the coast of Georgia—I read to Col. Johnstone the other day under the chestnut-trees at his beautiful place near Waverley. He declares it is the greatest poem written in a hundred years."

If you should see an APPLETON'S JOURNAL for the curren
month – November – you may be interested in an experimen
of mine therein with logaœdic dactyls called " The Revenge o
Hamish."     Another freer treatment of the same rhythm by me
will appear in a book to be issued by Roberts Brothers in the
No Name Series (called " The Masque of Poets ") under the
heading " The Marshes of Glynn ": – though all this last is a
yet a secret and not to be spoken of till the book shall have
been out and been cast to the critics for a while.   I hope to find
a publisher for my book on English Prosody next spring; also
for my historical and critical account, in two volumes, of " The
English Sonnet-Makers from Surrey to Shakspere "; and I am
in treaty with Scribner's Sons for a " Boy's Froissart " which
have proposed to them and which they like the idea of, so far
By next autumn I trust I will have a volume of poetry (" The
Songs of Aldhelm") in print, which is now in a pigeon-hole
of my desk half-jotted down.   During the coming week I g
to Washington and Philadelphia to arrange, if possible, fo
delivering my course of lectures before classes in those cities. [9]

There!   I have reported progress, up to date.   Who bette
than you – who looked so kindly upon my poor little beginnin,
– has the right to know how far I've gone?

Give me some little account of yourself, if you are not too
busy.   My wife and I send grateful and affectionate message
to you:   adding cordial postcripts for Mrs. Taylor and Mis
Lilian.

God bless you and keep you ever in such fair ways as follov
the fair wishes of

Your faithful

Sidney L.

To GIBSON PEACOCK

180 St. Paul St.<br>Bo. Dec. 21st 1878

My dearest Mr. Gibson:

If love and faithful remembrance wer
current with the wish-gods I could make you a rare merr

---

[97] None of these classes materialized. Neither "The Songs of Aldhelm" nor th
two volumes on sonnet-makers were ever published.

Christmas. – I wish I had two millions: I should so like to send
you a check for one of 'em, with a request that you make a
bonfire of *the Evening Bulletin*, and come over here to spend
Christmas – and the rest of your life – with me, – on a private
car seventy-seven times more luxurious than Lorne's or Mr.
Mapleson's. I really *don't* desire that you should spend your
life on this car – as I seem to, on reading over my last sentence –
but only that you should *come* on it.

The great advantage of having a poetic imagination is herein
displayed: you see how the simple act of enclosing you a check
for twenty five dollars – that twenty five which has been due
you so long, dear friend! can set a man's thoughts going.

I have a mighty yearning to see you and my well beloved
Maria; it seems a long time since; and I've learned so many
things, – I almost feel as if I had something new to show you.

Bayard Taylor's death slices a huge cantle out of the world
for me. I don't yet *know* it, at all: it only seems that he has
gone to some other Germany, a little farther off. How strange
it all is: he was such a fine fellow, one almost thinks he might
have talked Death over and made him forego his stroke. Tell
me whatever you may know, outside of the newspaper reports,
about his end.

Chas. Scribner's Sons have concluded to publish my " Boy's
Froissart ", with illustrations. They are holding under advise-
ment my work on English Prosody.

I saw your notice of the " Masque of Poets ". The truth is,
is a distressing, an aggravated, yea, an intolerable collection
of mediocrity and mere cleverness. Some of the pieces come
so near being good that one is ready to tear one's hair and to
beat somebody with a stick from pure exasperation that such
narrow misses should after all come to no better net result, – in
the way of art – than so many complete failures. I could find
only four poems in the book. As for " Guy Vernon " [98] one
marvels that a man with any poetic feeling could make so many
stanzas of so trivial a thing. It does not even sparkle enough
to redeem it as *Vers de société*. This is the kind of poetry
that is technically called culture-poetry: yet it is in reality the

---

[98] A long poem by J. T. Trowbridge in *A Masque of Poets*. For a list of
contributors to this volume and an account of its reception, see A. H. Starke,
" An Omnibus of Poets," *Colophon*, Part XVI (Mar., 1934).

product of a *want* of culture.   If these gentlemen and ladie
would read the old English poetry – I mean the poetry befor
Chaucer, the genuine Anglish utterances, from Cædmon in th
7th century to Langland in the 14th — they could never be cor
tent to put forth these little diffuse prettinesses and dand
kickshaws of verse. . . .

God bless you both, and send you many a Christmas, prays

Your  faithful

S. L.

To Robert S. Lanier

180 St. Paul St.
Bo:  May 6th 1879.

My dearest Father:

. . . .

I have been going, night and day, at an Edition, for boys, c
Sir Thomas Malory's *History of King Arthur*, the old Englis
classic from which Tennyson drew the stories which make u
his great Arthurian poems.   I sent off my Froissart book abor
three weeks ago, and drove hard at this one in the hope c
selling it to the same publishers as a companion-work.   It wer
forward yesterday, and I await its fortune with interest.

If I had not learned to murmur at nothing, I should t
inclined to complain at the cruel fate which keeps me editin
other men's works to boil the pot, when my head is so full c
books of my own that I sometimes have a sense that I mu
actually fly into fragments if I do not lessen the inward accumu
lation.   If somebody with faith would only lend me two c
three thousand dollars for a couple of years !

I have an offer, from a girl's school, of four hundred do
lars to teach English literature for one hour each day durin
the next scholastic year.   I shall probably accept; but am wai
ing a few days before deciding.

A very gratifying invitation was telegraphed me a couple c
weeks ago to deliver the annual poem before the Alumni c

the Phi Beta Kappa society resident in New York city, at their anniversary exercises in Chickering Hall. Dr. Noah Porter, president of Yale College, delivered the address. I wished very much to accept; but my poverty compelled me to decline, for the writing of the poem would have taken me a week, and a week means fifty dollars. So I gave it up; and saw afterwards that Mr. Edgar Fawcett was chosen.

I send you an account of our old ancestor (as I suppose) Nicholas Lanier, and a lot of his descendants, about whom I had accumulated many notes, and whose history I wished to place before myself in the compact form of print.[99] It is a curious circumstance that I found, only a few days ago, the name of *Nicholas Lanier* among a list of the vestrymen of a church in Brunswick County, Virginia, given by Bishop Meade in his work on the *Old Churches and Families of Virginia.* It seems probable that this Nicholas points back to the elder one and constitutes the link between him and us.

Have you ever yet seen my " Marshes of Glynn " and my article on Bartholomew Griffin (called " A Forgotten English Poet ") in the INTERNATIONAL REVIEW?

Let me hear how you are all faring. The glimpses of green leaves give me a mighty yearning towards Macon, which I suspect is now a pleasant grove and a garden of roses.

God bless you.

Your son,

S. L.[100]

---

[99] Lanier sent his father a literary " letter " addressed to J. F. D. Lanier, dated Apr. 2, 1879, privately printed as a supplement to the second edition of the *Sketch of the Life of J. F. D. Lanier*, the pages numbered in continuation of that book (VI, 361).

[100] Ten days later Lanier wrote his father that Scribner had accepted his *King Arthur* and agreed to pay him $700 for the two boys' books. The letter concluded: "I wish I could tell you how delightfully my life seems to be expanding, and how completely I am gathering in to myself all that I want for my growth and activity. The way in which the events of the past year have fitted into my special needs is almost startling; it really looks like a pre-arrangement made Elsewhere."

## To Robert S. Lanier

*Rockingham Mineral Springs.*
*Near*
*McGaheysville,*
*Virginia.* [101]
July 22nd 1879.

My dearest Father:
                   We left Baltimore – Mr. Day and all of us,
bag and baggage – on Saturday, and reached here at supper-
time same day, our journey including a drive of twelve miles
through the mountains from Harrisonburg, where we got off
the cars.

It seems quite like emigrating into some of the stars; this
cool, peaceful, upper story of a fresh cottage, with the wooded
ridges running off at all odd angles about us, and the noble
Blue Ridge reposing, farther off, in fair view from either
window of our room, while the air is invigorating and sweet
in all the channels of the breath and the children leap about
the brook and hill-side all day like young fawns: – all this,
instead of the stifling furnace of Baltimore, and the grim fric-
tion of iron wheel and cobble-stone that goes ever therewithal.
It is a beautiful enchantment: how I wish the spell included
you and Mama !

I have a grand little library, culled from the Mercantile and
Johns Hopkins of Baltimore; and the long mornings make my
books grow rapidly.  I expect to carry back three, ready for
the printer, when I go home on the first of September.  Mary
and the children will remain here until October, probably.

I am thoroughly pleased with our location.  The establish-
ment is small; there is no " ball-room ", no band, not the least
attempt at dress, and no interference with one's privacy or
quietude.  We are in a cottage to ourselves.  The fare is tolerable; service thoroughly clean, and water delightful.  Only
thirty or forty people have come, so far; indeed, there are not

---

[101] During the two months Lanier spent at this resort he completed *The Science
of English Verse.*

accommodations for more than twice that number; and so the opportunity for hard work and for thorough rest is perfect. . . .

And now I'll stop writing, for the day. We all send a thousand messages of love to you both.

Your son,

S. L.

To Robert S. Lanier

435 N. Calvert St.
Baltimore, Md.
Oct. 29th 1879.

My dearest Father:

It seems a long time since I have written you, though I cannot now think of any minute when I *could* have done so in the last two or three weeks.

My Johns Hopkins Lectures began yesterday. I had a large and fine audience: indeed the President tells me that twice as many tickets were applied for as could be given out. It is pleasant work, and I hope it may be lasting. I enclose a copy of the " Outline " printed for the use of the students who attend, and send you a copy of the Sun noticing the opening of the Winter course and giving a tolerable summary of my lecture.[102]

---

[102] Lanier's first course at the Johns Hopkins University consisted of sixteen public lectures on " English Verse, especially Shakspere's " (III, 311-410), delivered at Hopkins Hall from Oct. 28 to Dec. 19, 1879, on Tuesdays and Fridays at 5 P. M. The printed announcement stated: " The object of these Lectures will be to awaken and develop an interest in modern literary criticism by special studies in Shakspere. His moral and artistic growth will be compared and the metrical tests recently proposed by scholars will be investigated. The course will begin with an examination of the Laws of Verse." As actually given, the first nine lectures dealt with Lanier's theory of English verse; and the remaining seven were divided between a study of the pre-Shakespearian drama, the metrical tests as applied to Shakespeare, and a comparison of *A Midsummer Night's Dream*, *Hamlet*, and *The Tempest*. Copies of the " Outline " here mentioned have survived (Charles D. Lanier Collection, Johns Hopkins University). The notice in the Baltimore *Sun* here referred to was on Oct. 29, 1879. The average attendance at Lanier's Johns Hopkins lectures was 170, in comparison with an average of only 113 at ten other series of university lectures. His salary for the academic year was $1000. He had moved to Calvert Street in September.

These lectures — two a week — and the seven which I deliver to the school-classes each week,— keep me pretty busy in addition to the other work upon which I am engaged....

I am obliged now to close hastily.  Loving messages go to you from all of us.

Your son,

S. L.


To Clifford A. Lanier

435 N. Calvert St.
Bo; Jan'y 25th 1880.

My dear Clifford:

I fear I have not written you in a long time: but it is because I have written so much to less dear correspondents.  A serious illness, which was good enough to wait until the holidays before quite incapacitating me, kept me in bed during that season, and I have thus had to make up two week's work, besides keeping my regular round.

I ran over to New York last Monday night and gave Tuesday over to negotiations with Publishers and Magazine-editors. I completed the sale of my Boy's King Arthur to Scribner, which he is to publish next Xmas as companion-book to the Boy's Froissart.  I also arranged to sell him my Boy's Mabinogion – a collection of Welsh stories about King Arthur – as a companion-book to the others for the next year.[103]

We completed a bargain for my Science of English Verse, and he is to push the book at the utmost possible speed so as to bring it out by the first week in March.  I left with him, too, the *ms.* of "How To Read Chaucer," which he is to examine and report upon immediately.  I hope he will see his way clear to bring it out at once, upon a ten per cent copyright to me, he assuming all expense.[104]

[103] *The Boy's King Arthur* (IV, 355) was published in Nov., 1880; *The Boy's Mabinogion* (IV, 370), in Nov., 1881.
[104] The publishing contract for *The Science of English Verse* was dated Feb. 12, 1880. It provided that Lanier should pay the cost of composition and stereotyping, the plates to be his property. Scribner's agreed to publish the book and bear all

I have sent my two papers on " The New South " to SCRIB-NER'S MAGAZINE. They will probably appear very soon, being just now very timely to the agricultural passion which is possessing the magazines.

I'm working on an interlinear redaction of THE BRUCE of John Barbour (Scotch poet, 14th century) and of The WALLACE of Blind Harry The Minstrel, which I hope to sell to ST. NICHOLAS for illustrated papers.

I send you a Johns Hopkins official circular on p. 18 of which you will find an announcement that will show the nature of my class-work at the university.[105] On the next page is a very gratifying notice of the attendance upon my public lectures, which ended about the middle of last December. The numbers surprised every one.

I think I have not acknowledged yours containing check for $100 which arrived while I was ill.

Have you seen a poem of mine called " Opposition,"[106] just out in GOOD COMPANY, a monthly published at Springfield, Mass.? . . .

My poor Mary is wholly sick. Nothing is right within her. Her sufferings are scarcely tolerable to witness. I am wholly at a loss to know how to help her, – without money.

All here send love to you. Write me of your home affairs.

Your bro.

S. L.

---

other expenses, giving Lanier a royalty of 15% of the retail price (two dollars) on all copies sold. None of the other prose mentioned in this letter was published during his lifetime except "The New South," which appeared in the October 1880 issue of *Scribner's*.

[105] *The Johns Hopkins University Circulars*, No. 2, p. 18 (Jan., 1880), announced that Lanier would give " ten expository readings of Chaucer's Knight's Tale and Shakspere's Midsummer Night's Dream in connection, beginning in the middle of January. . . . The aim of the lecturer will be to awaken an interest in the poems under review solely as works of art." The course was designed for students not majoring in English literature, and the instructor offered to give three or four preliminary sessions to familiarize them with the language of Chaucer. According to one who attended this course, it was postponed and did not begin until the week of Feb. 8 (Starke, p. 505, note 34).

[106] " Opposition " (I, 130) was published in the Jan., 1880, issue of *Good Company*.

## To Edmund C. Stedman

435 N. Calvert St.
Baltimore, Md.
May 14th 1880.

My dear Mr. Stedman:

Some days ago in searching for a special letter of our beloved Bayard Taylor I came upon one which dwelt on *you* so much and so tenderly that I felt myself moved to snatch a moment from the frightful bread-and-meat work which has owned me so long, for the purpose of sending a line that might bring me some little word of your health and personal concerns.

Herewith goes to you a copy of my *Science of English Verse*, just published by Messrs. Scribner's Sons, which may interest you, since, in finding physical principles of classification for all possible phenomena of verse, it seems to place those phenomena in their true relations, – for the first time, so far as I know. I hope you may find the book a sound one, – all the more because it was so indescribably irksome to write. To go back, and interrogate one's own artistic procedure, and formulate in cold propositions for the general mind processes which are so swift and instinctive as those of the poet's technic: none but the artist knows the appalling constraint of this task. Indeed I could never have found courage to endure it, save from the fact that in all directions the poetic art seemed suffering from the shameful circumstances that criticism was without a scientific basis for even the most elementary of its judgments, and I had some poems which I hope soon to print but which I could not hope to get understood generally, without educating their audience.

I will be very glad to know of your work and your welfare, and am always

Sincerely yours,

Sidney Lanier [107]

---

[107] Stedman replied, May 17, 1880 (Laura Stedman and G. M. Gould, *Life and Letters of Edmund Clarence Stedman*, New York, 1910, II, 154-155): " I

## To Annie A. Fields [108]

435 N. Calvert St.
Baltimore, Md.
May 30th 1880.

My dear Mrs. Fields:

Your invitation to Gambrel Cottage is very pleasant and tempting, but – remembering other possible guests – I ought to send you word immediately that my visit to Boston cannot be very definitely fixed, and that even when I come I can't hope to do more than dine with you, or some· thing of that sort, as I shall be working like a beaver, – and ought therefore naturally to be in a dam, – which is certainly an expressive synonym for a hotel.

Don't therefore make any allowance for more than a pop-call from me, unhappy ghost as I am and must be for yet many days.

I am astonished – and, I confess, a little taken aback – that you, and several others who have written me about my book, find it abstruse. Almost every one refers to the "patient scholarship" of it; – and you can fancy that this is perplexing, when I add that the book was planned and written from beginning to end during the five weeks of my last summer's vacation, in the mountains of Virginia, where I had no works of

---

always have borne you most tenderly in mind, and am now doubly indebted to you– for your letter and for the early copy of your volume. . . .

"Let me congratulate you, & all of us, upon the heroic industry, & the profound rhythmical analysis, which have enabled you to render so complete this most scientific– this wholly unique work."

But he added: "I should much prefer recognizing the truth of your novel and wonderful analysis, in my own works, after having written them by instinct, than to attempt, *a priori*, to sing in accordance with laws which govern the poet willy-nilly "– thus indicating the same misunderstanding that was to annoy Lanier from all sides: the assumption that *The Science of English Verse* was a handbook of rules for writing poetry.

[108] It is not clear when Lanier became acquainted with James T. Fields, the Boston publisher, and his wife, a famous literary hostess. On Mar. 9, 1880, she had written Lanier: "I have a room ready for you here which I trust you will occupy when you come to Boston. Then perchance we can have some music too! As well as talk about the divine art of poetry." Lanier's trip to Boston, in connection with the boys' books, took place in September.

reference save what I carried in my trunk. I have no more claim to " scholarship " than to the throne of England, and you cannot imagine how it embarrasses me to find newspaper notices thus shoving upon me responsibilities I can never hope to support and am even unambitious to deserve. To be an artist, and preach the gospel of poetry: that is the breath of *my* life.

Mrs. Lanier sends you cordial messages, and we both hope for more meetings, and longer.

Faithfully yours,

Sidney Lanier.

## To Waldo S. Pratt [109]

435 N. Calvert St.
Bo; July 19, 1880.

My dear Mr. Pratt:

It is a genuine pleasure to have a word from you, and particularly to know that you have been looking for me.

It is now nearly six weeks that I've had a villainous fever, which has finally become the disgust of my doctor and the opprobrium of all medicine. Nothing seems to have the least effect on it. If it goes on it must result in overturning the most fundamental concepts of philosophy: for it is apparently without cause and without end, – though it certainly had a beginning, – and it is self-existent, – though a parasite.

Day and night it remains, calm, inexpugnable. I am satisfied that nothing ever acquired a state of existence so wholly imperturbable and elevated beyond the powers or the prayers of men, – except perhaps one of the grand gods of Lucretius, whose nature

[109] Pratt, a fellow in art history at Johns Hopkins, had attended Lanier's lectures and classes during the past academic year and was often a guest in his home. In June he became an assistant curator at the Metropolitan Museum of Art. He later distinguished himself as an author and professor of music history.

Ipsa suis pollens opibus, nihil indiga nostri,
Nec bene promeritis capitur nec tangitur ira.[110]

In truth this last line seems almost allegorical, in this connection; for *bene promeritis* may well enough symbolize the
mild homoeopathic suasives with which my Fever has been
appealed to; while *ira* admirably represents the heroic doses of
allopathic truculence with which it has been fought; but with
the former *nec capitur*, with the latter *nec tangitur*.

Seriously, I've been ill enough; and your imagination is all I
can rely on – for words are here simply exasperating – when I
tell you that about three weeks ago, thinking a change might
help me, I managed to crawl down to Charles Street Station
and *went* to New York, – and took to bed as soon as I reached
the hotel, there, – and tossed thereon for four days with a fairly
flaming fever, – and finally had to crawl back to Baltimore,
without having accomplished a single stroke of business, without having seen a single picture or friend, without having
heard a single crash of the horns and violins, – for which I
longed unspeakably.

Since I reached home, I've been very hard at work. I had
promised the Scribners to have ready for the printer by July 15,
the *ms.* of my " Boy's King Arthur " – an edition, for boys, of
old Sir Thomas Malory's *Morte d'Arthur*, which they are bringing out for the next Xmas holidays as a companion book to
my " Boy's Froissart " of last year. I could not bear to be
behind time, and so in spite of the fever I buried myself in
the work and triumphantly forwarded it on the appointed day.

But the doctor has decisively ordered no more of this; and
so on Wednesday, 21st, my wife and Mr. Day and I are to
leave for West Chester, Pennsylvania, a pretty little town about
thirty miles from Philadelphia, where we will spend a couple
of months.

But I keenly wish to run again to New York, – largely drawn
thereto by you and your wonders fair at the Museum; and you
need not be surprised at seeing me, any day in a couple of
weeks from now. It depends entirely on the disappearance of
my fever, which today seems to be flickering a little as if it
*might* go out.

[110] *De Rerum Natura*, Book II, 650-651 — inaccurately quoted.

The boys were sent to Virginia three weeks ago, and appear to have become a sort of combination of monkey and centaur already; for, by all accounts, they live either in the tops of trees or on the backs of horses.   They are at a farm-house, among the mountains; and declare that they are in Paradise.

Mrs. Lanier enjoyed your letter with me, and sends you all manner of cordial messages.   To us both, Baltimore seems to have lost a great many inhabitants since you left.   Pray send us something about your goings-on, often: although we saw much less of you than we desired, when you were here, still it was a comfort to know that you *were* here; and we find it a great *dis*comfort now that you are gone.

Letters will reach us addressed to " West Chester. Pa."   I am sure the boys would send you affectionate messages; whereto pray add those of

Your faithfully,

Sidney Lanier.

To Oliver W. Holmes[111]

West Chester, Pa.
Aug. 3, 1880.

My dear Sir:

Some time ago I made a note of your interesting remark upon the relation between the octosyllabic line and the average respiratory rhythm, of which I happened to see a short account in a newspaper.   I did not know — as your letter now informs me — that you had written a paper on this subject.[112] I had expected to quote your observation in my *Science of*

---

[111] This letter and the one to Holmes on Nov. 7, below, were first published in *American Literature,* XVIII, 322–324 (January 1947)—being unavailable for the *Centennial Edition* because of the war. This one answers Holmes's letter of July 24, thanking Lanier for his *Science of English Verse.*

[112] "The Physiology of Versification," *Boston Medical and Surgical Journal,* XCII, 6–9 (Jan. 7, 1875), conveniently reprinted in Holmes's *Works* (Riverside Edition), VIII, 315 ff.

In his letter of July 24 Holmes had said: "I printed a short article a few years ago on the relation of the length of verse to the natural rhythm of respiration. I traced the 'fatal facility' of the octosyllabic verse to the circumstance that each

*English Verse,* and to discuss it at some length, as connected with a confirmation — or rather with an extension of its bearing — which had come within my own notice. This extension is: that the whole body of instrumental music — though of course such music is wholly independent, so far as stringed instruments are concerned, of those limitations of vocal music arising from the singer's need to take breath at intervals — is nevertheless found to be segregated into rhythmic divisions whose length varies only within just such limits as are determined by the breathing-places in ordinary songs. In other words, instrumental music is rhythmized as if the instruments — even the stringed ones — had to respire.

It may interest you if I mention two, out of several, important bearings of this fact when taken in connection with your own principle. One is: that, since these rhythmic divisions which we are in the habit of calling "lines" in *verse* prevail also in *music,* we are necessarily driven back to a common origin for this remarkable rhythmic determination of what would seem naturally the most *un*determined and lawless of human feelings; and that common origin seems necessarily *the Song.* If now we widen the argument by taking in the fact that *prose* speech is determined into segregations more or less plainly rhythmical by the same limitations of breath-taking, which segregations must have been much more uniform when both syllables and emotions were less complex; we seem to find an explanation of the fact that poetry arises earlier than prose in all literatures; and if we go on to consider that the simple should precede the complex, and that poetry *is* rhythmically simple — so simple that its larger divisions are even automatic, being merely the respiratory rhythm — while prose is rhythmically complex in the highest degree; we are, I think, bound to conclude that men *sung* their most ordinary communications to each other long before they *prosed* them. Thus M. Jourdain's astonishment is not without grounds: for although he *had* been talking prose all his life, it would seem that the world has not, all *its* life.

---

line, in reading it, consumed one natural expiration. Even in unarticulated—or rather mentally articulated—reading, we follow something of the movement of articulated reading. All other verses but the octosyllabic will interfere with the ordinary rhythm of respiration in average individuals—so my experiments indicated."

The other remark is: that a proper application of *the Song* as type of all aesthetic uses of sound in verse as in music really sets at rest the whole question of "Programme Music" which has so bitterly divided the musical world for many years. The Song, in which every idea is accompanied by an appropriate tone or variation in pitch, is merely Programme Music carried to its utmost logical development; and such music, instead of being a modern invention as many have hastily supposed, is really the primal type of the whole art of sound. In my chapter on THE TUNES OF VERSE I have deduced some of the historic results of this view. I feel sure that when the fact of tune in ordinary speech — the fact that in all our every day talk we convey our meaning quite as much by tune as by articulate word — comes to be fully recognized, philology will find a new world for its investigations.

—        As I say, I had expected to quote your observation in my book and to discuss it with some detail; but there seemed no chance of getting a publisher for such matter, and I was compelled to make the work a semi-popular treatise, at the expense of leaving out a great part of what was to me the most interesting material of all that I had collected for the book.

I cannot help adding — since my book has been so universally misconceived in this respect — that its object was *not* to teach people how to make verse. — God forbid! but to present a *scientific* account of all those curious phenomena connoted by the term "Verse" and to refer these to purely physical principles of classification. Almost every one has taken the work to be a collection of rules for making verses; but it is not this any more than a work on the Science of Geology would be a collection of rules for making rocks.

Your "Last Leaf" has indeed a charming movement, and I do not wonder that Poe praised it. Your verse shows always a fine feeling for rhythm. Besides this, I find in your work a quite notable sense of the relations of tone-color in words. Many of your combinations in this particular, arranged as they are evidently by a pure instinct, give me great pleasure. There are persons, I find, who consider enjoyments of this kind finical; but I discover myself growing daily more and more rigorous in requiring the poet, if he use any forms at all which appeal to the sense, to use them so perfectly that his forms shall cast my sense into the same ecstasy that his conceptions cast my spirit.

I hope, in another edition of my book, to indulge myself with an appendix where I may discuss your rhythmic observation, along with other omitted matters. Meantime, where may I find the article to which you refer, for I have seen only a very unsatisfactory newspaper-account of it.

— Pray believe that it is not with malice prepense I have written such an unchristian letter. I began with the intention only of letting you know how important I think your filiation of the two great facts of human breath and poetic rhythm.

Very truly yours,

Sidney Lanier.

To Robert S. Lanier

West Chester, Pa.
Aug. 10, 1880

My dearest Father:

Your letter of Aug. 7 is just arrived, and I hasten to assure you that in a hasty reading of Mary's letter – which was probably written, indeed, under some momentary lowness of spirits — you have received an impression of our state of health much more dark than the facts warrant. It is true that I have not succeeded in breaking the singular fever which has caused me such daily distress for two months past; and the necessity, or rather the desire, of nursing me has added a very heavy weight to Mary's condition, which will soon require all her attention to be given in other directions; yet a quiet view of the whole situation does not present anything more than reasonable ground for some regret that both of us should be under the weather at once. My fever holds on; yet I am up at my usual hour every day, have as much appetite as ever, am apparently as strong as ever except in the periods of exacerbation, and show not the least sign of any more trouble in the lung than has existed for five years past. My doctor thinks the fever a result of overwork, not of *mental* overwork but simply of the continued strain of muscle and nerve involved in sitting at the desk for a great number of hours a day through a long period; and he declares that with absolute rest he has no doubt of my pulling through.  My own belief is nearly the same; but I am aware of an element which I feel sure has a great influence in the matter, indeed I would not be surprised if it were not the cause of my woe.  This is the nervous strain of *waiting*.  For two years past – since I have become in health to study at all – I have had such a rush and storm of ideas demanding immediate expression, and have had to put aside such an enormous proportion of them in favor of small daily duties which physically limited me to a book or two a year, that I have been continually jarred and shaken with ever-recurrent shock and resistance, like a steamboat's frame with the pull and push of the walking-beam. Especially wearing has it been, to do the work for which I care least, and to be continually crushing back poem after poem – I have several volumes of poems in the form of memoranda on the backs of envelopes, odd slips of paper, and the like! while I addressed myself to such work as seemed to offer more immediate return in the way of money.  This may seem intangible; but an amount of nervous strength is given out in mere dumb endurance of this sort which far exceeds that lost in physical labor.  If I could write nothing but poetry for the next two years — which means if I had five thousand dollars — I would be in vigorous health by October next !

— But the chances are strong that I will be, anyhow.  While, as I have said, my fever still gives me great distress — it is attended with a peculiar *malaise*, a misery in every bone — yet I seem to have lost no ground, but on the contrary am a little better than a month ago.  I have had three or four horseback rides within a week past, though of course short and easy ones.  As soon as Mary is safely past her crisis, which should occur now at any day, I expect to run over to New York and consult the best physician I can find there, – unless, of course, I should be then decidedly better.  I went to Philadelphia last week, and gave Dr. Lippe a full account of my case.  He is the physician, you remember, who treated me when I was so ill at the Peacocks' in '76, and who sent me to Florida from there.  I am taking his medicines daily, and the *malaise* seems on the whole somewhat lessened. . . .

Your son,

S. L.

To Charles D. Lanier [113]

West Chester, Pa.
Aug. 15, 1880.

My dear Charley:

A young man came to our house yesterday morning who claims that he is a brother of yours and Sidney's and Harry's, and that he is entitled to all the rights and privileges appertaining unto that honorable connection. You will be surprised to learn that both your mother and I are disposed to allow his pretensions, from the fact that he looks a great deal like Sidney, — and from several other circumstances which I need not detail. Indeed your mother has already gone so far as to take him on her breast and nurse him exactly as she did you three young scamps somewhere between twelve and seven years ago. I write therefore to ask whether you and Sidney and Harry are willing to accept our opinion of this young person's genuine kinship to you, or whether you will require him to employ a number of lawyers, like the Tichborne Claimant in England, to assert his rights in due form before the courts of the United States. If the latter, you had best give him early notice of your intention: for the fact is he has taken such a hold upon our affections here, by the quietness and modesty of his demeanor and by the beauty of his person, that if we were summoned into Court as witnesses in the case of

Robert Sampson Lanier Jr (so called), Plaintiff,

*Versus*                                Action on
                                         a Bond
Charles Day Lanier                       (of broth-
Sidney          " Jr.  } Defendants      erhood),
   and
Henry           "

we would be obliged to testify that we feel almost as sure — f not quite — that he is your brother as that you are our son.

---

[113] Lanier's oldest son Charles, born Sept. 12, 1868, was spending the summer with the two other sons) at a farm near Orange Court House, Va. His youngest on, Robin, was born Aug. 14, 1880—the subject of this letter.

As I have said, he is a most exemplary young man. He never stays out late at night; neither chews, smokes, nor uses snuff; abstains from all intoxicating liquors, and does not touch even tea or coffee; however much preserves and fruit-cake there may be on the supper-table, he never asks for any; he does no kind of work on the Sabbath; he honors his father and mother, particularly his mother; he plays no games of hazard, not even marbles for winnance; and I am positively certain that in the whole course of his life he has never uttered a single angry or ungentlemanly word. I am bound to admit that he has his shortcomings: he *isn't* as particular about his clothes as I would like to see him; he has a way of trying to get both fists in his mouth which certainly does look odd in company; and he wants his breakfast in the morning at four o'clock — an hour at which it is very inconvenient, with *our* household arrangements, to furnish it to him. But we hope that perhaps he will amend in these particulars, as time rolls on, and that he will become as perfect a gentleman as his three brothers. In fact we attribute these little faults of his to the fact that he appears to have been in a Far Country — like the Tichborne Claimant —, and the manners and customs of peoples are so different that we really don't know whether it may not be considered a sign of good breeding *There* to cram one's fists into one's mouth, and perhaps the very highest circles of the nobility and gentry in that Region take their breakfasts before daylight.

Earnestly hoping that this lovely little (for I omitted to mention that he is small of stature) brother Rob may find a good warm place in your three hearts without being obliged to resort to extreme measures, and with a hundred embraces for you, my dear big Charley,

I am

Your &c &c &c.

## To Oliver W. Holmes[114]

435 N. Calvert St.
Baltimore, Md.
Nov. 7, 1880.

My dear Sir:

Some very pleasant meditations result to me from the contact of the title of your book and the genial thoughts within it. We know what a beggarly crack we have made between the edge and the jamb of the Iron Gate, with all humanity at the crowbar and with at least six thousand years to work in; but all the more does it seem to me that to make so pitiful a crevice yield such wide prospects and suggestive fragrances as your book does is a very pretty achievement, and one which is never accomplished save by the true and earnest poet.

I find indeed a very precious and firm quality amid all the airiness of your verses: in spite of their sudden bringings-to, and gyrations, of thought, they always manage somehow to remind us that there are depths below; as, when we watch a sea-gull coming about in the wind and wheeling hither and yonder, we do not need to look downwards in order to know that the Sea is beneath him. I think a time is lucky to have a man in it who can without flippancy make us smile over questions that made Hamlet fumble at his heart and his bodkin for a quietus.

I have had quite special occasion recently to contrast this quality in true and large Humor with its opposite in many notable English works of old renown. In excogitating a series of lectures I am to deliver at the University here on "The English Satirists," I have been brought fairly up against the fact that I have never read a Satire in my life without feeling uncomfortable when I had finished. I always find a bad taste left. No enjoyment of the cleverness, the stroke, the irresistible laugh, however great, avails to prevent this after-tang of discomfort. And now that the exigency of lecturing on these matters has led

---

[114] This letter was prompted by Lanier's reading of Holmes's new volume, *The Iron Gate, and Other Poems,* and by his plans for lectures on the English Satirists—never given.

me to analyse what was before a merely vague sensation of mis-
ease (I wish we could use that dear old word, since you doctors
have appropriated "disease" to your horrible private purposes)
I find that it arises from the lack of the very quality I have mentioned as inherent in all your verse that I have seen, the quality
of somehow making us feel that though we *have* laughed at the
Image of Things in the cracked mirror, there is nevertheless a
great and beautiful Figure of which this Image is but a partial
representation.  This reminder of a dignified Whole while immediately suggesting only an absurd or grotesque Part, this
sending us off gentle Christians instead of smart duellists, appears to be the root of the matter.  From the *Golias* of Walter
Map — if he wrote it — down through all the Hudibrases and
Dunciads and Fables, — I can never read one without feeling
that whatever additional contempt they may have bred in me
for the villanies [*sic*] they satirize is after all but a heathen's
contempt, and is all lacking in love and largeness and a proper
relation to things.

I have examined this feeling, too, to see if there is not something a little morbid and nineteenth-centuryish about it.  But I
can not think so, with the most honest balancing of arguments.
I'm not constitutionally averse to a square fight — "fair fist and
skull" as my schoolmates used to call it — when things have
come to a point where some kind of clearance has *got* to be
made; but in the Satire I have a sense that the Satirist has an
unfair advantage; and though the fight here *is* against the devil,
I do not want to take advantage, even of him; the devil himself
is unfair and, heaven help us, he's the last creature *I* want to
set up for a model; particularly now that he has turned out to be
such a nobody.[115]

---

[115] This letter is unique for its full exposition of Lanier's views on satire. The
paucity of references in his published writings and letters to either the great satirists
or their works (see Index to the *Centennial Edition*) indicates that for the most part
he passed them by as uncongenial to his temperament and repugnant to his theory
of literature. He may have done some small reading in this field during the last
year of his life, but even in the prudish attack on the eighteenth-century novelists in
his lectures of this winter (IV, 152 ff.) his criticism is directed at what he calls
their "naturalism" rather than at satire as a literary method. The basis of his attitude towards the satirist is, however, stated in an aside in the same series: "The
great artist never can work in hate, never in malice, never in even the sub-acid,
satiric mood of Thackeray; in love, and love only, can great work . . . be done"
(IV, 176).

Hoping, and believing, that there will be no solution of continuity between the fine faith with which you now stand outside the Iron Gate and the fine vision with which you will some day stand inside it, I am, dear Sir,

Very truly yours,

Sidney Lanier.

To Paul H. Hayne

435 N. Calvert St.
Baltimore, Md.
Nov. 19, 1880.

My dear Mr. Hayne:
I have been wishing to write you a long time, and have *thought* several letters to you. But I could never tell you the extremity of illness, of poverty, and of unceasing work, in which I have spent the last three years; and you would need only once to see the weariness with which I crawl to bed after a long day's work, – and often a long night's work at the heel of it, – and Sundays just as well as other days, – in order to find in your heart a full warrant for my silence. It seems incredible that I have printed such an unchristian quantity of matter, – all, too, tolerably successful, – and earned so little money; and the wife and the four boys – who are so lovely that I would not think a palace good enough for them if I had it–make one's earnings seem all the less. . . .

For six months past a ghastly fever has been taking possession of me each day at about twelve M., and holding my head under the surface of indescribable distress for the next twenty hours, subsiding only enough each morning to let me get on my working-harness, but never intermitting. A number of tests show it not to be the " hectic " so well known in consumption; and to this day it has baffled all the skill I could find in New York, in Philadelphia, and here. I have myself been disposed to think it arose purely from the bitterness of having to spend my time in making academic lectures and boy's-books – pot-boilers all – when a thousand songs are sing-

ing in my heart that will certainly kill me if I do not utter
them soon.    But I don't think this diagnosis has found favor
with any practical physicians; and meantime I work day after
day in such suffering as is piteous to see.

— I hope all this does not read like a Jeremiad; I mention
these matters only in the strong rebellion against what I fear
might be your thought — namely, forgetfulness of you — if you
did not know the causes which keep me from sending you
more frequent messages.    I do not, and will not, forget the
early encouragements which used to come from you when I was
just daring to think of making verses. . . .

sincerely yours<br>Sidney Lanier.

To Clifford A. Lanier

435 N. Calvert St.<br>Bo; Mch. 7, 1881.

My dearest Clifford:

To take my pen in hand has been for many
weeks an enterprise requiring as much stoutness of heart and
concentration of muscular fibre as would have sufficed Sir
Launcelot to seize a great spear and unhorse six knights in one
sally.    Although my immediately-dangerous symptoms abated
months ago, yet the amount of unceasing pain seems to have
increased, and I've been working for the last two months particularly under such a load of physical distress that I have several times found myself *almost* at the point where one throws
up one's hands and cries My sufferings are more than I can bear.
The suffering is most peculiar and baffling: I cannot locate it
in any limb or organ, just as one cannot locate thirst which is
a lack in the whole blood; a severe fever comes — or rather
stays, it never goes — and therewith a general discomfort under
which I can scarcely refrain from such groans and shrieks as a
wounded dog gives, crawling off with a broken back and hind-
legs dragging.    To lie spread out and *repose* for one hour —
that is my dream; not old Aeschylus' Io, stung through the

orld by the unreachable gad-fly, ever longed so for a moment's
urcease of misery.[116]

Some infringement of heart upon lung, or contrariwise, seems
ɔ have occurred: I can lie but in one position, poised on my
ight hip and shoulder; and each morning finds me properly
tired.

To fall-to, each week, and begin the writing of a lecture
wherewith I am bound (or else lose my place) to amuse and
instruct some two hundred people in developing a continuous
line of systematic thought – is, you may fancy, forlorn enough:
particularly when I give a longing glance toward my desk
where lie two volumes of poems and some half dozen other
books in various stages of completion.

Yet, thanks to the great God of strength, I have never yet
quite lost heart; and have written and delivered six lectures, of
my twelve, which have been received with many pleasant tokens
of satisfaction. Moreover, amid all the distress, it seems clear
am better and stronger; no lesion of the lung appears to have
occurred, and the inflammation is still in the curable state; I
abound in plans and new books; and admit no ground-tone but
hope. It seems a miracle that I have weathered such a savage
winter as we have had, in which ice, snow, wind, sleet, and rain
have kept us whirling in one eddy of danger; and I look forward with joyful longing to the warm days when I can taste
some un-furnaced air and relax this tension of continuous re-
sistence to cold which we must all keep up through these
unfriendly blasts. . . .

I have been dreaming a little of Southern air in the spring:
but it is only a dream. Tell me if you prosper in the new single-
handed venture; keep out of speculation; and hold me always

Your loving

S. L.

[116] The allusion is to Aeschylus, *Prometheus Bound,* which Lanier had discussed
in his Johns Hopkins lecture on Feb. 16, 1881. His series of weekly lectures for
the academic year 1880–1881 had been postponed until after Christmas because of
illness, the first one being given on Jan. 26. They were announced in *The Johns
Hopkins University Circulars,* No. 8, p. 99, as follows: "From Aeschylus to
George Eliot: Twelve Studies in the Modern English Novel as a Development
from the Greek Drama."

## To Clifford A. Lanier

435 N. Calvert St.
Bo. May 5, 1881.

Dearest Clifford:

Mary and I returned from New York last night,[117] and I think I am a little less feverish this morning.

You will have received, I hope, a couple of days ago, my letter written you from New York. I send this scrawl merely to add that upon further thought it seems altogether more wise — instead of trying to make a horseback journey at once, which I do not at all see how I could do, in my present feebleness — to fit up a tent as soon as we get to Asheville and select some pleasant site near that place, (or some stream where we can fish, and on a mountain-side where we can get good protection against storms &c) with a view to my trying camp-life for several months. This is, indeed, what Dr. Loomis wants. Mary and the baby will come on as soon as necessary closing out arrangements can be made here, and if we should not find it possible, with our then experience of tent-life, to accommodate them there, I can lodge them pleasantly at Asheville, with daily seeing-distance. Our boys are to go back to their old quarters at Rapidan for the summer. I know so little of Wilsie's movements that I say nothing more thereof. If you could arrange to leave your little ones with Sissa, – provided she is well enough, – I think we could have a double wall-tent that would accommodate us four (you & Will, Maydie & me) and enable us to spend a royal summer. I hope to do some profitable study and to have your company therein. Perhaps I

[117] Mary Day Lanier had joined her husband in New York on April 28. Lanier's letter to his brother written from New York, mentioned in the following sentence, has not been found; but the important details of their week's stay are given in two letters from Mary Day Lanier to Sarah Farley. On May 1, 1881, she wrote: " Saw Dr. A. Loomis. He says the out-door life, on a *high* level, is the *one* hope, with no time to lose in trying it. Three months will decide the possibility, but not place out of danger. Heart trouble secondary will lessen if lung heals. He has to-day fresh pleuritic inflammations & lose ground. Too much noise." On May 3 she added: " Sidney has been enough worse to see that *he* ought not to attempt one thing unnecessary. . . . We leave here at 3:40 P. M. tomorrow."

may start you in some branch of scholarship which will give you just the ballast and specific actual freightage of facts which every man needs, as against a certain vagueness of general culture that I do not doubt you have already felt the disadvantage of.

But I am overtaxing my arm, which is now as it were but a rope of sand. I intended to put herein a P. O. order for twenty five dollars, – to pay your expenses here, – but cannot now get it in time for the mail, and will hand you that amount when you come. God bless you, dear soul, and all yours, – [118]

Bro.

S. L.

## To Mary Day Lanier

Eagle Hotel, Asheville, N. C.
Saturday, May 21, 1881.

Dearest Soul,     I am somewhat rested today from the fatigues of our journey, which were somewhat trying to my small modicum of strength. I much desired to write thee yesterday: but our morning was spent in a horseback excursion to Richmond Hill, – otherwise known as " Pearson's View," – and when we returned I was too weary for anything but the lounge during the rest of the afternoon, and so begged Clifford to give you some account of us.

We have decided to pitch our tent at this Richmond Hill. It is about three miles from town; secluded enough, yet within a short distance of Mr. Pearson's house, where we can get milk and butter, and other occasional supplies; we have arranged for communication with the city, so as to get fresh beef and mutton and the like, – a " Market ", or butcher's shop, is just across the street from this hotel; and I have the prospect of a saddle-horse, to be hired by the month, and kept at Pearson's stable near our camp.     I will not now descant upon the natural

[118] The members of Clifford Lanier's family referred to here, and above, were his wife Wilsie and his and Sidney's sister Gertrude.

beauties of our location.   In some particulars it is far from
being the ideal I had brought with me: but it combines so
many conveniences which we could not hope to find in any
other that we consider ourselves lucky in discovering it so soon.
The Mr. Pearson who owns the land is a young man, son of
Judge Pearson – a prominent lawyer of this state – who, after
having practised law a while and after travelling extensively in
Europe and in the West, has bought this beautiful tract of
land lying almost entirely enclosed by the Swannanoa and
French Broad Rivers, and is devoting much money – with which
he seems to be abundantly supplied – to making it a sort of
mountain Eden.

We have just engaged a cook, black as to the countenance
thereof like the blackness of Erebus, but an old hotel cook and
evidently used to taking care of people.   As good luck would
have it, young Penniman, – who very civilly called with his
father, Miss Carrington's relative, as soon as we arrived, and
has been unceasingly attentive since, – is in the hardware business, and by further good luck we found in his store, a second-
hand cooking-stove scarcely used.   This we have bought: the
whole affair, with outfit of cooking utensils, costing us only
nine dollars and some cents.   You had better bring with you
knives, forks and spoons, and such little matters of table-ser-
vice as may occur to you: but, as to all cooking-things, we are
supplied. . . .

I can think of nothing more to ease thy path.   God come
with thee – help and grace and love always *do*, for me – and
have special charge and bring thee in peace and gravity to thine
always

lover – [119]

[119] Clifford Lanier left for Montgomery on May 27.   Mary Day Lanier had
reached Asheville on May 25 with her youngest son, the three older boys having
been sent to Virginia in care of Mrs. S. M. Maxwell.   On May 28 she wrote to
Lawrence Turnbull: " Sidney has had to conquer a fresh pleuritic attack in the
opening of his stay here, and his nights are– as he says– abnormally bad; yet
he is confident that he has gained strength of limb and of lung– working in the
face of this new inflammation, which must speak volumes for the fine air and
for out-door exposure."
    Awaiting the arrival of furnishings shipped from Baltimore, the Laniers re-
mained at the Eagle Hotel in Asheville for about two weeks before removing
to " Camp Robin."

## To Richard M. Johnston

Camp Robin, near Asheville.
July 5th 1881

My dear Colonel (but why should I not spell it *Kernel*,— as being one to whom other men are but as shells or husks?):

I was just beginning to dictate this to May when she was called away, and so I scrawl on, as well as I can, to tell you that your sweet letter came in upon me through my circumjacent woods like a rose peeping through the leaves, and that I should long ago have sent you my love for it if either work or health had permitted. Our camp-outfit required endless small labors, and as soon as we moved into our tents — which was about five weeks ago— I had to set very hard to work at completing my *Boy's Percy* (a redaction of Percy's *Reliques*) which I had promised to furnish — along with the Introduction to my Mabinogion — by July 1st, complete and ready for the printer. Although in the greatest bodily distress I have ever known,— I managed to get through in time, and had the gratification of fulfilling my contract in spite of old Chang Lung, the tyrant. [120]

I am sure you will be glad to know that I am now comparatively free from pressure of work, and will be so for four or five weeks to come. It is too glorious for any words to sit under my great trees, here, and fold my hands, and lie fallow to the thoughts that rain down from God and from the mountains.

I have improved a little, I think, in one or two particulars, and my appetite is better; though my leg is certainly the most ridiculous object I ever beheld, and as for the muscle of my arm, there is none. Nevertheless, I shall get well, and look for great things in the next four weeks.

Tell me how the novel fares,— for I shall brood anxiously over each character. [121]

[120] *The Boy's Mabinogion* and *The Boy's Percy,* Lanier's last two volumes in this juvenile series, were published posthumously, in the autumn of 1881 and 1882. He was paid $350 for each.

[121] The allusion is to *Old Mark Langston* (1883), Johnston's first novel; it was apparently prompted by Lanier.

But here comes May; (who takes her rebel into custody, with a reprimand) and as this is the longest letter I have written in a great while I will allow her to close for me.   Please give our love to Dr. & Mrs. Browne, and tell them how completely hard work has barred both May and myself from putting on paper the kindly thoughts of them that continually dwell with us.

With as many sweet wishes for you as there be leaves in all the valley betwixt this mountain that my tent is on and yonder blue range twenty miles away that I glimpse across many an intervening lesser hill whenever I lift my eyes,

Your friend

S. L.

## To Charles D. Lanier [122]

Asheville, N. C.

July 20, 1881.

My dear Son Charley:

I have been for several weeks lying at the very gates of death—so close that I could almost peep in upon the marvels of that mysterious country — and it has been long since I could write a letter with my own hand; but your mother has read me Mrs. Maxwell's report of your ever-increasing manfulness and of your gentle disposition toward your brothers, and this has brought me such deep gratification that I cannot help devoting a part of my very little strength this morning to the pleasant work of sending you this brief line of thanks and love which will enable you to share my pleasure with me.   It would require a great many more pages than I can now write for me to tell you how earnestly I admire the sight of a man fighting his own small failings, as a good knight who never ceases to watch, and war against, the least blemish or evil: you may therefore fancy how my heart warms with loving pride in you and for you as I learn from Miss Mary the patience and generosity and large conduct which you daily exhibit towards your brothers, the gentlemanly thoughtfulness which you show

---

[122] Lanier's sons Charles, Sidney, and Harry were at the same Virginia farm where they had spent the last few summers.

for the comfort of all about you, and the general advance and growth which your whole nature appears to be achieving.

This makes me much more easy in mind when I think of the possibility that death may at any time compel me to leave my dear wife and my three beautiful boys (you should see Robin at this moment! with his great shining blue eyes and his milk-and-roses complexion, and magnificent limbs, he is like a young inhabitant of a morning-star just caught among the rhodo-dendrons of these mountains) in your charge as head of the family; for I well know that as long as you behave like a man you will never lack men for your friends.

But, – over and above all this, – I take the gravest pleasure in seeing you unfold what I know to be your natural qualities; I have always known that your character is strong and fine, but I have feared that your beautifully-sympathetic disposition would sometimes be apt to persuade you that you liked people or things which were really unworthy of you, and that you might have trouble with entanglements or stains thus arising, even after you had yourself perceived the unworthiness: but I rejoice to find in you a reasonableness and good judgment which I think will always bring you out safely at the end.

This is but a dry and didactic letter: nor will you know how much pleasure, how much hope, and how much affection go with it, until you yourself, my dear, dear boy, shall have a son who seems as fine as my Charley and whom you love as loves

your own

father.


To Charles Scribner

Lynn. Polk Co. N.C.[123]
Sept. 3rd, 1881.

My dear Mr. Scribner:

About four weeks ago a desperate attack of illness suddenly rendered me unable even to correct proof.

[123] Early in August Lanier's camp had been moved to the "no-frost" belt on the side of Tryon Mt., about 50 miles southeast of Asheville, in search of a better climate.

In the hope that abatement would come I held over from day to day such parcels of proof as arrived from Boston; but I find that this may involve more delay, as well as a constant burden of responsibility which works against the speediness of my recovery.  I write therefore to say: (1) that I yesterday managed by pure *tour de force* to revise the proof of the Introduction, (which you had kindly sent at my request, and which I found greatly disfigured by printers, and proof-readers' errors), and to send same to Boston with a marginal note explaining cause of delay; (2) that I send you, at New York, all the other proof which has reached me up to date, asking that you will have it read by some person competent in the premises, and will charge expenses of same to my account.  I had hoped, indeed, that by the time we should have reached the point where I stopped four weeks ago — I had then corrected about 150 *pp.* of page-proof — the proof-readers would have caught my very simple system of punctuation so clearly as to make any further supervision by me unnecessary; but I find them still sprinkling commas over the page as these country cooks in North Carolina sprinkle black pepper over their unspeakable chicken-pies, out of pepper-boxes whose holes have run together by liberal use and wont until they often give down three grains for one.

I am entirely ignorant, however, of dates, of necessity for haste, &c, in your plans for the book; and if such farther proof-reading as I suggest involves delay or inconvenience I beg you to disregard all said in that connection and to go forward as seems best to you.

Your little check for balance due on account copyright *Science of Verse* was received with joy and merrymaking by my little circle who are about me here in the mountains.  You will observe that my P.O. address is " Lynn, Polk Co. N.C."  This will continue for at least a month.  I shall pull through the present crisis and write many another book, whereof the germs have already been born in this strange and beautiful Tryon Valley.

With earnest thanks for the inquiries as to my health which I
find in your last letters, I am always

Sincerely yours,

Sidney Lanier.

by M.D.L.[124]

---

[124] Scribner replied, Sept. 5, assuring Lanier that he need give himself no
further anxiety about the proofs, which would be corrected by Mr. Burlingame
without charge, and that *The Boy's Mabinogion* would be published at the end
October, as planned. But his letter probably reached Tryon too late. Lanier
ed on Sept. 7, 1881.

# INDEX OF POEMS

# INDEX OF NAMES

Fo